Full Circles,
Overlapping Lives

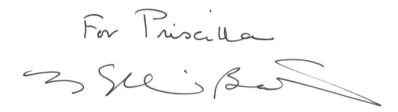

FULL

Culture

CIRCLES

and Generation

OVERLAPPING

in Transition

LIVES

Mary Catherine Bateson

Random House

New York

Grateful acknowledgment is made to Harcourt, Inc., for
permission to reprint an excerpt from *Murder in the Cathedral*
by T. S. Eliot. Copyright © 1935 by Harcourt, Inc., and
copyright renewed 1963 by T. S. Eliot. Reprinted by
permission of the publisher.

Library of Congress Cataloging-in-Publication data is available.

ISBN 0-375-50101-0

Random House website address: www.atrandom.com
Printed in the United States of America on acid-free paper
98765432
First Edition

Book design by J. K. Lambert

Contents

As her centenary approaches,

I dedicate this book to the memory of my mother,

MARGARET MEAD, 1901–1978,

*for her pioneering work on the relationship between culture
and generation and her openness to friend and stranger.*

*In her memory, I hope this book reflects both caring
and the possibility of change.*

Full Circles,
Overlapping Lives

1 | Overlapping Lives

We live with strangers. Those we love most, with whom we share a shelter, a table, a bed, remain mysterious. Wherever lives overlap and flow together, there are depths of unknowing. Parents and children, partners, siblings, and friends repeatedly surprise us, revealing the need to learn where we are most at home. We even surprise ourselves in our own becoming, moving through the cycles of our lives. There is strangeness hidden in the familiar.

At the same time there is familiarity hidden in the strange. We can look with curiosity and respect at the faces of men and women we have never met. Learning to recognize these strangers with whom we share an increasingly crowded and interdependent world, we can imagine ourselves joined in a single family, perhaps by a marriage between adventurous grandchildren.

"I loved him, but I couldn't really know him. So I learned to stop and think before I let myself get all upset." This was my sister Nora, who had lived in Thailand with a Thai partner. "Then, when I married an American, I found I had to keep on the same way." Living with someone from another culture had taught her not to expect to understand her husband. Strangeness and love are not contradictory; to live at peace we need new ways of understanding these two realms, each one embedded in the other.

Strangers marry strangers, whether they have been playmates for years or never meet before the wedding day. They continue to surprise each other through the evolutions of love and the growth of affection. Lovers, gay and straight, begin in strangeness and often, for the zest of it, find ways to increase their differences.

Children arrive like aliens from outer space, their needs and feelings inaccessible, sharing no common language, yet for all their strangeness we greet them with love. Traditionally, the strangeness of infants has been understood as temporary, the strangeness of incomplete beings who are expected to become predictable and comprehensible. This expectation has eased the transition from generation to generation, the passing on of knowledge and responsibility, on which every human society depends. Yet the gap between parent and child, like the gap between partners, is not left behind with the passage of time. Today, in a world of rapid change, it is increasing, shifting into new rhythms still to be explored.

I have learned to work on the assumption that my daughter and I were born in different countries—not according to our passports but because our country has changed, making me an immigrant from the past. But she, in her twenties, has the same comment about today's teenagers: they have grown up in a different country from hers. She cannot look inward, drawing on memory to understand them, but must learn from them, warned only by her own wry memories of the incomprehensibility of adults.

Differences of age and sex crosscut all human lives with the experience of Otherness, that which is different, alien, mysterious. These differences, occurring within the household, offer a chance to learn about strangeness in a familiar setting, so we can say with Annie Sullivan in *The Miracle Worker:* "Oh, strangers aren't so strange to me. I've known them all my life." In a world where waves of strangeness rise or enter constantly, these are important lessons to learn. When we encounter new immigrants from other faiths and continents, we can reassure ourselves by remembering the utter strangeness that coexists with love within every household. We can even learn to look at the sun or the moon, a tree or a snail or a forest pool with affinity and greeting, then look again and acknowledge their strangeness.

When you pass strangers on the street, the unfamiliar faces blur. When you let your lives touch and make the effort of asking questions and listening to the stories they tell, you discover the intricate patterns of their differences and, at the same time, the underlying themes that all members of our species have in common.

I have tried in this book to suggest a way of thinking about differences by setting the heightened differences between generations, produced by social change, alongside other kinds of differences, all in stories and fragments of stories, lives in motion. The strangeness of others is most off-putting when it is experienced as static, most approachable when it is set within a narrative of continuing development. The people in this book, named and unnamed, will strike the reader as both strange and familiar, individuals growing through their own eras of knowing and unknowing, as they work out courses through an unknown landscape, the changing shapes of lives.

For nearly a decade I have taught a course at George Mason University on the way lives differ from culture to culture, using autobiography and ethnographic life history. There I get a cosmopolitan medley of students, from eighteen-year-olds to those returning to school at midlife for a second career and sixty- and seventy-year-olds pursuing learning in retirement. Reading the papers my students write, stories drawn from their own lives and from the interviews they conduct, I have had the privilege of moving through multiple lives. In the spring semester of 1996, I was invited to Atlanta to teach a version of my life history course at Spelman, a historically black women's college. During the planning for my visit, however, I balked at the probable makeup of my class, the lack of a kind of diversity I needed, that would allow members of the class to learn from one another. What I balked at was not that all the students would be female or "of color" but that they all would be at the same stage in their lives. Instead of worrying about whether I was the only white person in the room, I was worried that everyone else there would be less than half my age. Since I would be teaching about life histories, I wanted students who had experienced aging and childbearing, but I had another concern as well. I wanted to use differences of age within the group to set the stage for learning from one another and opening up further differences within the group, even as we read life histories from other times and cultures.

I went to George Mason University, and later to Spelman College, to have the experience of teaching in unfamiliar regions and kinds of institutions. Mason is a newcomer to Virginia's state university system. Located in Northern Virginia, just outside the District of Columbia, where more and more immigrant groups have come to live, it attracts a wide variety of students—Dominicans and Somalis, Cambodians and Iranians—echoing the upheavals of recent history. Washington was a small town until World War II, when it became a community of migrants within America, and it is still full of transients passing through or recently returned from service overseas. The Mason campus is ringed with parking lots, and the student center is reminiscent of a mall, drawing in a population on the move.

Spelman, by contrast, represents over a century of tradition. It is one of a cluster of historically black institutions in Atlanta that affirm the commonalities of the African American community while at the same time providing a sheltered place to explore the variety within that community. Spelman's whole existence is a reminder of the values and dilemmas of difference that must be addressed in an interdependent world.

I first visited Spelman a decade ago, when a close friend, Johnnetta Cole, became its first black female president. I wrote about her in *Composing a Life,* using a series of conversations with four friends to explore the creativity of how women and men increasingly live, without scripts or blueprints, composing and learning along the way.

Spelman fits a model familiar to anyone who has explored American education, the elite liberal arts college, designed to select promising young people after high school, give them both depth and polish, and prepare them to go out and live their adult lives, often with a stopoff in graduate school. Spelman has struggled to give its students confidence as women and as African Americans, to help them claim and value their own variety and draw on the models and achievements of people of color in other countries and especially throughout the African diaspora.

Often white Americans lack a sense of the diversity within the black community, and becoming aware of that diversity with curiosity and respect is a first step into familiarity. Those who repeat the old alibi "They all look the same, you can't tell them apart" often leap to conclusions about an entire community from a single anecdote or the remarks of one person, assuming other kinds of homogeneity, economic, social, or political. No wonder the encounter feels uncomfortable—natural human groups are not monolithic, and the illusion of uniformity is daunting to outsiders. At the same time one of the great burdens on members of any minority in an integrated setting is the expectation that they will be interchangeable, with an implied obligation to represent the group.

There is a more subtle dynamic than similarity when groups withdraw from the majority and hang out together, and this is the pleasure of differing among themselves. It is true that social scientists can predict much of what each of us is likely to think or do from a set of descriptors—age, gender, class, ethnicity, and background—but there is a core that is distinctive and individual for every person. That core of individuality shines out when I am with others who are similar but not the same. Ironically, we seek out similarity to discover and celebrate uniqueness. In any group that has been subject to prejudice and stereotyping, members need to look newly and clearly not only at themselves but also at one another, finding not only strength but also variety.

There is a bewildering array of genetic and cultural diversity on the Spelman campus. Although most Africans brought to the Americas as slaves came from West Africa, Africa is the seedbed of all human diversity, including to this day a wide range of ecological adaptations and traditions as well as different physical types, from the smallest stature to the tallest, from the very thin and long-boned to the most ample of curves, across a range of coloration. The ancient diversity of the continent has been amplified in the diaspora by the reunion with other human strains long dispersed to Europe and Asia and the Americas.

No human skin is either truly black or truly white, but some of

these women are so dark that their skin almost matches their graduation robes, while some come closer to the white dresses beneath
them. Here, where social convention defines almost everyone as belonging to one "race," the students play with their differences from
one another and enhance them by their choices, using variations of di-
alect and pronunciation to set different moods. It has been important
to learn not only that black is beautiful but that there is a whole spec-
trum of African American beauty. The poet Langston Hughes saw it
and found it sweet: chocolate, brown sugar, caramel, peach.

This variation, which is ignored by the crude oversimplification of
the color line, is the basis for another kind of bias common in non-
English-speaking countries and within the African American community itself. Differences of shade can be a source of pain as well as a
delight, and I heard this repeatedly in the stories students told me. A
husband accuses his wife of unfaithfulness when a child is darker—or
lighter—than expected. A dark-complected girl teases her fairer
younger sister, saying that she is really an abandoned white child, not
part of the family at all. A young woman dreaming of applying to Spelman hears the old cliché from her neighbors that only the very light-
skinned are wanted there. Yet the most telling differences may have to
do with upbringing. Once, at a northern college, I sat with a group of
faculty interviewing a series of applicants for a traveling fellowship,
and a mahogany-colored young man, adopted in East Africa, began his
presentation by saying, "As you can see, I'm a German Jew." There are
students like him at Spelman as well, who have come there to explore
the counterpoint between their skin color and the people they have
grown up to be.

Spelman is full of surprises. It reminded me of Israel, where Jews
from all over the world believe they are more similar than they really
are and where a common origin and a common pain offer a way to

bridge huge cultural differences. Spelman students are all bright, but backgrounds and qualities of mind differ and there are many different intelligences reflected here. Many belong to the traditional black Protestant churches, but these range from strict fundamentalism through the many expressive forms of Pentecostalism to the upscale "high sididdy" stereotype of propriety—the frozen chosen of African American high society—and openness to other traditions, references to Mother-Father God and to the Yoruba deities and the ancestors. There are Muslims on this campus and agnostics, those who would welcome lesbians and those who would exclude them, those who admire Farrakhan and those who abhor his racism. There are those who are warm and responsive when I strike up conversations on campus, and others who turn away from this aging white outsider with barely muted hostility. Historically, Spelman has been associated with privilege, with the black bourgeoisie, but it struggles to broaden that base, offering as many scholarships as possible. Some parents send their daughters with designer clothes and jaunty sports cars, while others have scrimped and saved devotedly to raise even a portion of the tuition.

So there was plenty of diversity for me to work with at Spelman, but I wanted something more. I have come to believe that human beings can learn to accept and work with differences most richly from the differences that go with age and generation, differences that occur naturally within households. This learning is short-circuited when age groups are segregated as they are by schools and retirement communities, eliminating the chance to use age as a model for understanding other kinds of difference.

There is a familiar saying, "Never judge a man until you have walked a mile in his moccasins." It is through the passing of time that this adage becomes most accessible. I can spend a lifetime knowing men as friends and colleagues, lovers and kinsmen, sharing some of their changes, but I will never live out the experience of being male. I can explore what it feels like to be isolated or to be an outsider, but I can never know what it feels like to have grown up as an African American. In the normal sequence of events, the young will become older and the old can recall being young, and therefore all of us know what it feels like to live in changing bodies and meet the world with changing minds; there is no comparable way of exchanging moccasins across lines of race and gender. Some years ago, working on a memoir of my parents, Margaret Mead and Gregory Bateson, I became sharply aware of how my capacity to understand them has increased since I reached my forties, for this is how old they were when I became able to observe and remember them with the limited understanding of a child. Now I grow older with their maturing spirits beside me, reinterpreting their later years as I encounter my own.

Reaching across a gap of strangeness, all parents draw on the memories of childhood—the games they played, the nursery rhymes they heard, the punishments they feared. Because the world has so greatly changed, however, we cannot re-create that world for our own children and probably would not want to. No one today can walk the same mile as a parent or a mentor, for the landscape has altered. But we can learn to talk about the shifting contours. Awareness of these differences may still be helpful.

Teaching anthropology on American campuses, I am well aware that college students have a world at their fingertips, but I know all too well that often they taste it only in little nips, like giveaway samples in a supermarket. I try to propose the wholeness of other ways of living or seeing by assigning full ethnographies or the book-length narratives of individual lives: better a book unfinished but still on the shelf beckoning than an excerpt quickly forgotten. Teaching in Massachusetts and Virginia and Georgia, in Manila and Tehran, I have tried to enter the classroom as a participant observer, hoping to learn from my students, even though they see me as the one who is supposed to know the answers. In a world of lifelong learning, whatever the task or role to be played at a particular moment, participant observation can become a way of living. More—because it calls for a stance of humility and wonder, learning can be pursued as a form of spirituality.

Curiosity and respect. We all fall short in these disciplines. I like to go into unfamiliar contexts and watch and listen, but I cannot attend at that depth all the time. No one can. In the same way, I cannot discipline myself, either spiritually or professionally, to look with wonder at every person on a bus, saying, This is my sister or my brother who is also profoundly different, trying to understand the complex mix of stress and contentment, estrangement and kindness in the faces. Even in the classroom, where I often have more students than I should in courses designed as seminars, some of the faces blur. We have become accustomed to hearing about culture shock, but it is also useful to think in terms of culture fatigue. I feel it too and treasure solitude. The familiar is comforting. It is easy to understand the temptation to blur one's eyes and work with stereotypes, to put aside the effort of response and recognition.

We carry with us from the far past, when such things often made for survival, the potential for rage and competition, the habit of suspicion and dislike of the unfamiliar. Certainly the capacities to learn and to create, the need to love and to be loved, are deeply rooted in human biology, but each of these has built into it an affirmation of the known that stands ready to reject what is new and strange. Social convention smooths over differences, providing scripts and costumes that allow us to meet one another in familiar roles, to say what we are expected to say and to anticipate the responses of others, but some of this harmony is illusory. Freedom reveals the underlying differences and allows them to develop. Particularly today, familiar gender roles and stages of the life cycle are shifting, so that it is no longer possible in families to rely on assumptions about the behavior of a son or a mother, a twelve-year-old or a fifty-two-year-old. A rapidly changing world requires improvisation as we find ourselves onstage without a script, perhaps with grace, perhaps in awkwardness and anger.

Over time, as human numbers have increased, we have arrived at a necessity for interdependence and empathy that goes beyond any selected for during evolution. Today the challenge is to learn and affirm new kinds of recognition both within the species and outside it. We cannot cure our estrangements and the suspicion they bring with them by ignoring difference or by imposing similarity. Somehow we must find the wisdom to live together in peace, cherishing a new generation of strangers. The homes in which we raise our children are parts of a single home we all share, for *home* does not refer now only to a household; the word can be extended to a landscape or a nation or the planet we inhabit, any one of which could be turned into a wasteland. Crowded together and struggling to survive, we risk growing to depend more and more on ancient biological impulses to dominate and to react to the unfamiliar with fight or flight, instead of that other ancient impulse, curiosity.

My sister gained insight into strangeness at home by living abroad, but Americans do not need to travel abroad or even to walk out the front door to find themselves struggling to balance the impulse to reject and the willingness to learn. Diversity is native to every household and countryside. Home is the heartland of strangeness; perhaps, then, we can learn to think of home as the best place to learn to live with strangers.

Prejudice and stereotyping are ways of making intellectual and emotional sense of a puzzling world, easy solutions to the challenges of difference. They offer the assertion of commonality with one group, denying the differences that are there, and the definition of another group as inimical and Other. When a diverse community is caught up in turmoil and uncertainty, as Yugoslavia was with the breakdown of the Eastern bloc, tribalism is the great simplifier. Serbs and Bosnians and Croats, who had lived at peace, simplified a confusing world by projecting every threat onto the other groups, hoping that ethnic cleansing could create a home that was orderly and intelligible.

Similarly, Americans often deny the strangeness within the household by projecting its threat outside the walls, outside the town limits, across national borders. Statistics show, however, that danger lies inside the boundaries: within the secrecies of family life or in the crimes of neighbor against neighbor, black on black or white on white. Again and again we hear about the surprise and shock of family members and neighbors, unaware of living side by side with potential violence. We deny the ordinary violence between young and old, male and female, and fantasize instead about supercriminals and abductions by extraterrestrials.

Even as we deny the deep unknowing of the familiar, all boundaries are increasingly permeable to the unfamiliar. It enters, day after day, in news and music from around the world, through speakers and computers and televisions, and carried by the movements of peoples from place to place. The extreme example of trying to exclude all outside influences was the terrible bloodletting in Cambodia, but efforts to block immigration or to prevent schools from teaching about other cultures are expressions of the same impulse. The rise of fundamentalist movements in our day is, among other things, an effort to make behavior more predictable and orderly, to enforce a commandment not to grow or change or question.

Other kinds of rejection are less extreme but still costly. A lack of curiosity about new neighbors has often gone in both directions and been experienced as a lack of respect. We smell other people's cooking, find their garbage more offensive than our own, and take refuge in the suburbs, where differences of class and race and even age are sorted out by geography, as if into separate nations. When a new group enters a community, kinds of dissonance that have always existed may begin to be blamed on simple but deceptive concepts like race. A girl who would have achieved only average grades under any circumstances may become a bigoted adult if many of those who surpass her have a different color skin. A boy who might have been harassed for his expensive clothing whenever he walked into a working-class neighborhood will cherish a different anger if he is harassed in a foreign accent. No wonder we project differences outward.

There is a necessary counterpoint between accepting new encounters with the strange and acknowledging the intimate strangeness of the known. In Atlanta before the Summer Olympics were held there, the city worried about how to welcome visitors from all over the world—but at the same time it was forced to become more sensitive to differences already present between rich and poor, racial antagonisms, and the possibility of homegrown terrorism. Bridging the new South and the old, becoming steadily more cosmopolitan, the city offered a test case not for unity in diversity but for civility in diversity.

When I have lived abroad I have learned to be apprehensive when someone says, We've invited the Smiths—you'll like them, they are Americans too. When my daughter was young I learned not to say, You'll enjoy playing with Bobby, he's just your age. Just because someone shares some characteristic—has the same color skin, speaks the same language with the same accent, recalls the same kind of education—does not mean that she or he sees the world in the same way. Likeness does not mean liking.

Yet we do use our similarities as links, and rely upon them. It can be painful to find that someone who seemed familiar and trustworthy has become a stranger—or has always been one behind the mask of familiarity and convention. Family members shock one another by revealing conversions or drug addictions, sudden violence or unsuspected talents and longings. Husbands or wives come home to discover that a spouse has packed and moved out; grandparents fall in love or take off on global travels; sons and daughters, claiming new sexual identities and preferences, inform their parents that now they have discovered who they really are. Because we deny the constant possibilities, we have few conventions to deal with them. The myth of mutual understanding transforms the evolutions of others into occasions for guilt—how could I not have known?—or rage.

We could instead learn to temper love like steel, with curiosity and respect, both softening and strengthening it. We could come to revel in how little we know of one another, harvesting insight, transferring it to other contexts. A New England couple, living and gardening in voluntary simplicity, once described to me the annual vacation they allow themselves, always to someplace new, carefully researched and studied in advance. Every day of their trip, they keep separate journals, and during the months that follow they read them aloud to each other, each discovering that what the other saw and noted was different— and perhaps surmising differences of experience in familiar surroundings as well, to enrich the simplicities of home. For them this is a way of recycling the luxury of travel.

Travel can be used to open eyes to the mystery of what is close to home, as it did for the generation of Americans who served in the Peace Corps and brought back a new understanding of themselves and their own traditions. Often in my writing and teaching I use examples drawn from places that seem remote, from my years of living, as an anthropologist, in Iran or the Philippines or Israel, or from the research and writing of other anthropologists. But I have come to realize that this practice is deceptive unless I also propose the discovery of difference a single breath away. The exotic is fascinating, but my examples are no more than travelers' tales unless we use them to discover—and be enriched by—the strangeness that lies closer to home. It is a mistake to think travel is necessary in order to encounter the vivid heterogeneity of humanity, or, having encountered it, to reaffirm those things that unite all human beings more fundamentally than their individual and group diversity.

All of us live today at a crossroads where the most ancient of human paths converge. Parting and coming together is the story of our species, a small group that grew and slowly spread across Africa and around the planet, diverging and inventing different ways to survive in different environments. For millennia our species became more scattered, changing gradually so that pockets of population in different places diverged, both in the way they looked and in the skills and knowledge they passed on. But virtually as soon as this process of divergence began, the reunions also began, as groups long separated met, in either conflict or new learning.

In this time of accelerating convergence we have access to a greater range of what it means to be human than ever before, but the willingness to learn and to be changed is still fragile and vulnerable to fatigue and fear. It is this willingness that we need to conserve and foster above all. We need to evoke and support it in early childhood and in the classroom. We need to affirm its continuing presence in the responsibilities of adulthood, and in the estrangements of dying. Above all, we need to understand how we can learn from one another.

Today lives move in new contours and follow unaccustomed rhythms. Their overlapping patterns offer challenges both to participation and to observation, the interwoven disciplines of curiosity and respect. The risk is that by denying so much of the strangeness we see close to home, we are caught off guard and meet it gracelessly, finding it inimical. Everyone has the chance to discover the patterns that order multiple ways of being human: through the arts, through the media, through conversations with the neighbors. At the same time one becomes aware through reflection of a more intimate diversity: within the self, now and across the life span, and within the household.

I went to Mason and then to Spelman to learn: above all, to learn more about myself. Learning, I become someone new. Now we need a new definition of the self: I am not what I know but what I am willing to learn. Mystery waits in the mirror. Curiosity and learning begin before breakfast. Growing, we move through worlds of difference, the cycles and circles of a life, fulfilled by overlapping with the lives of others.

2 | *Once Around*

At Spelman the solution Johnnetta Cole and I reached to providing age diversity for the seminar on women's life histories was to make it cross-generational, with a mix of Spelman undergraduates and older women connected in some way with the college, including Johnnetta herself.★

On the first day of class, impressions were superficial, but I could guess at the ages of the women around the table and learn a great deal from their chosen appearances. Sometimes human beings try to erase differences and sometimes we accentuate them, but everywhere we play with them, and even the superficialities are twisted, like dreadlocks, into declarations of identity. On the day of our first meeting, looking around at my Spelman students and colleagues, I could see, in

★The members of the seminar are listed in the Appendix, along with the pages on which each one is introduced or quoted extensively.

their different hairdos, ranging from a few sixties-style Afros to the windblown look of blonds in shampoo ads, with every variation in between, a freeze-frame collage of ideological and technical choices imposed on a wide variety of shades and textures, with just about half the class choosing one of the "natural" looks. Many dos, I later learned, are costly in time or money or comfort: braids are purchased and painstakingly attached, while dreads—or Nubian locks—demand care and can recall the saying I too heard as a child, "You must suffer to be beautiful."

It would be the third week of class before I had everyone sorted out, names matched to faces. The youngest member of the class was a sophomore, Hillary Ferguson, an enthusiastic tennis player, breezing in from practice with a baseball cap worn backwards, lifting spirits with fresh and quirky perceptions. It was Hillary who told me about the discomforts of being the lightest-skinned member of her family and about how important it was to her to affirm her blackness. Some of the juniors or seniors were much more clearly ideological in their style, with dreads or overalls, inclined to make theoretical arguments. My eye hesitated when I reached Pat Bakr, not sure where she fit in, for at forty-three she was older than most Spelman undergraduates, a single mother back in college after a marriage to a Muslim man ended in divorce. The older women ranged from the youngest, Fleda Mask Jackson, a Spelman faculty member often sporting a bright red beret, to Marymal Dryden, an alumna approaching seventy, consistently elegant in a parade of Afrocentric outfits.

We were eighteen women, clustered by age, so that most of the members of one group could have been the mothers or grandmothers of the others. In the end, there were two other white women in the room, one in each age group, an exchange student from Scotland and

Cree Durrett, who had become a long-term friend of Spelman after her marriage brought her south to Atlanta.

This way of putting together a class sounded interesting, though I by no means understood the implications when we started. I had not thought through the fact that these two generations would meet across an especially great gulf of historical and cultural change. The older women would all have experienced legal segregation and would remember demonstrations and assassinations, sexual revolution, the antiwar movement, and the resurgence of feminism, while the under-graduates would all have been born since the years of the Civil Rights Movement and would be looking ahead to new kinds of uncertainty.

I have struggled for a term to use for the older members of the class. They were not technically enrolled, so they could be called *auditors,* but they did far more than sit and listen. Instead they plunged in, arguing, making presentations, and writing papers. I scoured the thesaurus and toyed with the idea of calling them *veterans* and the undergraduates *recruits,* or calling them *oaks* and the undergraduates *saplings.* In the end I have called them *elders,* which resonates with the traditional African American respect for age, but I hope every reader will bear in mind as well that these were stylish, energetic women of the modern era, in no way over the hill.

During my semester at Spelman I got to know the members of the seminar and many other women on the campus. Some appear here only in brief vignettes, while others appear with longer narratives, stories they shared that counterpointed the ones we read together. Anyone telling a life story evokes a world and refers to overlapping lives, the parents and friends and lovers who come into the telling. But when women write about their lives, they typically speak of relationships more than men do, and they often describe themselves as responding to others and to circumstance rather than acting alone. To be good mothers women have needed not only to teach but to learn how to respond to the unfolding mystery of each successive child. Such continuous learning carries over to other areas and blossoms into skills of adaptation and improvisation.

Similarly, anyone telling a life story uses ideas about the shape and punctuation of lives, which are often clearer in the lives of women than in the lives of men. All the students I meet now have a dawning awareness that the shape of lives is changing, creating new dissonance between generations. Lives are more variable and unpredictable than ever before, demanding new ways of entering adulthood, new eras of maturity, a new approach to death. These topics are especially urgent for women, for whom no past culture provides adequate models. Women today read autobiographies from other times and places in the awareness that in the richly diverse world they will live in, they must try to understand their neighbors and improvise their lives from a world of possibilities. It is good to have a wealth of models, for sometimes local ways of thinking about lives interfere with the ability to live them well, turning those that do not conform into perceived failures.

We practice the art of living in telling stories, whether spoken or written or imagined in secret, dreamed or planned, past or future. I have come to think of the composition of lives as an art form, and of families and communities as artful tales in progress. In some societies the arts hold to familiar forms and lives are largely predictable. But in the modern era individual artists are expected to invent distinctive styles, with an uneasy eye on the critics, or to borrow eclectically across distance or time. There are lives that resemble artworks planned in detail in advance, but for most of us, even though we persist in telling the young that they should have clearly defined goals, the improvisational arts are more apt. The creations of working artists, still in progress, some lives seem more beautiful than others, regardless of fame, regardless of suffering. We do judge ourselves and others.

We practice the art of living as we read also, picking our way past similarities and contrasts in the writings of others. The women whose life histories we used in class were with us in that room.★ A few books turn up on the reading list virtually every time I teach. Marjorie Shostak's extraordinary *Nisa,* about a San (Bushman) woman in Africa, offers the words of a woman as distant as she could possibly be from us in the material facts of her hunting-gathering life and in the way the stages of her life unfold, so different that we hardly feel we share the same biology. In *The Woman Warrior,* Maxine Hong Kingston, as a daughter of Chinese immigrants, uses fantasy and folklore to show how it is possible to see the familiar American social landscape through totally different eyes—and demonstrates that life history is not always constructed from literal truths. *Coming of Age in Mississippi,* by Anne Moody, describes the struggle and self-affirmation of a young black woman, writing at the age the students are now but living in the era when the elders were that age. I assigned one of my own books, *Composing a Life,* the story not of one life but of five. I always include at least one "novel" that raises the question of the autobiographical sources of all writing, so we read *Nervous Conditions* by Tsitsi Dangarembga.

There is a temptation to teach with excerpts, but these cannot show how a particular author frames her story, where she begins and where she ends. When whole books are assigned, not everyone completes them all by the date of discussion—but then no one gets all the juice out of a complex story on the first reading. I like to imagine the

★The readings for the seminar are listed in full in the Appendix.

books revisited and then lent out to friends, part of developing dialogue.

In order to read life histories with intelligence and sensitivity, it is
important to try one's hand at autobiography as well. Six weeks into
the semester, members of the seminar handed in portions of their
own life stories to set beside the ones we were reading. Hillary re-
called my preference for whole books and evoked a manuscript a hy-
pothetical 480 pages in length, even though she handed in only two
"excerpts," labeled pages 13–19 and 244–247. Because the group was
small enough to do so, I asked several of the women to read us sections from their narratives; they included Marymal Dryden, the oldest member of the class, who described her youth and her first
marriage, and Imani Romney-Rosa, one of the undergraduates. Their
willingness to share what they had written marked the distance we
had come from our first meeting. What these two women, five
decades apart in age, wrote and later said gives a sense of the range and
vitality in that room and the contrasting voices of two generations exchanging experiences across a great gap of cultural change. Both writers surprised the other members of the class and, in the writing,
surprised themselves.

It was Marymal, with her billowing, exotic robes and waved white
hair, who reminded me of an oak tree in full leaf, so "that the birds of
the heaven come and lodge in the branches thereof." Her writing
made a vivid impression not only on me but on the students in the
class, who felt she had given them a glimpse into the lives and times of
the elders.

When Marymal spoke about her life, she started by describing a
much protected seedling. "I had some very strict rules and a great deal
of emphasis on being a lady. You represented your family, so how you
behaved was a reflection on your family, and you did not want to do

anything to disgrace them. I always had that in mind, and I never got too far off the beaten path. The kind of fella that asked to kiss or— God forbid—anything else was not a good man to know, not the kind of fella my mother described as the kind to listen to. One of the courtship rituals at Spelman was to walk around the oval, and there was this fella who would come by very dutifully on courting days and we would walk the circuit. He made no demands, and he always had this friend with him. Then about twenty years later I met him again and I said, Aha! He and this fella who was walking with us all the time were lovers. Well, he'd just seemed like the epitome of what my mother approved of.

"I'm kinda glad that I lived the way I did, because when I see people I knew when I was at Spelman they can look at me and say I was always a lady. Mom's warnings about my virtue, her expressed fears, were always paramount in my mind: Do Not Get Pregnant! But no advice about the facts of life was offered. 'Just don't do it!' She literally scared my legs together. Sexual activity was viewed as fearful, unfulfilling, not very satisfying, and full of risks. Now I realize that my mom's sexual life must have been filled with frustration. I wish we could have had more open discussions."

Marymal's first marriage lasted for nine years of social, prosperous living with her lawyer husband, George. She had graduated from Spelman and gotten a degree in social work at Atlanta University, following the insistence of her mother and grandmother: "Get your education, and you will always be able to take care of yourself and not be dependent. You won't have to take any *stuff*!" When she married, no one would have thought her choice inappropriate; within a few years she could say, "My husband is a brilliant, handsome, up-and-coming, successful young attorney at law; I have three adorable sons, all born within a four-year period, a lovely home, and status in our community. Don't I have it all?" But then she had to ask herself, "Why am I miserable?" Like so many other women of that era and since, Marymal woke up to the fact that she had become trapped in the conventional roles of wife and mother and become a stranger to herself.

Marymal's father had gone to Tuskegee when George Washington Carver was there—arguing the appropriateness of practical, vocational education for the Negro—and later he had worked as a railway porter and then as a teacher at a vocational school. Her mother had two years of college and worked as a matron in the county jail. Marymal herself was a catch, educated, beautiful, refined, and her husband often teased her about being a "Spelman woman."

Although they moved in separate circles, women like Marymal followed the patterns of white middle-class society—what black Atlantans sometimes refer to as the "majority culture"—in assuming that marriage and childbearing would be the center of their lives. Often they married right out of college and had children while they were still unformed as adults. Many of my classmates at Radcliffe in the fifties followed the same pattern as Marymal, marrying men who would be expected to provide for them and would, in turn, expect them to reflect credit back on them by entertaining and maintaining a glamorous image. In the black community, however, it was the norm for women to work. "I wasn't marrying to settle down and not have a career," Marymal emphasized to me. "I have met friends from other racial groups for whom marriage *was* their career. That was their goal in life, but they weren't ending up happily ever after. They were so frustrated, but they still had the attitude of being rescued. I never had the attitude of being rescued.

"I tended to do what they expected of me. I finished high school, college, got my master's, got a job, had my children. It was all in a progression. A social work degree in that time was like an MBA, so when I was married to George, wherever we went, I just got a job. But when the children came I didn't work, they came in rapid succession."

As Marymal wrote the story and read it in class, the inspiration she needed to take charge of her life and her future came not from her mother, concerned with what the neighbors might think, or from the friends who surrounded her and her husband, but from a portrait of a woman named Rosalee. Marymal and her husband had begun to build an art collection as part of being among the "beautiful people," but this time their guests rejected her taste: "What do you see in this painting? She looks really depressed, as if she had a really hard life." This set Marymal wondering, "Am I that different, my tastes so different?" With her paper, she included a copy of the portrait, part of the final art school project of the artist Herman "Kofi" Bailey, who described the subject as a black tenant farmer in rural Alabama.

"Once while looking at the picture of Rosalee, I saw something in her expression. It was as if she was speaking to me. As if she was quoting snippets of Langston Hughes's classic poem 'Mother to Son': 'Well, Son, I'll tell you./Life for me ain't been no crystal stair.' In Rosalee I saw determination, hope, a willingness to fight against the odds, working from sunup to sundown, in conditions akin to slavery. Always tired, with few comforts, little money." But Marymal's husband and their friends did not respond to what she saw, so the picture brought into focus not only a neglected part of their reality but Marymal's realization that she was living with strangers.

Against her mother's urging Marymal decided she had to leave. Realizing she could not take her children until she could get her own life together, find a job and housing, she set out for Cleveland with one suitcase and fifty dollars from her housekeeping money, and found a job in child welfare. "George would send postcards and address me as the 'mother of my sons who has abandoned them.' It was just so ludicrous. He wanted the kids, but I knew him well enough to know that wasn't going to last, not three children, three little boys. That's a big responsibility." It was not long before the boys arrived in Cleveland. "Once he realized that I wasn't ever coming back and his ego was massaged enough, we were able to communicate more. He knew I was totally unprepared for taking care of three little boys, 'cause I had just rented a room and I had no furniture, so one weekend he brought the children to visit. He said, 'I really think the boys need to be with you,' so he just left them." Marymal improvised and coped.

Later Marymal told me that after their divorce, she found out George had been having an affair with a woman in his office. "I knew he wouldn't ever marry this woman, but she didn't know that. He was the kind of man who liked trophy wives. . . . I'm glad I found all this stuff out after we were divorced. Anyway, that young lady worked for him, and I did know she would take very good care of the children. A lot of this stuff was so painful I had actually blocked it out and didn't really recall it until I started writing my story for class."

Marymal today has multiple versions of her résumé, one a summary, one focusing on international programs, and another on domestic. Happy in a third marriage, she now has five grandchildren. She said to me, about halfway through the seminar, "I've been thinking over what you've said, and I've decided that I really have had a very successful life." Marymal was one of the students who reported in class on *Blackberry Winter*, the autobiography of my mother, Margaret Mead. Like Marymal, my mother was married three times and had to deal with the cultural bias that suggests that the termination of any marriage is a failure on the woman's part. My mother did not regard her marriages as failures, though I think she grieved for the rest of her life about being rejected by my father, and she prided herself on maintaining a friendship with each of her ex-husbands. Whatever the understanding of divorce, Marymal's life is impressive as a record of decisions taken about what wasn't working and the adaptations she was able to make, not a straight line but a series of chapters, a zigzag development.

Marymal described her encounter with a piece of art as providing the framework for rethinking her life; now she had the task of composing it in a new way in a new place. At first she was very much alone, and it took time to put her life together and make space for her children. Like an artist gradually adding different shapes and colors and bringing them into relationship on a canvas, she found ways to fit together the pieces of her life. Many women today, with greater resources, are similarly preoccupied with the problems of composing lives that include both child rearing and career. The most common way of describing this complex composition is the cliché of juggling, a pernicious metaphor because it suggests a frivolous trifling with what is most precious—and constant anxiety about dropping something, perhaps a baby. The metaphor of composing suggests instead a search for distinctive ways of fitting diverse elements into a unity, combining the familiar and the new, as artists work within their traditions and blend in materials from other cultures in novel ways. One advantage of aesthetic judgment is that we are accustomed to the idea that fashions change and tastes may vary.

Music is composed in a different sense, unfolding through time with interwoven continuities and discontinuities, development and resolution. More and more people today have to find meaning in lives like Marymal's that do not follow a single clear plan. We face interruptions, downsizing and layoffs, returns to school for retraining, time off for childbearing . . . but we want to recognize all the twists and turns as parts of a single life, as expressions of a coherent identity, finding the familiar in the strange. How are the periods between transitions to be understood—as chapters? the movements of a symphony? the verses of a poem? Tastes change. Often we interpret the unexpected as a sign of failure, but we no longer expect each new generation to be an overlapping repetition of the previous one like the lines of a canon or round.

When new works that artists offer seem inharmonious or unsatisfying to a particular generation, as they have again and again, they may prefigure a change in the shapes of lives or in the way lives interconnect. Lives that seem admirable in one setting may be rejected in another, and the most puzzling behavior of a neighbor or family member may express an unfamiliar sense of grace or balance. Yet a comparison with the arts is a reminder that curiosity and respect do not necessarily entail imitation.

Composing suggests a continuing search both for harmony and for dynamic dissonance, the many elements never brought into perfect balance, certainly never completely merged. Within the last generation old metaphors of community, especially the metaphor of the melting pot with its suggestion of homogeneity, have been rejected. As a child I imagined a melting pot as an old-fashioned stewpot and rather liked the image of myself simmering in a wonderful spicy bouillabaisse, not homogeneous at all. In fact the reference is to the melting down of scrap metal, often enough to make bullets. More common today is the metaphor of a salad, in which the different elements remain recognizable, tossed up in a common dressing. But no single dish is an adequate metaphor for a diverse community. Good cooking, in my view, involves composition and often improvisation. The elements that give a meal its distinctive zest are sometimes mixed and sometimes not, sometimes side by side and sometimes in sequence.

There are other metaphors that pervade discussions of human lives, and these too can be expected to change. It has often been useful to think of lives as having a shape, outlined by biology but modified again and again by culture. The image underlying discussions of development or education is often a ladder or flight of stairs: the ascent must be made in sequence, with each step seen as an achievement providing access to the next, a foundation underlying subsequent progress. Today, however, such continuing progress seems uncertain and foundations seem infirm.

The stories our children need most to hear are not the stories of daunting success, achievements so impressive and final that they are hard to identify with, but the repeatable stories of composing and improvisation, in which adaptation is more central than dazzling accomplishment. Learning occurs in stages, but the process never completely ends for the individual even as it is repeated from generation to generation. In a world of accelerating change every graduate needs to understand that much of the shiny new learning is obsolescent, while the authority of elders is contingent on their willingness to continue to learn even as they teach. When society is fluid, young and old alike need to improvise and to teach each other. Wisdom is gradually revealing a whole new meaning, traced out through the life cycle. Today we do well to think of wisdom as depending on the flexibility, playfulness, and willingness to learn that are sometimes lost or denied with age, the kind of intelligence that includes self-criticism and the habit of reflecting on experience.

Narratives focus on dramatic events and transitions. But within our repertoire of ways of thinking about human lives, we need ways of thinking of the plateaus between transitions, long periods of little obvious change or learning, when maintenance and continuity are paramount, even as we remember that all such periods are temporary. We are skilled, in this culture, at talking about change and transformation, not so skilled at thinking about sustaining what follows. We deal with ongoing problems with quick campaigns promising spurious victories: crash diets instead of new habits, urban renewal by bulldozer, or such a flurry of simultaneous experiments in schools that parents and children are simply bewildered. Excitement about change leads all too readily to short-term efforts that are abandoned as quickly as they begin to show results.

Some diagrams of lives move straight across the page while others rise. In most human cultures age has been respected, and often an ascent continues even beyond death, for "now we see through a glass, darkly, but then face to face." "He will go from strength to strength," in the words of the Anglican burial service. In some traditions there is a progression from one life to the next, while in others the authoritative voices of the ancestors weaken slowly over time.

Other traditions see a similarity between the end of life and its beginning, and depict a rising trajectory turning downward into a declivity, just as our accounts of history often deal with an ebb and a flow, a rise and a fall: of a movement, an empire, a fashion. Americans have been all too ready to take the metaphor of ascent only through middle age, and to regard the rest as over the hill. The curve may even be reversed, falling and rising again, tracing the loss and recovery of innocence: for the Balinese, infants and old people are revered as closest to the gods.

When aging is seen as a return to the beginning, the young and the old are brought closer together and everyone is aware of a cyclical repetition from generation to generation. Erik Erikson, perhaps the most insightful recent thinker about the life cycle, used diagrams that seemed to suggest a sequence of *steps* but usually spoke of lives in terms of *cycles,* one of the most common metaphors of pattern through time, although he never drew them. Linear diagrams seem simply to end at the margin of the page; a cycle, by contrast, returns on its path.

The model that I find most comfortable is a spiral, which suggests both development and return. From above it looks like a circle. From the side it looks like a zigzag. A spiral models both a temporal movement and an internal process of reflection, revisiting experience through new eyes. But any of these models plays out differently today because the timing of lives is so changed and because the new timing puts generations out of step with one another.

Marymal had a kind of charisma for the young women in the class, for even though she did not fit their assumptions about successful lives, she had an unmistakable aura of success. If she was like the generous oak tree, firmly planted, then beside her Iyabo Morrison, the tallest of the students, was like a slim, resilient sapling. When Iyabo talked to me about why she valued the cross-generational structure of the group, she was especially grateful to Marymal for telling us about her first marriage because she was not used to hearing older people she admired acknowledging the losses and failures in their lives. "You know," she said, "I guess we expect, when we graduate from Spelman, we're gonna be successful, have a husband. I guess Marymal sharing about her divorce and eventually having three different marriages, that surprised me. That story could take place at any time, in the nineties or whenever it happened to her. The things that were kept quiet might not necessarily be kept quiet now, but our problems seem to be the same, just different time periods that they take place. It's really useful to talk to people who have done a beautiful job with their lives with what they found, and to know they've had to struggle." Stories like Marymal's encourage the younger generation to do some growing up before they commit themselves to marriage.

Iyabo was twenty when she took the course, a junior at Spelman, the only child of an academic family in Syracuse, New York. She had all the uncertainties that surround the end of college, even though she had lived a year in Europe with her parents and spent a year as an exchange student in San Diego, where she felt she carried the burden of representing not her family but the black community. I have a snapshot of her with an Afro that must have been taken then, but by the time I met her at Spelman she was enjoying the freedom of wearing her hair in an unideological pageboy cut.

"I feel like I'm getting old," she said, "and the real world is approaching. I'm not really ready to be a senior." For one of her papers she interviewed a Libyan friend who had married at nineteen and was about to have a baby. Then at the end, she wrote, "Someone asked me, if someone proposed to me now, would I do it? A hearty *no.*" Yet the following fall she said, "I'm in a Mecca for intelligent black men, but my mother fears I'll be lonely for the rest of my life." Sheltered behind thick-rimmed glasses, Iyabo was reserved in class, but when she and I sat down together she took the initiative, systematically quizzing me about my life and my own marriage.

Cheryl Chisholm, another one of the elders, a writer and filmmaker, had also had to struggle, but the students found themselves admiring her poise and independence even as they occasionally detected the pain in her voice. She said to me later, "One of the things I *didn't* talk about in the seminar was exactly what the students are about to go into, that I wouldn't go back to for anything—my twenties, which were the worst decade of my life."

For many women marriage is a mode of self-definition that is singularly hard to escape. When Erikson described a crisis of identity as the central issue of adolescence and youth, he wrote about the risk of foreclosing identity, getting locked too early into a particular understanding of who to be. Marymal's early marriage and childbearing had locked her into a social position she found uncomfortable, and it took great courage to escape, since it looked so desirable, so successful. Cheryl, at that age, faced the same kind of problem, success that could become a trap.

Imani Romney-Rosa was close to fifty years younger than Marymal. She had been awarded a coveted Presidential Scholarship to Spelman, but like many members of her generation she had brought with her a complex set of issues of self-definition. Imani's parents are both from the Caribbean, her mother from English-speaking Trinidad and her father from Puerto Rico. The hyphen in her name seemed to carry a weight of symbolism, at once an inverted echo of Spanish custom and a claim to the non-Hispanic side of her ancestry, a feminist assertion of the right not to be named by a man and a claim that her divorced parents are united in her. Imani's hair and golden coloring would identify her as "black" anywhere in North America, but the surname Rosa identifies her as Hispanic—as coming from a community that draws no sharp line of race. She would be one of many who would be uncomfortable with the categories of the U.S. census.

Imani has a quality of great sweetness, gentle eyes, and a soft voice. She camouflages her weight in shapeless casual garments, unlike some of the older women who used their weight and curves in majestic self-assertion. By the time of this writing, Imani had dropped and then restored the hyphen. She described herself as "Black, Puerto Rican . . . bisexual, womanist, overweight." Moving between two households, she grew up "between Happy Valley Amherst [where her mother is a psychotherapist and teaches at Hampshire College] and the South Bronx, where people get shot every day."

Whereas Marymal's early life was overdetermined by convention and the expectations of those around her, Imani has had to find a path through ambiguity. When the class wrote about their lives, Imani wrote not about the enigmas of ethnicity that affect her but about the enigmas of sexual orientation, describing a transient romance with a friend she had met in high school. Like Marymal, she read portions to the class. "I began to become drawn to Alison [not a real name] at the Gay Pride March in Northampton, without my even knowing it. It was the first time I had gone to the Pride March since I was five years old, but the emotions of that day would not be like those of thirteen years before. It was a brilliant day! There was laughter in the air, and energy whirling around us. Towering above us was the balloon rainbow that would lead the parade down Main Street.

"Throughout the day she slowly pulled me in. Seeing all the same-sex love that was surrounding us, we were comfortable holding hands, showing a different kind of love. We, in fact, spent the entire weekend together attending different events, her drawing me in the whole while, with her charm, her flirtation, and her true love for me as a close friend.

"We'd been friends for a few years, having met in peer education and counseling training, and we did a few workshops together, mostly on self-esteem, for elementary school students. She knew how to make absorbing information fun for the kids. Alison was a kid herself among all the little sixth-graders. We were also both part of the Women's Collective and a program called the Gender Series. The WC was a group of high school women who met every two weeks, over a meal, of course, to talk about ourselves. We discussed current events, studies, lectures, and ongoing programs in the area. We talked about sexuality, abortion, racism, the Women's Movement, being a woman at our high school, and a plethora of other things. Sometimes we agreed, sometimes we disagreed, but we were always respectful of one another and our multiple opinions.

"Alison was one of the first two women to come out as bisexual to the Women's Collective during one of our meetings, the other being a friend of mine also. She and I were what I would call close friends then. The Women's Collective forged friendships that were like no others. Our weekly meetings were sacred to us, me especially. This group of extraspecial women had formed a relationship that was safe, that was comfortable, and that was homey. I acted as facilitator of both the WC and the Gender Series. They had become my babies. They were my heart.

"It was into that environment that I also came out as bi, later that month. This brought Alison and me closer together, on a new level. Over my last year in high school, my friendship with Alison grew. She became one of my closest friends. It was to her and another good friend of mine that I passed on the responsibility of facilitating the Women's Collective, while I made strides toward my dream of going to Spelman College.

"At Spelman I decided to join the Lesbian and Bisexual Alliance, hoping to find a 'Black Women's Collective.' In my mind, it could only be better. Instead, what I found were black women who were afraid for their safety, black women who were angry at straight women for ostracizing them from the Sisterhood, and blaming the straight allies who were in the room. There was neither the warmth nor the cohesion of my Women's Collective. Furthermore, I was not presiding and in control of the direction the meeting took. I was disgusted with the proposal, made in the presence of the straight people, to have separate meetings for the lesbian and bisexual women. There was clearly an issue of trust in play here.

"By this point I had denounced my bisexuality. Being bi meant something different to my sisters than to me. This network would not be supportive to me, so I took my own path, leaving the Spelman LBA behind. At that point, I was unable even to make suggestions as to improvements which could be made with the group.

"Was my definition of bisexuality white? Was it Amherst? Or was it just mine? I was not afraid to let others know. I was not angered by reactions of uninformed/misinformed straights, I was disappointed, and saw where I had work to do. I dropped—the title at any rate. Having only been attracted to, and not involved with, one woman, the last few months of my senior year, perhaps I had been too quick to label myself. Besides that, I preferred playing the ally rather than the targeted; it made more of a positive statement about the greatness of the lesbian, bisexual, and gay communities. Anyway, no sense in getting myself involved with a group that would add to the other oppressions I experience from being Black, Puerto Rican, a womanist, and a woman, right?

"That was only the beginning of many issues I would have at Spelman. Though I thrived in the classroom, I had trouble finding my niche. I felt far from the people I loved and trusted most, the people I'd gone to school with the last thirteen years of my life, with whom I had made solid bonds. Now, in this new environment, not quite knowing how to reach out, how to make new friends, or how to truly trust people, both in my sadness and in my victories, I felt lost."

As I worked on this book, I became concerned about using Imani's story about Alison and other material from her childhood, and about whether she was comfortable with all this as a permanent part of her public identity. Imani had recently become engaged and then broken her engagement to a young man from Kenya, and no one can know what lies ahead. In my years of reading student autobiographical writings at Mason, I have encountered stories of self-discovery as gay—

and, more recently, stories of falling in love with a member of the opposite sex after years of a same-sex relationship. People change. Greater openness in society has produced greater fluidity, flow in both directions, but there are plenty of prejudices still. Her response was, "I think it's important in the book to say that I'm bisexual. I think throughout people's lives they tend to lean more one side than the other . . . most everybody is along a continuum. I don't think it's something I'll go back on and try to hide like they do smoking pot."

"You're saying that whatever choices you make later, the fact you've had a woman lover has shaped you in important ways?" I asked.

Imani nodded emphatically. "I think that the emotional connectedness that women have, even if they're never physically intimate, is so much deeper."

Imani's relationship with Alison had developed but did not follow a steady course. "I tried to express some of my frustrations to her, but without really telling her what they were. I mean, at the time I wasn't comfortable saying, 'I'm attracted to you, but I think you're the world's greatest tease,' not only because it wasn't such a nice thing to say, not only because it didn't totally convey my message, but because *I* didn't want to know I was attracted to her. Alison is the kind of 'guy' your mother tells you to look out for: she's sexy, she talks a great line, and when she's sucked you dry of all attention, love, and whatever else she's needy of at the moment, she's gone like the wind. Anyway, I didn't want to imagine that I was falling for such a person, a person who I knew would make me feel on top of the world for a moment but in the end, hurt me deeply. So, I postponed it, at least consciously."

Imani and Alison experienced the same kinds of tensions that heterosexual couples experience, seeking intimacy across a gap of unknowing and trying to satisfy desire without threatening friendship. After returning from her freshman year at Spelman, Imani pressed Alison to sort out with her what was happening between them. They used the conflict resolution techniques they had learned in peer counseling to try to find their way and traced their history together as each one saw it. Then, "I explained to her about how hurt I was," Imani wrote. "She was such a tease. She'd say things about how much she really cared about and was attracted to me, then the next minute she was shutting me out. We would have the most intimate moments, I mean from our hearts, not from our libidos, and then she'd push me away. I knew she was afraid of being hurt and loving too much, but I wouldn't hurt her. I did love her, and I would never do anything that would put her heart at risk. I told her, 'I love you. I want to make love with you.'

" 'I don't know what to say.'

" 'Good. Neither do I.'

"We looked at each other, nervous, aroused, and confused. 'What if we just date?' Alison suggested.

" 'Sounds good, and if anything happens we promise it won't be a one-night thing.'

" 'No. Definitely not a one-night thing.'

" 'Okay.' So, now what? I'm thinking to myself. What does dating a woman, Alison, mean? Does this mean we get to hold hands and cuddle the rest of the night? Does it mean we look at each other with the Look? Well, I'm happy no matter what it means. We spent the rest of the evening kickin' it in her room with her friends, and mostly trying to figure out what dating did mean.

"Sleep time came. The anxiety with which this hour had approached was unprecedented. After an entire evening of waiting, wishing, hoping, and being disappointed, this would be the determining factor, or so I thought then, of whether or not we were truly dating, and whether or not Alison's proposal to date was simply to placate me.

" 'Where should I sleep?' I asked, hoping she would pull back the covers she was under, looking so delectable.

" 'Anywhere.' Gulp. 'No, here,' Alison said, pulling the covers back, 'but I have a cold.'

"*Yes!!!* I was psyched. I had high expectations, but I knew I could be satisfied just lying next to her for the night. My expectations, however, were not only met but surpassed. Alison and I traveled to a different world that night. We were oblivious to our surroundings, including her roommate. We were inside each other and exchanging places. We were moving in and out, among and around, consciousness and fantasy. After months of anticipation, this was more than I could ever want. This was the best and remains the best physical experience of my life. I felt every part of her body against my body, with my hands and with my tongue, as she did mine. I held her, close to my body and close to my heart, wishing for forever.

"Lying in bed with her, the next morning, I said, 'I love you, Alison.' She distanced herself, closing her emotions off from me. It was the end, if there had ever been a true beginning. I'd seen the signs, all of the signs, which had told me the night before that it wouldn't last, wouldn't work, and couldn't, but I wanted it so badly, wanted her so badly. So, this was how it ended, the end of the pretense of some sort of relationship."

Imani and I were having lunch together in Amherst, where she had transferred to the University of Massachusetts to be closer to her family, when I explored with her for this book her current views on bisexuality. "I think probably if I hadn't been around the Valley so long I wouldn't have been bisexual. It's very trendy to be bisexual now. The women I knew in Amherst said, 'Care for who you care for. The most important things are, Do you like them, do they respect you . . . and after that it's, Oh, are they male or female?'

"I think being bisexual is an important part of who I am," she continued. "It's also connected to my experience of sexual assault when I was a kid." Imani had not spoken about this experience in the seminar, even when we discussed rapes occurring in the readings, but she told me about it the following fall and later said that she realized this too had been so important in shaping her development that it was a necessary part of her story. "A really good friend suggested that because I was raped, I have an emotional shield when I have sex with men, I'm not as emotionally vulnerable. When I am with women I'm completely in it. That pushed me into a lot of thinking about my sexual relationships. Since I broke off my engagement, I haven't had sex. Now that I am in this place where I'm thinking about my sexuality, I seem to be choosing not to be with anybody, not to be in a relationship. After that night with Alison, I realized that I had exchanged a relationship of four years of building, and struggle, and love, with a boy, for a one-night with a fantasy."

Imani's choice of story from her life could not have been more different from Marymal's, but each wrote fluently and generously and each said she had come to understand herself differently in the process of writing. In some ways Imani seemed more sophisticated as a high school girl than Marymal was as a young bride, not only about sex but about how to discuss and resolve issues, but she was also more perplexed. Both were reaching for intimacy and commitment at a time when they could not really imagine how much they might still change and develop.

I had raised the issue of openness with Imani because the group that reported on my mother's autobiography had compared it with my memoir. I had spoken to the class then about how I had struggled with whether to discuss my mother's bisexuality, which she had hinted at but never revealed directly. Understandings of sexual orientation have unfolded over time, and we had traced this process in the seminar after we read *Zami,* the autobiography of Audre Lorde, the black lesbian poet. When my mother was building her career and Marymal was taking discreet walks around the Spelman campus, Audre was growing up in Harlem, and any hint of homosexuality was a deep secret. After the beginning of Gay Liberation in 1969, people started to be more open, but the African American community continued in denial and the gay community tended toward polarization, treating claims of bisexuality as disingenuous. Only in the mideighties, under the spotlight of the AIDS epidemic, did bisexuality become a matter of general discussion, though people of different generations still approach these issues very differently and have some difficulty trusting each other. My mother had talked to me about bisexuality, but never about her own orientation, so when I came to understand it after her death, I too had that experience of finding a stranger in place of a familiar figure and of starting again to try to understand.

Trust was an issue when my Spelman class first met, not only trust of me but trust of one another. The undergraduates were diffident and skeptical, expecting to be dominated by the elders. They had been well drilled in classroom courtesy and the habit of hand raising, while the older women treated the class sessions as conversations, speaking up when the spirit moved them. One student complained of "adultism" and described courtesy as "internalized oppression." Meantime, the older women from outside the academy worried because they had not been in the classroom for so many years, had not written papers. I paired the groups off to make presentations. We could not know when we first met that within weeks we would be sharing stories like these, that Marymal would describe leaving her first marriage, Imani her sexual orientation, and I my coming to terms with my mother's reticence.

In some ways I had more in common with the black women of my generation than the older and younger black women had with each other, but I did not know that when we started. On the first day of my class at Spelman, I was more concerned that I would have difficulty getting the students to engage with me across the gap of race than I was about the gaps of age and experience in the group. I had met four of the elders, but the women I came to know as Marymal and Imani, Iyabo and Cheryl, Hillary and Pat were still strangers. I had names and faces to learn, but more important, I knew I had to do something immediately that would put the seminar outside expected classroom patterns that encourage deference and might edge over into sullenness. At the same time I was concerned that the older women would be easily affronted, and that if we did not connect quickly they would politely drift away.

I wanted to bring the class together and find a way to mark what we were doing as something new. With my heart in my mouth, I opened with an exercise I had learned from my daughter, Vanni, who is an actor and sometimes teaches workshops with me, where we use the techniques of theatrical improvisation to explore the meanings of improvisation in life. Risk. Speed. Commitment to a chosen course. Creativity without a script.

I got them up from their chairs around the seminar table. It was 5:30 in the afternoon, and I pointed out that they had come from other classrooms and from offices and traffic jams where they might have been sitting for a long time, and that we would be there until 8:30. First I led them in some rudimentary stretching exercises, just enough to suggest that this course would engage a different set of muscles and that I wanted them present as whole persons. Then I mimed plucking an invisible wisp of something from one woman's shoulder, kneading and shaping it, explaining that this was a "ball of energy" that we would pass around the room, giving a sample of what could be done with it. The ball of energy began to vibrate in my hands, shaking my whole body until I could no longer hold it, and I passed it to the woman on my left.

Around the circle it went. The group got quickly into the spirit of it. Some of the women grew the protean "ball of energy" to massive size and weight, staggered with it, and passed it on. Some treated it as small and delicate, holding and rocking it like an infant, entrusting it to the next person like a gift. One—was it Hillary? I no longer remember—served it like a tennis ball. The last woman in the sequence, from whose shoulder I had plucked the first notional wisp of energy, kneaded and rolled it out like dough on the table. Then, taking up an invisible knife, she sliced it in strips, putting one back onto her shoulder and passing one to every member of the class. The piece she passed to me turned into a butterfly and flew away. Then we sat down.

Only then did I start acting like a professor. This was more than a game, I said, pointing out that each one had found a creative solution to the problem of how to act in an unfamiliar situation, had improvised in a context where she had no script. Nevertheless, I said, they had all drawn on cultural models to behave in ways that would be meaningful to others without additional explanation. They had also been influenced by one another, picking up and reshaping ideas but each one trying to offer something distinctive and individual nonetheless, not a bad model for the way we all learn to project membership and individuality at the same time.

We had also created a circle, not just by sitting around a table but by watching one another and attending with respect, sharing something passed from hand to hand. We had each become a part of something larger than ourselves, unknown and unpredictable. There is no more powerful symbol of unity than a circle, and no more powerful symbol of the stages of life, cycling from generation to generation. "Let the circle be unbroken," in the words of the spiritual, so that no one is lost or excluded.

3 | Youth–Dancing the Limbo

After we had passed the "ball of energy" around the seminar room, I pointed out that our improvisations had amounted to a round of self-introductions, versions of "Who am I?" "Now," I said, "I would like us to go around the table again, in a different way." Since we were going to be reading and writing life histories, it would be useful to explore the difference between what individuals can say of themselves and what they can say of others. "Imagine," I said, "sitting in a café with a friend, describing a third person who is about to join you. She—the absent person—is yourself." Again we went around the room.

I was blown away as the women in that room took up the imagery of communion that had ended the previous exercise and combined it with the idea of metamorphosis, symbolized perhaps by the butterfly released into the air, metamorphosis both for students and for elders as continuing maturation and freedom to change. Very little factual history was given in these introductions; I had to go back for that later. Instead, each woman spoke of her sister self in a process of change: where she was emotionally, what she was going through in the present, what her hopes and aspirations were for the future. "She is really struggling with . . . she has had to change her ideas about . . . she is excited about this class, about graduation, about next year."

One of the elders said she was excited about a new man in her life, and her best friend, across the room, dropped her jaw. Two women in their final year spoke of their approaching graduation and leaving Spelman. Of the elders, the one most clearly in transition was Ama Saran, who had just returned to live in Atlanta after many years. Ama is a handsome and dramatic woman, with the intense gaze of a sibyl, but what I remember most vividly about her is her voice. Now, in a musical crooning, she spoke of her long involvement in the dying of a friend and her sense, working with AIDS patients, that coming to Atlanta for renewal had meant being surrounded by dying. Others spoke of approaching menopause, applying to grad school, threats of bankruptcy, losing weight, moving to a new house, being excited but intimidated by the course. Some chose self-revelation, while some were more self-protective, vague, or funny. Cree Durrett, the only white woman among the elders, described herself diffidently as too defined by her family and hoping she would be more than "just a homemaker" in her obituary, although she has in fact played a highly effective part in many areas of Atlanta life, working to build connections between the different communities. Several women toward the end spoke with such intensity that they lost track of the pronouns I had asked them to reverse. I was both excited and scared. When the circle came around to me, my nerve failed and I took refuge in describing how my "friend," newly arrived in Atlanta, kept getting lost. At that stage I was less able than some of the others to be open, but this metaphor too was accurate for the uncertainties I felt as a newcomer, an outsider. On that first day of our conversation, the speed was taking my breath away.

The seminar was not intended as a consciousness-raising group, but neither was I willing to lock us into the conventions of the academy. I hoped to bypass the artificial divisions of thought and feeling, objectivity and subjectivity, so we could all reflect on and use our own experience of where we were in our lives. At the same time I wanted to encourage the students to listen to the voices we would hear in the readings, responding to women of other races and cultures at different stages of their lives and comparing the situations of others with our own in a disciplined way, entering into dialogue. Members of the Spelman class became so fascinated with the sense of being in conversation with the various authors that as the seminar progressed they began to track them down to question on the telephone.

When someone tells her life story, she necessarily addresses the experiences of change and contrast. In this sense every autobiography deals with the play of similarity and difference, and with the emergence of a sense of uniqueness. Marymal wrote about discovering that she was unlike the people she lived with, Imani about a shifting framework of likeness and unlikeness. There are immigration stories, conversion stories, stories of isolation and exclusion, and stories of breaking away into extraordinary achievement, all efforts to unravel the questions How am I different? How have I become different? When cultural anthropologists collect first-person narratives and life histories, they are often looking for examples that can be seen as representative, but this is never really possible. The awareness of difference is amplified by the ethnographers' own curiosity, and their "informants" are never simply representative, because the willingness to spend time with an ethnographer or oral historian often stems from a kind of loneliness. Even those who say their lives have been "just like everybody else's," "nothing special," are unique individuals and live their lives in imperfect understanding of and by those they are closest to.

Sometimes life histories are directed to an audience profoundly different from the teller. The authors of slave narratives were offering their stories to touch the hearts of slave owners or of Northerners who might be persuaded to become abolitionists; today they are read by later generations who would understand the American past. Life history is often intended as a cross-generational genre, especially during times of change, when older people may be urgently trying to tell their grandchildren what their times were like and why they acted as they did, to give life to the memories that will remain after they are gone. The genre has conventions, too, for every narrator wants her story to sound the way a good story should sound.

The assignment I had given as we went around the table for a second time asked for a focus not on the past but on the present, yet all stories of the past are also filtered through the circumstances of the present, looking ahead to the future. What the women, students and elders alike, produced was a description of themselves in transition. The students spoke of hopes and plans for the semester, but when they looked further ahead they were full of uncertainty.

The "she" of our conversations would be someone different every week of the semester. I explained that we would, in reading life histories and autobiographies, most of which start with childhood, use the first names of the authors, who had chosen to share their private experiences, to discuss them. This got nods of agreement—after all, African Americans often speak comfortably of Langston or Malcolm or Martin, while the whole country calls Oprah by her first name—until I followed up on the logic. When I pointed out that the class would be reading my book *Composing a Life,* which would mean referring to me as Catherine and to the president of the college as Johnnetta in our presence, this was obviously a matter of deep discomfort. From the very beginning of the seminar, I was challenging the group to move with and around the conventions of age as a way of exploring the unfolding stages of lives. But in asking the undergraduates and the elders to function as equals, I was asking for alien and even discourteous behavior. Thus, "she" would be Maxine or Sarah (Sarah Rice, a struggling black woman in the rural South) or Tsitsi Dangarembga's heroine, Tambu, her life and deepest friendship divided by conflicting cultures. "She" would be Audre and Nisa and Margaret (my mother, Margaret Mead, becoming an anthropologist). "She" would be Zimbabwean, Vietnamese, Australian.

This was not a frivolous thing to ask, for I hoped that learning would go in both directions. With elders, including a couple of professors, as students, I wanted to model the learning process myself and to encourage students to take on a teaching role, while the elders, who were impressively faithful in attendance, modeled a free commitment to learning. The question that stayed with us was whether we were an anomalous group of girls thrown together with matrons, or a group of women facing similar issues. Each group had conventional expectations of the other that no longer fit.

There is a growing ambiguity in American society about when young people are ready to meet the challenges of adulthood and about whether those challenges are resolved or left behind as older adults move into the home stretch. As the semester progressed I realized that we were all women in transition into life stages which, because of demographic and social change, are newly ambiguous. The undergraduates were moving into an extended youth, while the elders were dealing with an extended adulthood that posed the questions of growing up all over again at an age when our ancestors would have been growing old. None of us could fully understand where she or the others stood or rely on traditional assumptions about the life cycle. Because tradition defined us as so far apart, it took a while before we could recognize in each other the hesitations of moving into uncharted waters, still deciding who to become.

Celeste Watkins was a senior, a slim, self-possessed young woman who had served as student trustee on the Spelman board. One day, after she had graduated and gone on to graduate work at Harvard, she commented on the makeup of the class. "Sometimes I felt like the women were taking on a motherly role, like when Cree made us brownies and we were so excited, and other times it was like, This is my girl, my running buddy. I wouldn't have expected *both* of these to occur. I stopped paying attention to the differences and started paying attention to the similarities." Even in the process of discovery the traditional gap affected her. "Having faculty and administrators in the class made me reserved," she continued, "because I knew what they had done in their careers, and to be in a class with them was just, like, wow. Oftentimes I would sit and wait for one of them to say something. But I didn't mind the 'adultism' that was alluded to, I was prepared to take on the role of listener. These people had been composing for a lot of years."

"My girl, my running buddy." This was something Celeste might have felt disrespectful saying at the beginning. Dominance along lines of race or gender has often evoked the inequality of parent and child, so the need to resist that dominance, to question alien authority, can resonate within the family as well. The words *girl* and *boy* have become awkward to use even of twelve- or thirteen-year-olds, because of their histories of misuse. Calling a white woman a "girl" is no longer flattering but belittling. Calling a black man a "boy" is more than belittling, it is an unforgivable reminder of racism, so even five- and six-year-old black males start addressing each other "Hey, man." Young women, white or black, still often refer to each other as girls, but college faculty make a conscientious effort always to speak of students as women, and I noticed Imani referred to her high school friends as women. We steer different courses around these sensitivities. Later I noticed that Ama avoided the term *girlfriend,* which Johnnetta and I use playfully to each other, and graciously referred to me as her "sister friend," while Hillary once spoke of being offended when a white woman at her summer job too glibly called her "girlfriend" in an exaggerated accent. As for white males, they have long insisted on being "men" in college and after, except when they are "good, old" or "out for a night with." Or forming and using a network.

Of all experiences of human difference, the experience of being an infant, encountering an adult who is able, for better or for worse, both to nurture and to exercise control, must be the most basic, a source of ambivalence throughout life. Adult strength vis-à-vis childhood vulnerability starts out as a self-evident fact and gets amplified into many kinds of symbolism. College students are caught in the middle. In most human cultures inequality is projected right through the life cycle, with older people dominating younger, and is also projected onto gender relations. All too often we evoke the helplessness of infancy deliberately, whether to convert or to heal or simply to control. Among the many liberation movements of the sixties and seventies, we should count a youth liberation, partly reflected in new kinds of respect, partly repressed. Every shift in the shape of lives proposes new understandings of freedom and shifts in the intersecting geometries of obligation and dependency. Young people today often speak of the future with anxiety. They continue to believe they must make the right plans and decisions now, "get on track," and get on with their adult lives, but they are finding these tasks increasingly difficult. They are caught in a contradiction between traditional expectations of self-sufficiency and changing possibilities.

What the older women had to say was also a kind of refutation of tradition, as a woman of fifty or of sixty spoke of what she wanted to do or take on next in her life, new relationships, new projects, new learning. Perhaps this was comforting to the undergraduates. After all, through most of history young people have had at best a single shot at a desirable life, a moment of possibility that has been especially brief for women. In much of the world, among peasant villagers like those in traditional China or India or Iran, unmarried women the age of these students might already be approaching spinsterhood, fearful of losing their one and only chance of happiness, while women at the age of the elders are already dealing with the losses and withdrawals of old age. As lives are slowly shifting into new shapes, adulthood is lasting longer than ever before, but its beginning is becoming less and less clear, leaving young people in a limbo, neither this nor that. The transition from childhood now seems to go on and on, surrounded by ambiguity and tension.

We speak of "children" and "adults" as if these were self-evident categories, but surely if this were so there would not be so much conflict around adolescence. When children reach puberty parents have an especially vivid sense of encountering their children as strangers—a father does not have to be a pedophile to feel stirrings of desire for a daughter suddenly become a woman, and a mother may feel overwhelming irritation and threat at a son towering over her, spreading chaos through the household. A familiar embrace dissolves suddenly into the discovery of a stranger clasped close in one's arms. Around the world there are rituals that recognize and celebrate a new affinity beyond this strangeness as a boy is recognized as a man and a girl as a woman, but the timing and meaning of such rituals vary greatly.

In some places, especially for girls, adulthood is defined by physiology. Many American women my age seem to have arrived at their first menstruation with virtually no preparation or warning, as many young males found themselves having erections and wet dreams without knowing what was happening. Ama's mother died when she was twelve, but she was fortunate that her mother had still been with her when she reached menarche. "My mother was very excited about it," Ama told me, "and prepared me, you know, said, 'That's a wonderful thing that can happen.' I had no idea that most other people didn't take that view. Such a good preparation. She liked being a woman and would always talk very freely and openly about all that." Audre Lorde's mother seems to have acknowledged Audre's first menstruation as creating an almost mystical bond between mother and daughter, but what she actually spoke about was hygiene and propriety. In many cultures menarche is the time when girls lose their freedom and must become docile and demure, which one of our authors refers to as "acquired insipidity," the time when they are lectured about necessary sacrifices. "This business of womanhood is a heavy burden. . . . How could it not be? Aren't we the ones who bear children?" A responsibility but not a time of freedom.

Struggling to find meaningful definitions, cultural or biological, I have to remind myself that even the biological facts to which our categories refer have changed. In the seminar we used *Nisa: The Life and Words of a !Kung Woman,* by Marjorie Shostak, to provide a baseline for contrast. Among Nisa's people, who lived during most of Nisa's life by foraging in the Kalahari, as among other hunter-gatherers, girls began to menstruate between the ages of fifteen and seventeen, but this was followed by two to three years of infertility. By contrast, in the industrialized world there has been a steady *drop* in the age of menarche, with fertility quickly established. Different diets and different lifestyles. For boys, too, with no such clear marker as menarche, the bodily changes of puberty begin early, along with the insecurity and urgent drive to experiment. Junior high is no longer a shelter from the sexual preoccupations of high school.

In most times and places, even if a woman conceived at the first possible opportunity, she was unlikely to give birth before she was eighteen, while conception at twelve or thirteen has become an increasing concern in the West. Where menarche defines the transition between childhood and womanhood, "children having children," as current political rhetoric would have it, is impossible by definition, for a body capable of bearing a child is by definition a woman's body, even though she continues to grow in stature and understanding and continues to need support.

In the United States the transition from child to adult has become more problematic as physical and social maturity have become disconnected and the responsibility that the one proposes cannot be fulfilled by the other. Writing in the present tense about her life in Charleston, West Virginia, the summer before she started college, Hillary reflected on the search by her high school classmates for the next step in their lives. "There is nothing to do but get in trouble. My guy friends are either selling drugs or are whores having sex with any white girl they can get their hands on—it's just a phase. All of my girlfriends are having babies . . . with the drug dealers. I am friends/associates with about twenty teenage mothers. . . . This place is Loserville."

"Guy friends" is the phrase that allows her to avoid the word *boy* and to speak of friendship without the suggestion of romance.

These young people have left childhood and been released from the classroom, yet they find very limited paths to the next stage of their lives. Hillary may have exaggerated the number that are dealing drugs, but the reality is that there is no way most of them can live up to their own and their peers' expectations to become legitimately self-supporting without further schooling or marking time in some other way, for decent jobs are often closed to them and viable and socially accepted independence lies years ahead. Sexual activity, childbearing, and the risks and profits of the drug trade seem to prove adulthood, but they are filled with irreversibilities. The young people who continue with schooling, the students I encounter in my teaching at Mason or Spelman, seem very young and sheltered, but as I listen to their stories I realize their good fortune in finding a productive way to spend these limbo years without drifting into dependency and alienation. I hear stories of cousins or childhood friends that remind me that in families who have only recently found their way into the middle class, these are especially dangerous years, for poverty or prison are still too close for comfort.

The girlfriends Hillary was speaking of are sexually mature and sexually active. Living in an environment that offers few roads to adulthood, some welcome an early pregnancy because no alternative future, calling for planning and self-discipline, lies invitingly ahead. In contemporary society the teenage mother will not be stoned or banished, and she and her infant will not be allowed to starve; they will be demeaned by welfare bureaucracy, however, trapped by the lack of alternative child care, and finally cut off from benefits.

In American culture we still have assumptions of self-reliance after high school or college, even as times change and the graduates are un-

able to fulfill them. Identity is expected to be newly forged by each individual, just as each is expected to separate from the family, choose a
career, and start a new household, without waiting to inherit from the
previous generation.

We place expectations on youth that Nisa's people do not. For a San
woman, marriage may precede maturity, but the responsibilities of
adulthood come later, with new wives still seen as children growing
up in their older husbands' care, and with their parents nearby. When
she bears her first child, it is customary for a young wife to be with her
mother, and it is understood that she needs the guidance of older
women who are more experienced and ready to help. Whoever it is
that stands by them, young mothers around the world are rarely expected to cope on their own, isolated all day with infants or toddlers,
or to be fully self-sustaining while they have young children.

Bearing and caring for young children has been the most common
career for women, combined with virtually all the tasks that can be
carried out simultaneously with child care, either near the home or
within walking distance, with a child fastened to the body: food preparation, foraging and gardening, raising small animals, handicrafts, care
of the sick, and training of older children. Hunting or fighting or trading across great distances, along with the leadership of such enter-
prises, have become the preserve of centrifugal males, focusing on one
kind of effort at a time. The tasks of males and females have dove-
tailed, leaving women productive but not independent. Because San
women contribute more than two-thirds of subsistence through their
foraging, they are more nearly self-sufficient than women have been
almost anywhere, so they are not forced to remain in marriages that
have become distasteful.

It seemed to me, reading Marymal's autobiographical writing, that
even though she had been in her twenties, with a bachelor's and a

master's degree, she had married and had children without having had an experience of independent adulthood. Leaving her first husband was about growing up, claiming the right to be a full person, and she recognized that, even with her training and work experience, making that transition with young children would be virtually impossible until she had a new job and a new place to live.

Marymal's early social work career in Cleveland involved a pioneering effort to keep unmarried mothers in school and on the path to economic maturity and independence. "I was responsible for developing programs to enable the youngsters and their mothers to stay together, to enable them to survive and not become statistics," she told me later. "This meant I had to meet with the boards of education, and I was involved with a lot of political turmoil. At that time people were very adamant that they didn't want unmarried mothers to go back to school and taint their children. Of course they didn't worry about the unmarried fathers! But they wanted the girls to be punished and have to go to night school. The pendulum has swung now, so that's no longer an issue, but in the sixties it was a serious fight. That was my last big achievement in Cleveland, that they were finally accepted to where they could go to school. They could bring the babies to the center where we provided services, and we could deal with them and with the mothers so they would have some insight into their responsibilities."

It is not only that physical maturity now comes earlier than in the past. The sexual revolution actually reduced the choices and sense of autonomy of young women, opening the doors to an immense increase in sexual bullying: males, generally older and stronger, pressing females to put out by arguing that there are no longer significant costs. Restraint and respect were once tokens of love, and the preservation of virginity was an accepted reason for saying, "I'm not ready." Today the answer is likely to be "Aw, come on, why not?" "Who are you saving it for?" or "You owe me." Hillary writes, "Guys just don't like to be rejected, they say I'm stuck up." Even having a boyfriend does not protect her from pressure, yet traditional protections have come to feel like constraints.

Most of the elders were already married by the time of the sexual revolution. One day, outside the class context, one of the graduating seniors posed the question to the older women: "So come on, tell us, did y'all fool around before you got married?" "We were giggling," Hillary told me, "like, She's crazy." That "y'all" drew a line between the students and the elders. But the query was not addressed to any particular person, and no one said a word, leaving the question hanging in the air.

In Western societies there is a long tradition of trying to postpone first sexual awareness and then sexual activity for years beyond puberty, to an age of marriage that coincides with economic maturity and differs for boys and girls. In this sense economic maturity involves more than contributing labor or even holding a job. Throughout human history almost everyone—men, women, and children—has worked. Without being fully self-supporting, children have been responsible for some work—gathering and weeding, herding sheep, fetching and carrying for their parents, or working beside them— from very young ages, contributing to real needs. One of the most important tasks done by children has been caring for younger siblings and for the elderly. In Western societies today leaving a two-year-old in the care of a nine-year-old has come to be seen as irresponsible and even abusive. But caring for younger siblings offered a framework for exploring issues of responsibility and gave girls direct training in the tasks they would do later, training that is unlikely to be replaced by courses in home economics. Everywhere much of childhood is spent imitating the grown-ups, so that work and play and learning overlap. Nisa's childhood playmates watched the adults and rehearsed the skills of adult life, stalking game and building huts and imitating sexual intercourse without consequence.

In most cultures the economic emphasis in defining adulthood has been greater for boys, delaying it by several years after puberty and after girls are regarded as ready to bear children. Manhood was celebrated for a San boy when he killed his first major male and female game animals, with tattooing and scarification, generally between the ages of fifteen and eighteen—but he was unlikely to marry for another ten years or so, until he had proved the consistent hunting skill needed for economic maturity. This made him a valuable son-in-law, who would join his new wife's band for several years and contribute his hunting to the household. In general the status of an adult male is likely to involve skills that are not practiced, perhaps not even visible, while a boy is in his mother's care, so he needs extra time before he can make a full economic contribution. A potential son-in-law has either had to have access to resources, what used to be called expectations, or had to prove his adult capability by bringing down game, building a canoe, seeking a vision, or killing an enemy in war. These are activities that allow young males to use their new strength and stature, matters for pride.

Nisa, like many of her playmates, was married off even before she began to menstruate, by parents eager to acquire a son-in-law. A bride would continue living right next to her parents, would be allowed to play with other children, and would not be expected to have sexual relations until menarche. Such marriages were easily dissolved as young women matured and made their own choices. In fact, Nisa kept running away to her parents' hut during the night. In first marriages inequality was established by the difference in ages, but these rarely lasted. Later marriages were more symmetrical in age and experience and more likely to be based on mutual attraction, and Nisa was not shy about expressing and pursuing her preferences.

Both for boys and for girls then, among the San, there was a blurring of what might seem like a clear transition between childhood and adulthood. The full weight of manhood or womanhood was assumed gradually. This pattern seems to be developing in our society also as males and females seek similar kinds of economic maturity, which is more and more deferred. Men and women who are challenged to continuing development often outgrow their early marriages, and we have an emerging pattern of couples living together or with a series of partners, still dependent on parental subsidies, for several years before making a long-term commitment and growing into a full adult role, privilege before responsibility. At every level of society, sexual activity is preceding full economic maturity, whether support comes from the family or from the state. But when that early sexual activity brings children, the transition to full economic maturity becomes much more difficult for women.

In many parts of the world adulthood means responsibility without privilege or independence. A young husband may have committed himself to years of bride service, hunting or laboring in other ways for his in-laws. Often he must have borrowed heavily to afford a brideprice, and paying that back will keep his nose to the grindstone for years to come. In a fixed economy married offspring may be obligated to continue as unpaid workers in a family enterprise until death or retirement offers space for independence.

In the United States in the booming fifties, however, early self-sufficiency was possible and early marriage was the route to independence and sexual access, even to a "starter house" in the suburbs, and this is the ideal that now haunts us: privilege and responsibility in tandem. Today even the best public education does not lead to employment offering security for a family and the prideful satisfaction that eases the acceptance of obligation. Under those circumstances fatherhood, which includes the social expectation of support, presents males with cruel ironies, a loss of freedom without the independence that could make them truly responsible. The beginning jobs available to high school graduates are generally minimum-wage or part-time, and even these are often not available to young black men. High school today is like a ladder leaning against the side of a cliff, yet when you reach the top it proves just too short for climbing up to level ground. Why try to finish a course of studies if it leads nowhere? Even military service is an option for very few. Yet we go on expecting young people to follow patterns that might have worked a generation ago and no longer do. All over the country grown children are living at home and working at jobs that lead nowhere, while their parents, bewildered by changing patterns of courtship and the job market, waver between resentment and wondering if they should blame themselves.

Marriage, sexuality, and adult responsibility are everywhere offered as a complex series of trade-offs, but the package deal looks less and less attractive to many Americans. Today young men no longer have to get married or have regular employment to become sexually active. They do have to strut their stuff, however, and in a consumer society this takes money, not just for expensive running shoes and leather jackets but for boom boxes and cars as well.

The inadequacy of the transition is not resolved by graduation from college. Young black men at Morehouse College, across the street from Spelman, have made it through high school and into college, but I wonder whether they and their parents, dedicated to making them self-sufficient, realize that graduating from college also falls short of meeting their aspirations. Among the middle class the four under- graduate years are increasingly seen as preparation for professional training, while in many institutions students work and study part- time, half child and half adult, extending the four years to five or six, compiling a work record combined with a student lifestyle so they enter the serious job market at an age closer to thirty.

At one time in Western society everyone still in training or in school was regarded as a minor not yet ready for free choice. Only heads of households or landowners were truly adult. Until the liberation movements of the sixties, colleges stood in the place of parents—*in loco parentis*—indulgent of the high jinks of boys who will be boys but concerned with protecting the virtue of children, especially girls, en- trusted to their care. One of the by-products of the Vietnam War was giving the vote to eighteen-year-olds, making them legally adult at the age when they could be drafted and sent to war, ostensibly inviting them to participate in societal decisions. Eighteen became the legal age of majority even as the possibility of full adulthood was becoming later.

Nothing brought out the degree of change at Spelman more vividly than the anecdotes the elders told of Spelman parietal rules in the past. Beverly Guy-Sheftall is an alumna and a faculty member, and she tended to remain in her academic persona in the seminar. ("I don't think I ever allowed Dr. Guy-Sheftall to be a student," Celeste had told me.) Beverly wears glasses with big, bright-colored frames, her hair shoulder-length with the ends turned under, and a great variety of colorful clothing, but she made a careful distinction to me one day, pointing out that her clothing is ethnic but not narrowly Afrocentric.

"Spelman was cloistered when I was a student, unlike now, so even when my mother came to visit, I could not go to her hotel room. We had curfew and chapel, we couldn't ride in cars, and we could not leave the campus except in groups of three, even to go to the library. The goal was to keep you on that campus and to keep you so busy that . . . I don't even remember reading on my own or having any extra time to do anything. It was stultifying—you know, rigid rules, not much time for reflection or exploration. You really were encouraged not to leave those gates."

Most especially, Spelman students were not encouraged to get involved in the Civil Rights Movement. The little exposure Beverly found to contemporary struggles for racial justice in the curriculum was through courses taught by Staughton Lynd and Howard Zinn, progressive white professors from New England. There was virtually nothing about women's issues. "When I got there, Spelman was totally discouraging about participating in demonstrations. I remember going on two marches that King organized. I remember King telling us about nonviolent political strategy. It was very scary." That was about my own level of involvement, I told Beverly, up in Massachusetts, where it wasn't scary—a couple of marches and hearing Dr. King speak once, at a time when I was already getting involved in the peace movement. "I was not in that very tiny group of Spelman students who were committed to this full-time," Beverly continued. "I was in a category of kids whose parents told them, You are in college to be doing your work." The authority of those older than oneself and the requirement of expressing deference to that authority are very strong in the black community. Yet during the years of the Movement it was essential that young people defy the cautions of their elders and their warnings of danger.

The discontinuity caused by change, however welcome, however incomplete, has produced a generation gap not unlike the one that occurs in immigrant families. In the seminar we would be discussing historic events that look different from the vantage point of different dates of birth. The Civil Rights Movement, the Vietnam War, all the liberation movements and reactions since then, each one would be approached through the lens of personal narrative. All of the age-related issues we would talk about—sex, schooling, puberty, marriage, parenthood, aging—would pass in double images before our group. Divided by some twenty years, like mothers and daughters, we would be talking about stages of life that continue to shift and change.

The second book we read together was *Coming of Age in Mississippi* by Anne Moody. Anne begins in early childhood, with an account of what it was like to grow up black and poor and smart in rural Mississippi. She carries the story up through high school and college and her intense involvement in the Civil Rights Movement. She ends in May of 1964, with her graduation from college. One of the things Anne emphasizes is the determination of the adults around her—including her family and the administration of her college—to keep her from becoming involved. The older generation was both protecting the younger from the very real dangers and protecting their own prerogatives and what they had managed to build, but Anne was unsparing in her judgment.

The undergraduates were startled to realize how much fatalism and opposition to the Movement there had been at that time among African Americans who had grown up under segregation. "I think we barely have a clue about the profound generational differences among African Americans," Beverly told me. "When I think about most of my students now, who have absolutely no idea what it was like to grow up in the Jim Crow South, it amazes me. Young black people are so cut off from that fairly recent past. The Anne Moody book was a perfect way to get in touch with that."

After the discussion of Anne Moody's account, in fact, Hillary said, "I'm gonna call my daddy and tell him I do finally understand what he's been talking about." But when she called home she was disappointed; she shouldn't have had to read a book, she was told. I had already encountered that particular generation gap. Walking onto the Morehouse campus for the first time, trying to find my way to an event on the King holiday, I asked an elderly guard for directions, and he replied with a harangue about how "these kids" won't trouble to remember the past. Yet an older generation for whom the past represents suffering may be unaware of how much they limit their reminiscing to avoid recalling pain and humiliation.

Since the sixties new ways of enforcing conformity in the young have emerged. In the middle classes higher education has come to be organized around debt. The rising costs of tuition and the creation of multiple categories of student loans ended the sense of freedom to experiment, and the pell-mell issuance of credit cards to college students created a spurious sort of economic independence. In American society, debt and concern about credit ratings enforce conformity in the same way that long-term bride payments did in some preliterate societies. The contemporary system of student loans effectively damped down for most the experience of college as a carefree moratorium. Higher education now is not the sheltered continuation of childhood it once was, but neither does it initiate the expectations of adulthood.

Young people have both lost and gained rights. It is becoming more and more common to hear demands that children who commit crimes should be tried as adults; eighteen-year-olds are now liable for crimes that used to be excused as youthful folly, but these same adults are not allowed to drink until age twenty-one. Increasingly, parents find themselves offering house space to grown children who are not yet self-supporting, but they also find them no longer willing to be governed by their parents' rules.

The "generation gap" of the sixties marked a new way of encountering the transition from childhood to adulthood, with freedom offered well before responsibility. We are still trying to sort out the strands of freedom and responsibility within our definitions of adulthood. By the end of the seventies colleges had more or less given up the struggle to control sexual activity, and on many campuses dormitories had become coed. Other changes went along with these—most colleges ceased to enforce other kinds of civility; rooms ceased to be inspected for cleanliness; dress codes and "quiet hours" were abandoned. Dormitory rooms were no longer sanctuaries for reflection or places where students could slough off some part of their self-consciousness. Freud may have been right in connecting civilization to sexual repression.

Spelman is still less permissive—more sheltering—than most non-denominational white institutions. Rules have been relaxed, and "bifurcated garments"—slacks and jeans—are permitted, but there is still a rare demand for civility, and there are still checks on anyone entering the walled campus and limited times for visits by the opposite sex. "These are very precious packages entrusted to us," one administrator said to me—often the first members of their households to attend college, carrying the hopes of entire families.

What is it that makes a girl into a woman or a boy into a man? What kinds of responsibility can be expected at various ages? What difference will it make as the vast numbers being born in Egypt or Mexico, Indonesia or Zaire, become full participants in society—whatever that means, and whatever base of socialization that requires? And how will they carry out the tasks of preparing the generation that comes after? Today, in much of the third world, participation has come to look more like exploitation, with children of six scavenging in city dumps, guarding cars, selling lottery tickets, or even working in factories. Twelve- and thirteen-year-old boys were sent to fight in the Iran-Iraq war, and little girls in parts of Asia work in electronic assembly plants or are even sold into prostitution.

At the same time the very concepts of schooling and education are changing in meaning, as we recognize more and more clearly that education increases societal assets—human capital, as the economists say—and logically requires continuing societal and corporate investment. Logically we should pay young people for the "work" and "public service" involved in becoming educated, protecting them and us from their unemployment and dependency later. Schooling as a preparation for "real life" is never complete, while real life has long since begun.

The age at which a San youth was regarded as ready for marriage, some ten years after his initiation into manhood, was not so different from the age of economic maturity in our society, and women who intend to have the ability to support themselves are putting off childbearing until about the same age, somewhere between twenty-six and thirty. This looks like a trend among the affluent, but research has shown that if girls from poor backgrounds delay childbearing only until twenty or twenty-one, they do not do better economically than teenage mothers, for graduation from high school or junior college is still not enough to guarantee self-sufficiency. Teen pregnancy is dropping, but early pregnancy is not just a teenage problem. We are not entirely candid about how long they may have to wait when we tell young women to just say no.

The changing shape of the life cycle and the changing job market have combined to create a gap from about age fourteen to about twenty-six that has to be rethought, used productively, and protected without simply extending childhood. We used to have a socially supported transition from childhood to adulthood called high school. It no longer works. Gradually college, or at least junior college, has replaced high school, but it too is proving inadequate. Within this ambiguity schools and colleges have a mixture of goals almost as confusing as those of families: to protect and challenge, nourish and judge; to impart factual knowledge, skills, critical thinking, cultural literacy; to build character or emotional maturity, uphold standards, prepare for citizenship; to raise self-esteem and prevent risky experimentation. At one moment students are treated as mature, at the next they are treated like children, for we are still struggling to find ways to teach that consistently evoke maturity.

Extended education has long been a way to keep young people occupied and off the labor market while separating them from their families, but it is no longer sufficient. Spelman is proud of the numbers of its students who go on to graduate school, more than a third of seniors who fill out questionnaires about their future plans. Even after four years of college, Hillary could find herself in a limbo not unlike that of her high school classmates. Middle-class and affluent people now know that their children cannot "work their way through college" and that most will not find stable jobs even with a B.A., so realistic parents are learning to anticipate tuition for graduate school, grown-up children living at home, and continuing subsidies or health insurance premiums—no end in sight. Ideas of discipline and family roles are shaken by the return of educated, sexually active offspring who just don't quite seem to be adults. Meanwhile, educators at every level are being scapegoated for the fact that graduates are not adequately "prepared"—for a developmental step that has been drastically altered and a job market no longer ready to absorb them.

It is a mistake to regard young adulthood, when most hormonal

transition is complete, simply as a prolonged adolescence or as a sus-
pension of the normal sequence of events. This period has its own
characteristics and turns up for males in many cultures where adulthood needs to be honed and practiced. It has become equally important for women entering the workplace. It seems clear that there is a
need to acknowledge a life stage here with substance and social value,
challenge and a sense of achievement, and to make it productive for
both males and females.

A good model can be found in Israel, with near universal military
service. Parents still regard their eighteen- and nineteen-year-olds as
children and expect to pamper them and do their laundry when they
come home on weekends—there is a joke that the Israeli army has no
washing machines—but by the end of military service, these young
adults are ready to be mature workers or motivated students, citizens
literate in Hebrew and familiar with the country and its different
classes and ethnic groups, disciplined and physically fit. They still
need further training for most jobs, but they approach study differently, and many have gotten the training they need in the military.
Young Mormons get the same kinds of benefits from their missionary
years. The Peace Corps has offered a coming of age for thousands of
young Americans, but its numbers have been steadily reduced and
programs like Americorps have been under constant attack. National
service, followed by further education and reshaped for peacetime and
nonmilitary needs, is probably the best model available. These years
should be filled with useful and challenging activities, supported and
remunerated by the whole community.

The boundaries will continue to blur. As elders come back into the
classroom, especially if they are mixed in with traditional undergraduates, it is harder to think through the distinction between children
and adults. We cannot think of adults in our society as having arrived

at a definitive identity or as being beyond the need for guidance as they continue to improvise and reinvent themselves. Perhaps colleges and universities should begin to think of themselves as "education maintenance organizations," with new kinds of connections to alumni.

One of the ways contemporary society is attempting to ease the transition from childhood to adulthood is the invention and elaboration of rites of passage. It is not surprising that Spelman pays even more attention than most colleges to ceremonies like graduation, when young graduates receive their diplomas in the presence of relatives and friends. Commencement is a day of extraordinary excitement. Parents have made huge sacrifices to send children to college, but the ceremony goes beyond the parents to express the sense that the education of these young women has been a community effort, an effort that will need to continue.

At commencement one of the air conditioners in the Cathedral of the Holy Spirit, a vast modern church rented for that day—for no one is turned away and many graduates are accompanied by a dozen family members—failed. After a while several of us in the faculty section slipped our suffocating academic robes off our shoulders, leaving mortarboards and hoods in place for camouflage in the crowd. A young, attractive professor with a sleeveless and low-cut dress was sitting at the end of my row, and an elderly woman, some graduate's grandmother no doubt, slapped her lightly on the cheek as she passed, treating her as still a child of the community.

It reminded me of the way Bill Cosby brought down the house at the dedication of the Cosby Building on campus, when he switched, with an exaggerated double take, into the vernacular, saying, "What'chu do wit' your clo'es, girl?" to his svelte and elegant daughter in a spaghetti strap dress. That grandmother's action was a dramatic expression of the tradition in the African American community that it is appropriate for any adult to correct the behavior of any younger person—and to go on doing so. The huge assemblage was not about Spelman as an institution or about the granting of diplomas but about the involvement of individuals in the long growing-up of their children, the real meaning of the African proverb that "it takes a whole village to raise a child."

4 | In the Heartlands of Unknowing

Families are composed of strangers. The biological family, however it may be reshaped in a particular time and place, is always a potential school for difference, a classroom in which young and old, male and female gaze at each other in puzzlement. Sex and age differences mean that most human beings, even in apparently homogeneous and stable communities, necessarily live in intimacy with others who hold different values, whose needs and desires are not fully intelligible and never will be. Even siblings of the same sex and close in age fall into conflict, and so do gay and lesbian partners, discovering they are by no means of one mind. We need each other, but often we feel guilty about our failures of understanding, bound by love to Otherness.

The best way to learn about difference, including individual difference, is to grow up in a large family with several samples of every category and close ties to a diverse community. But in the modern West the emergence of a particular pattern of family life, one or two children isolated with one or two parents and no older adults, has meant a drastic reduction in our preparation for encountering and adapting to difference and for surviving the ups and downs of living with other human beings. Arguably we should see the nuclear family not as the ideal of family life but as a bare and fragile minimum. Virtually all human groups offer more interaction between different ages than we do in the United States, where the elaborate division of labor in industry sets the style, and neighborhoods are segregated by age and sometimes sexual preference as well as by race and class.

The larger the family, the more raw material for learning about difference, but custom also dictates how the raw material is used and who is worth learning from. Fathers may be absent. Male and female children may be reared separately after their earliest years. And everywhere there are assumptions, about gender or age, about what women want or how all men behave or what it means to be eight or eighty, that reduce the wonder that another human being could see the world so differently.

Celeste Watkins had an older sister who left for college when she was twelve, so during her teenage years she was almost like an only child. As she spoke about the ways in which a small family, even a very happy one, can be limiting, she slipped into the idiom of her teenage years. "My sister and I had this discussion Labor Day weekend about how our relationships go, and it's probably not gonna be like we expected. My friends call us the Huxtables, 'cause, like, I've never seen my parents fight. My mom is a great mom, and my dad is a great dad, and I don't have a lot of baggage or resentment. But the disadvantage to that is you kind of expect the same thing. I've realized more and more how rare their relationship is. When my sister and I date people, we tend to kind of measure them by whether they have the qualities that our daddy has, and we tend to be overly critical. We have this image of what marriage is supposed to be, and we're having a hard time finding guys who can fit into that. We're getting hit by this propaganda too, about black male shortage, black men in jail and so many are gay, and so it's easy to go, like, okay, I'm just gonna be single for the rest of my life. We're trying to figure out ways that we can be happy either way."

Perhaps every child needs more than two significant adult figures, more models of caring and hard work—and also telling examples of the failure to care. The removal from immediate experience of irascible uncles and gossiping aunts, of quarreling in-laws and indulgent grandparents, was a logical prelude to more frequent divorce, for it has simply meant that the small number of close relationships become increasingly fateful and intense.

Most of us are no longer used to sharing a household with a varied group of people. "My granma comes, and a lot of times it used to cause tension because I'd gotten used to being very autonomous," Celeste said. "She would come and stay a month, and she would want to know every aspect of my life: What did you do? Where did you go? and dadadada, and it would drive me crazy. So my mom would say, She just wants to be in touch with your life. I just was not accustomed to people asking me questions constantly, but now I'm definitely beginning to understand where she's coming from."

Because questions are one of the key ways generations can connect, I asked Celeste, who was in Cambridge doing graduate work in sociology by the time we had this conversation, whether she ever turns things around and asks questions herself. "I've started doing that," she said. "I'm just now trying to learn my family history. I got that from your class. I asked a lot of questions at my father's family reunion in

Tennessee. I'm getting closer and closer with them, and I'm appreciating them much more. I'd never interacted with them much because we lived in Michigan. This last summer I spent my time with my grandfather's brothers and sisters. It's definitely appreciated. These eighty- and seventy-year-old women started joking about who they're gonna get with and marry!

"I went through a little snobby period, like, I can't believe my family ever lived on a farm, but now I totally appreciate them and I so look forward to going. My father spent every summer on this farm. It's been in the family for decades. They just got indoor plumbing two years ago. You know, people say you should never forget where you came from and never get too proud, and that's it basically. My parents would send us down for a week every summer and then drive down and meet us." For Celeste the family farm was a place of indulgence.

Tambu, the Shona heroine described in *Nervous Conditions,* moved between two households, which offered her five different adult models of womanhood to work with in inventing herself—untold riches compared with the narrow choices offered to girls or boys simply told to emulate their same-sex parent, if they are lucky enough to have one. I remember as a child sorting out my impressions of my mother's parents when we visited them in Philadelphia. I found similarities between my mother and her father on the one hand, and between my father and my maternal grandmother on the other hand, which helped me detach the characteristics of individuals from gender stereotypes. But I never met my English grandparents.

With more than one child in a family, there are profound differences of developmental stage to learn from, and every child is born into a different environment with a different combination of genes and turns out differently. When couples have a second child they are often amazed at the differences, realizing that they have not "learned about babies" after all but only learned about an individual and unique baby, and the next one is a stranger.

All her life, Hillary has played the role of youngest, as she did in the seminar, for she has two older sisters, and although she describes them and her mother as her best friends, this has given her a vivid sense of similarities and differences between women, all four women standing in contrast to her father, of whom she says, "He is from the old school. He was raised that women don't whistle. He just has a straight way of thinking and he likes things a certain way and he doesn't like riffraff supposedly . . . although I've heard that he was quite a riffer and a raffer. He thinks we're not about business like we should be, we play too much. We know he loves us a lot, but he doesn't always glorify us in his presence. He's the type of person, you walk in and hear him talking to his buddy, That girl's sumthin else, she's so pretty now, she's this and she's that. . . . We're very liberated, so there's a lot of conflict in our household, but for the most part he wants us to be independent women." This is a familiar pattern—a man who feels free to criticize but expects positive feelings to be self-evident and voices them only to outsiders.

"My sister Gregg, now, she has the creativity; she's the writer and the actress and the dancer. Kathy is more structured. Kathy's an English major, but she writes about controversial issues, not about love and flowers and passion like Gregg. Kathy is a case manager for a house for troubled kids. She's very maternalistic, very structured. She's the one that will cause a little conflict, she wants resolution and change. Kathy is down to business, she wants a husband, she wants children, it's just mapped out. She's like, It's gonna be like this, I want a car, a nice apartment, then I want to move into a town house and . . ." I imagine Hillary's sister as brisk and directive, ready to tell troubled young people firmly how they ought to behave, just as she is ready to map out how her own life ought to be.

"Gregg isn't like that. If it happens it happens, if it doesn't work out, whatever. Gregg, she has no inhibitions, whatever she has on her mind she just talks about. Kathy heard me talking to a girlfriend once about sex and she got maaad. She's very, very Christian-oriented too. Gregg's spirituality is more on the me-sense . . . like, my body is my temple. It is Christianity, but you have to develop yourself and treat yourself right, love yourself and acknowledge your faults. Whereas Kathy is, you go to church, fan yourself, holler with the preacher, and bring the fried chicken. That's how I distinguish if you're a church member or a churchgoer: I'm a churchgoer, 'cause I don't cook. As soon as the service is over, I'm out the door."

Hillary described her mother, who is a civil rights lawyer, as somewhere between her two older daughters with regard to religion. "She has always had a spiritual base, but she goes in and out as far as going to church. She always tells us, Rely on God. Our whole family is like that, we love Jesus, we really do. We might not say it all the time, our actions might not . . . We just do. She's always instilled that in us." Hillary grew up in a household with a lot of argument and debate, strong opinions and laughter. "Our house is like a comedy circle, a joke."

As I looked at the undergraduates around the seminar table, I could see the greatest similarity between my family and Iyabo's, for we are both only children from academic families. But Iyabo's is an intact nuclear family, which means that at least it gave her the experience of two sexes and two age groups—a minimum start toward understanding humanity. My mother dealt with our tiny household, made even smaller when my father was sent to Southeast Asia during World War II, by linking our household with that of Lawrence and Mary Frank, a blended family in which the father had been widowed and remarried twice so that his oldest children were adults and the younger son, Colin, was my age. That linkage lasted after the war, when my parents were divorced.

Colin and I were like siblings, allies against the big kids—except when other children our age were around, in which case we split into rivalries and coalitions based on sex. When we were together we were curious and puzzled about the phenomenon of two different bodies. I can remember Colin, my dearest friend and playmate, taunting me from the top of the staircase that divided our living areas, "Ginasy, ginasy!" and myself shouting back, "Penisy, penisy!" against the background of the playground conflicts between the girls and the boys. One of the students in the seminar described being waylaid as a child by boys who would grab the girls crossing a vacant lot, shouting, "Catch a girl, kiss a girl," and how that taunt has been replaced in more recent times with "Catch a girl, fuck a girl." It is not a bad thing to discover early on that the opposite sex is not always caring and protective.

As a child I had honorary siblings while still feeling that when my parents were home I had them to myself. I also had a great many surrogate parents and never acquired the notion that there was only a single model for womanhood or manhood, for who I might become or what kind of person would be an appropriate partner.

Sex and age are related: the sexes diverge and then converge again; males and females are less different in childhood than they are in adolescence and during the reproductive years, and this may be one reason for the recurrent tendency to equate women and children, as if a man could understand his wife by remembering himself before the buildup of male hormones. It never quite works, and we can never really walk in each other's moccasins. Men and women also become more similar during old age, men mellowing and women becoming feistier. Development and aging, puberty and menopause, provide the experiences of internal change that mean that all of us know to some degree what it feels like to live in an alien body and experience unfamiliar emotions, to be strangers to ourselves.

When you try to understand difference, you can start from the facts of your own difference from day to day and year to year. These are made less useful than they might be by ways of thinking that dismiss change before adulthood as preparation (children as incomplete) and aging as adverse (old people as deteriorated). Under pressure, during adolescence or aging, and even in dreams and sleep, we can encounter ourselves as strangers, either dismissively or with curiosity and respect.

Valuing the multiplicity of the self, I see my students in the process of becoming persons still unknown, so I try to leave the seeds of alternative ways of thinking in their memories to sprout in changing seasons or as they encounter drastic change, like those species that reproduce only after a forest fire or a rare flood. In the same way I reread books that have been important to me in the past and enjoy the amazing discovery that because I have changed the book has changed. Living increases human variety, for while adolescents struggle to be like their peers, the elderly, under their practiced conformity, become a variegated treasure trove until this splendor is muted by failing health.

In childhood individuals are gradually distinguished and become familiar. We begin to love with very little understanding. The encounter with persons, one by one, rather than categories and generalities, is still the best way to cross lines of strangeness. Carl Rogers once said, "The most personal is the most universal." A small set of one-to-one relationships within the family—too few, perhaps, in many households—can become a model for thinking of the cosmos, which is then seen as reflecting familiar patterns of kinship structure and authority: hierarchical or pluralistic, chaotic or ceremonial. Visions of Mother Earth and Father Sky and claims that "all men are brothers" are colored by memories of actual parents and siblings as well as by the cultural construction of these roles.

Sex is perhaps the deepest of the visible and enduring genetic differences between people. There is always, in every society, a differentiation related to the biological differences between the sexes, which makes them mysterious to each other, learning to give pleasure but without ever knowing exactly what the other is feeling from a particular touch. Cultures elaborate the differences, but the relationship between sisters is always different from the relationship between brothers. Cultures also mandate a degree of standardization for members of the same sex and provide stereotyped interpretations for behavior. "Just like a man!" and "That's a woman for you" are handy camouflage for puzzlement but costly barriers in the path of understanding, while diverse men and women are constrained to fit cultural expectations, some more painfully than others.

"If I had known enough about men, I wouldn't have married my first husband," Marymal said. "I would have known he saw me as a trophy rather than as an equal partner. I would have known better with my second husband." But Marymal was not alone in the experience of falling in love with someone who remained a stranger, living for years with a spouse whose ways remained mysterious.

Marymal's second marriage also ended in divorce. "I can't remember how I met my second husband. He owned a funeral business two or three blocks down the street from where I lived. Somehow we got together. James was a very handsome man—all my husbands were very handsome—and he was wonderful with children. One day my youngest son said, 'Mommy, when are we gonna marry Uncle Jimmy?' Okay, why not? His father was one of the founders of the Church of God in Christ, and he wanted his oldest son to be in the church, but to my husband's credit he just could not be a hypocrite. So his father decided to set him up in the funeral business, and because his father was so well loved by people in the faith, everybody in that region that died automatically came to him for the funeral.

"James never really understood how to work for anything because it was provided for him. He only saw the successes of his father, he didn't realize . . . People would come from all around to hear his father preach, kind of like the TV evangelists today, and he would send a chauffeur and a big car to bring his sons just before the rallies. The money would come in by buckets, but Jim and his brother never saw how much preliminary work went into all this, so he never valued money.

"When I married him I didn't realize how irresponsible he was. He was so nice though—my first husband wasn't really all that nice—and the kids loved him. But then as I got deeper in this marriage, I found out the funeral business was surviving because of his father's name, while he was at the racetrack. I couldn't believe it. He didn't have to be responsible, there was always a chunk of money coming in, another funeral, but you could never get the money to the house because by that time he owed it at the racetrack. That horse-racing thing, it's addictive. Oh yeah. Later on I joked about all that, I said I went from one with two-legged fillies to one with four-legged fillies. You can't compete with a horse! I just visited with a friend from those days; she remarried her husband and they just got a second divorce. We started reminiscing about these men, and it sounded as if we were talking about the same man.

"Well, of course I did my bit, I got pregnant and I had my daughter,

Cornelia. I was thirty-seven when she was born in 1965, and she was the apple of our eye. I stayed in the marriage as long as I thought it was feasible, but I just couldn't afford being married to someone who couldn't handle money, so we were divorced in 1967."

Marymal moved to Atlanta with her four children and married Charles Dryden, who had been a Tuskegee Airman, one of the small group who integrated the Air Force. He had three sons, two teenagers living with their mother in Jamaica and one who wanted to stay with him and Marymal. "We had our ups and downs adjusting, but we were determined we were gonna blend this family, and to our credit we did. We function as a family. When one of our children had problems, we had faith that time would work it out. You have to persevere and you have to set limits. My sons all live here, and they're all wonderful men, very protective and respectful. Maybe they've developed that because they were with me when . . . we were just a team, we operated like a team. Each boy has tried to help as best he can. We've been married for twenty years. It's amazing."

Marymal and Charles have five grandchildren now. There are other young people as well, whom she described as part of their extended family, so she was observant of the younger women in the class and curious about their lives. But she also bemoaned changes in the younger generation with friends her own age. "I have a good friend with a handsome son at Morehouse, and he said he had to stop going through the malls because girls would walk up to him and grab at his privates. I couldn't believe it," Marymal said. She shook her head. "It's a different generation. I don't know how they're gonna survive. At least with celibacy you get to know each other better, become really good friends. These kids, they seem not to have any barriers at all. And the girls don't mind being very assertive, they call fellas."

Marymal had seen other changes too, over the decades. "After Kennedy's assassination, I was invited to teach here at the School of Social Work. I wasn't academically trained to be a college professor, but I had had wonderful experience, so I just kind of winged it. I had all this excitement about being a part of what was now called the Great Society—Atlanta was a target of the Model Cities Project. That was 1968, all of us really committed to social change, but by 1979 I saw a changed attitude in the students, only interested in getting a degree and getting it over with. I was sort of disappointed. I had come up through the era when everyone was excited about change."

Marymal's first two marriages seem to have been based on rather traditional expectations about the behavior of husbands and wives, and two divorces had not made her skeptical about the institution. Beverly, by contrast, had been in a marriage that seemed more modern in that it was framed outside of traditional expectations. Some twenty years younger than Marymal, she came into contact with feminist ideas after graduating from Spelman, and when she returned as a faculty member she played a leadership role in making Spelman a national center for black women's studies.

"My husband did not want children, and I was indifferent—we'd had that conversation before we got married. He had decided, as a little black child in Macon, Georgia, that he did not want to be responsible for bringing anyone into this world." Beverly drew the logical conclusion. "I said to him, Since we're not gonna have children, we don't have to have a traditional marriage. We can eat when we want to, with a big lunch in the faculty dining hall, and we don't have to have a schedule. I basically didn't cook. In retrospect I realize how shocked he was, because he had a housewife mom, who hardly left the house except for doctors' appointments. She cooked and cleaned and her whole life revolved around the inside of the house and motherhood. She had a wash day, she had a dust day. . . . I said, I'm not gonna do that, it's just the two of us."

The marriage lasted a decade and ended in an amicable divorce. Beverly spoke about her ex with appreciation for his clarity about what he believed in. "In retrospect I realized that my notions about marriage must have been antithetical to his." Beverly grew up with a divorced mother and two sisters, neither of whom has had children. "I was raised by a feminist mother. She was very clear about men. You know, they're useful but you don't feel in any way inferior. Who could feel inferior to men? They can't do but one thing at a time, and you certainly can't depend on them for your life, that's something you have to take responsibility for yourself, even if you're married. She certainly liked men, but she was just damn realistic: she said there are often good ones out there and you're fortunate if you get one. If you don't, you can still have a life."

Beverly had given me a copy of her anthology of black feminist writings, *Words of Fire,* and now I quoted back a saying of her mother's from the acknowledgments, "Stand on your own two feet and appreciate a good man when you find one." It struck me that Beverly and her husband had come to marriage with different understandings about what is natural to men and women, husbands and wives, understandings that did not match. They had to improvise instead of relying on inherited role definitions shaped to fit. Beverly has lived a self-reliant life rather like her mother's, while perhaps he has been able to find his way to a remembered ideal. Divergent ideas about manhood and womanhood, about marriage and family, are cultural rather than innate, and the households we compose today can never be more than approximations of those we observed as children, which once felt so completely natural.

It is not easy to distinguish between what is acquired through exposure and environment and what is innate. We know that culture, religion, and specific languages are learned, and could each be learned by any normal infant, regardless of sex or race. Yet when I learned to speak Hebrew in Israel, many Israelis asked me, "Are you *sure* you aren't Jewish?" I have wondered since whether there was not an attitude toward intellectual debate in my mother's family that led both of her sisters to marry talented and articulate Jews, a cultural style my Israeli friends were picking up in me a generation later. Even if I am reasonably certain that the characteristics my friends were responding to were learned, there is no way I can be sure what is mixed in my genes. There is a family story that the name Fogg (the maiden name of my mother's mother) goes back to a Jewish family that fled to Foggia, Italy, during the Inquisition. The story is one my mother told me to enrich me in my sense of connections. Who knows. All we really know is that eventually English Protestant Foggs migrated to New England and then to the Midwest. I know I have African ancestry because all human beings do, but there is no way I can be certain if there has been any more recent mixing. I can be certain, however, that some of my characteristics came as a surprise to my parents, for in each generation some traits are unexpressed and new combinations appear.

I selected one book from Australia to raise exactly these issues for the seminar: *My Place,* by Sally Morgan. Sally grew up feeling at odds with the white Australians around her, feeling that her family was somehow different. The household was poor, consisting, after the death of a violent and alcoholic father, of Sally's mother and grandmother and siblings. It was not until she had begun her studies at the university and gotten married that Sally finally understood that her grandmother, Nan, had been the child of an Aboriginal mother and a white man. Under Australian racial policies at that time, every effort had been made to sever these roots, so Nan had only fragmentary and traumatic memories and was terrified to share them. The interesting thing for me was that claiming this connection was so liberating for Sally, legitimating her impulses toward the arts and toward the natural world. Being what used to be called an octaroon made Sally special and gave her the license to be creative. She immersed herself in trying to understand the connection and reshaped her painting to echo Aboriginal artistic styles. "Is Sally a racist?" I asked the class. Resonating with her experience, they were unwilling to use the negative label, so I pressed them on the dangers of even positive racial stereotypes. Did they believe that Sally's talent as an artist (which none of her siblings shared) came to her as a genetic trait special to the Aboriginal gene pool? How about logical thinking or a sense of rhythm in other contexts, both positive, both likely to become invidious when applied to populations? What was important, we agreed, was that Sally used her rediscovered roots to become unique.

Looking back as a senior on the summer after her sophomore year, Celeste described the wrenching experience of traveling to Ghana, sure that her African ancestry would make her feel at home: "Was it obvious I was a foreigner? Surely I wasn't in the same category as the European tourists on the plane with me. I had dark skin, and my facial features were clearly African." Celeste found the Ghanaians kind and hospitable, but she felt devastatingly foreign. "I had never felt so Western, so American, so lonely . . ." She could not imagine living where she visited. "I mean, there are lizards all over the place! I am so prissy. I am so boojie . . . I am scared and I am lonely and I want to go home. . . . I was supposed to feel this bond because I was in Mother Africa. Instead, I felt like an outsider. I felt like an American." Other African Americans have had the same disconcerting experience. Celeste was the most poised of the undergraduates, secure in her own competence, and perhaps this made her more willing to talk about an experience that had felt like failure only two years in the past.

The same processes of learning that shape us into successful members of our own communities make us foreigners elsewhere, and this has little to do with genes or skin color. Even though Americans today are increasingly knowledgeable about cultural differences—a lot of journalists seem to have taken Anthropology 101—it has gotten harder, not easier, for Americans to encounter other cultures, because of the comforts we have become accustomed to and the sanitizing of the environment. I told Celeste that next time she goes to Africa she should learn to appreciate the little gecko lizards that cling to the walls of houses open to the climate, relentlessly pursuing insects, chirping from time to time, but girls in America are taught to fear reptiles, and the idea of wild creatures sharing the same house evokes roaches and mice.

Everyone we meet has used innate capacities to acquire differences from most of humanity, by internalizing local traditions. During this process, shared human potentials are shaped to fit contrasting expectations. Depending on environment, individuals learn to learn or, far too often, *not* to learn, so early perhaps that there are impacts on neurological development that may inhibit adaptation over a lifetime and may be passed on in the rearing of children and grandchildren. Subtle indicators of discrimination, deep pessimism in the behavior of adults reflecting the lack of meaningful opportunities later in life, may affect the learning process very early, so that a child may be primed to fail long before starting school. We underestimate the effect of any specific lesson on the continuing capacity to learn. When and how do infant girls learn not to be good at math, perhaps the last major disability remaining from the many they used to be taught they had? Because I grew up in an unusual and bookish household, I was sure that I could succeed in mathematics but deeply doubtful that I could or would acquire any athletic skills: everybody who mattered to me could handle abstractions, but none of them could catch a ball.

How long did it take, with the breakdown of the taboo on visual representation, for the emergence of the first visual artists in modern Jewish history? Modigliani, Chagall, Soutine, Epstein, and a score of others who came later are evidence that Jews had no innate inability to paint and sculpt, that the apparent lack had to do with potentials unexplored and unstimulated by a cultural environment. It took generations of living side by side for white men like Buddy Holly to begin to learn from black jazz musicians, instead of assuming that the sense of rhythm is a racial characteristic—and even longer before black women asserted their ability to be jazz instrumentalists as well as singers, so that one of the feminist innovations at Spelman is an all-female jazz ensemble.

Nevertheless, growing up within a community does not produce homogeneity, and neighbors are often at odds. The illusion of shared values, whether in nations or in households, is enhanced where there is a power structure in which only the values of a few are recognized while other divergences are concealed. In a patriarchal household or a monarchy, there may be the appearance of consensus, an appearance restored even after revolution in countries with autocratic traditions like Iran or Russia. "What I say goes" is a wonderfully easy way to resolve differences of opinion, echoing through the ages in the voices of fathers and mothers, husbands and teachers, bosses and dictators.

It is not easy to orchestrate highly diverse groups of people without a rigid hierarchy backed by possible coercion, like that of an army or a ship. Warfare almost always evokes authoritarian models of consensus, offering an easy way to decide whether to plan for guns or butter. The hierarchical structure inherited from Imperial Rome by the

Catholic Church and many other organizations was developed for military purposes. The Roman Empire included many peoples, polyglot and pledged to different gods, but diversity was, for a long time at least, a manageable problem. As distances and diversity increased, there was less and less room for discussion, while decision making was limited to a smaller and smaller group. Rome, like other ancient empires, was diverse but not pluralistic, and the same has been true of human families in many cultures. Later empires, like that of the czars, used forced acculturation or genocide to reduce diversity as well as limit its expression.

Human diversity makes top-down control easier, making it possible to divide and conquer while still getting the benefit of a variety of skills and talents. When members of ships' crews were lost and replacements shanghaied in any convenient port, the fact that they saw the world differently was actually an advantage for the captain. During the years of the slave trade, human merchandise from numerous tribes and regions was mixed together; the ordeals of the middle passage, of auctions and rape and labor in the fields, might not be shared with a single speaker of the same language, yet even under these terrible circumstances empathy and mutual comfort could emerge and differences did not preclude caring.

Diversity is never absent in any human community. In the early years of its history, anthropology focused on the commonalities within small and isolated societies, those ways of thinking and acting learned by each individual and held in common by the group. Any adult, it was thought, would give the same answer to such questions as how to make the past tense of *take,* whether it is proper for a man to marry his father's brother's daughter, or where the sun goes when it sets. So you often hear statements that "the Samoans" or "the Navaho" or "the San" share some opinion or kind of behavior. They do, and so do the French or the Russians, but at the same time they also share disagreement, and misunderstandings occur everywhere. Often these are part of a tradition as well, quarrels that come up again and again, part of a pattern, overt or covert, of agreeing to disagree, that allows cops and robbers to participate in the same battles and ballets, and prison guards to join the PTA.

In my own understanding of my intellectual (and real) ancestors, I locate this shift in awareness from emphasis on homogeneity to the recognition of culturally patterned diversity in the decade that followed Ruth Benedict's first descriptions of the cultural styles shared within certain tribes of Native Americans. Benedict described styles that men and women, young and old, clever and simple, seemed to hold in common, so that words previously used to describe personality might be used to describe a whole community. The next step was the discovery in research in New Guinea that such commonalities might apply to groups within a society, for example to the men, setting them in conventionalized contrast with women. Many of the differences between males and females are of this kind, with differing methods of child rearing used by the same parents to evoke complementary styles within a single family.

This thinking about the relationship between culture and personality, sex and temperament, set the stage for the study of much more complex societies during World War II. Even in the study of the enemy, it became clear that overgeneralization was hazardous, and this insight was epitomized by the contrasts and tensions in Ruth Benedict's title of her book about Japan, *The Chrysanthemum and the Sword*. Since the war anthropologists, like sociologists, have dealt with diversity in many dimensions, studying change and colonialism, minority-majority relations, and migration.

The problem of difference is not a new one, not an artifact of modern conditions. Every culture has a characteristic mosaic of differences and ways of both enhancing and suppressing them. We need to know more about the legacy of conventions and skills that human beings have developed to bridge or balance difference and embrace tension. Children need to be offered ways to express respect and pursue their curiosity simultaneously, to honor others by trying to understand them.

New patterns of diversity come into being constantly, like ripple patterns in a pond. The gradual acquisition of new cultural traits, often from another group, always creates a gradient of difference within a society, like high and low pressure areas moving across a weather map: those who grew up with New Math and those who did not, those who have learned to watch their cholesterol levels and those who have not, those who have seen the latest hit movie, learned the latest dance . . . When change affects one individual before it affects others, you see ripples of turbulence but also the starting points for new forms of adaptation, creativity at the margins.

American society has been engaged in an extraordinarily difficult experiment with its own increasing diversity: allowing every member of the polity to have *and express* opinions. This means sacrificing a great many conveniences and conventions that make a system run smoothly, so it is not surprising that many people think the experiment has gone too far. There has been a growing pattern of debate about how much diversity any community can tolerate. It is no accident that we can see a move to the right, demands for a more punitive criminal justice system to punish deviations and for the exclusion of immigrants and homosexuals, demands for programs to promote uniformity and English-only policies. As the millennium approached, Americans began to exaggerate the commonalities of the past, to be nostalgic for romanticized images of eras when values seemed to be shared, harmony was the rule, and everyone was content with his or her lot, accepting and living by a single set of values in a sentimental-ized TV world. Much of this nostalgia is delusory. Friction and mis-understanding have always been present. And again and again what seemed unthinkable at one point in time past has become a treasured part of the common wisdom.

We live in a polyphonic world, but not everyone listens. When my teaching at George Mason, a coeducational institution, focuses on women's lives, there is never more than a handful of men in the class. They are understandably unwilling to personify "the Other" or be asked for "the male point of view." They are welcome, however, for the rare opportunity to listen and be in the minority. Young men es-pecially, even though they have had women as teachers, often have difficulty learning from the experiences of women as these appear in life histories. But because the composition of women's lives has al-tered more rapidly in our time than that of men's, the implications of contemporary changes are most tellingly explored in the lives of women. Men today are aware of facing new discontinuities in their own lives and aware that the future may not match their expectations. Black men suffer from a mismatch between American values, which they grow up mostly to share, and the opportunities open to them, but more and more white men are facing similar dilemmas as traditional patterns of privilege shift and change. All young people, black and white, are facing problems as their elders decline to "stand down."

If the class had not been closed to cross registration, I probably would have had one or two male students from Morehouse College next door, and perhaps one or two older men, but there was no way I could have gotten parity. The process might have been more difficult if the group had included men, bringing in their own power struggles and a greater need to distance from me, but even more revealing.

When my daughter drove me down to Atlanta, she stayed over for a night, and she insisted, knowing that her mom is generally on the wrong side of gradients of awareness in popular culture, on preparing me by taking me to a film about love and marriage between prosperous black men and women, *Waiting to Exhale.* All semester long, jokes about the movie cropped up among students who could imagine themselves with the same kinds of futures, reminding me that gender still plays differently for African Americans. (My own favorite for Spelman? Waiting to excel.)

There is a kind of competition in the black community for the dubious honor of being at the greater disadvantage: black women, who say they suffer from two isms, a double whammy, and black men, who talk of becoming an endangered species. When I suggested late in the spring that black women have certain advantages compared with black men—they are less frightening to white people than men and less likely to be harassed by the police, and at least at the level of bare survival they are better off, even though the available work is demeaning—I got a chorus of disagreement. Nevertheless, black women have had to be resourceful and adaptable, so they are largely free from the "learned helplessness" that afflicts young white women, sometimes making me want to shake them. Being strong is an important theme for young black women, and tears are fiercely resisted. However, at a middle-class institution like Spelman, some kinds of "learned resilience" may be lost. It would be better if the learning moved in the opposite direction.

Highlighting cross-generational communication between women in our seminar instead of mixing genders allowed for a certain freshness of discovery. At another level, however, I feel regret, wishing I could go back and address the same questions with a group of young men. Too often when feminists speak of "patriarchy" they forget that this familiar term refers as much to generation as to gender and that young men suffer as well. Treating women like children may even set the scene for treating members of a different race or culture as chattel. Both age and sex may be connected to positions of power in which it is possible to avoid learning.

In a public speech I gave at Spelman I used a story I have told repeatedly in recent years, from a paper written by a student of mine at Mason, Chessalay Blanchard, now Zimmerman, a tall, blond young woman who had participated as a reservist in Operation Desert Storm. Chessalay described a series of interactions she had had as a seventeen-year-old with the grandmother, in her seventies, illiterate and speaking almost no English, of a Mexican immigrant family living next door. The grandmother, whom the children called Miaba, had come to live with a son who had found his niche and prospered in the United States, but she had chosen to spend her time in a small outbuilding built by her son to give her privacy and approximate the simple conditions she had grown up to be comfortable with. The two families became friendly through the friendship between Chessalay's little brother and Miaba's grandson. "One day," Chessalay wrote, "I came looking for my brother. As I walked around the corner of the house, there was Miaba, stripped to the waist and bathing under a makeshift shower on the side of her little shack. I stopped, quite startled and embarrassed by my intrusion into her private ritual. She saw me and motioned for me to come over. Gingerly, I walked nearer, until I realized that her ablutions were spiritual and that she was using something other than soap.

"I am sure that my fear and uncertainty showed on my face, for Miaba smiled and took my hand. Gently, she led me to the barrel under the lean-to. She unbuttoned my light summer blouse and pushed it off my arms. There were jars everywhere, all holding liquids with distinct colors and odors. I could see by this point that she had painted herself with these liquids. She began pointing to different jars and making motions, trying to explain the meanings they concealed. Slowly, she dipped a finger in the reddish jar and pointed to my belly. She folded her arms as if holding a baby. As I watched in complete fascination, she painted circles on my abdomen. Another jar held a thick blue mud. This she put on my temples and forehead, with the admonition 'No go crazy.' The green went on my breasts, perhaps for health or maybe good milk.

"She continued until the upper half of my body was covered with paint, and I realized that our colors matched. I tried to communicate this, holding our matching arms together. She smiled, nodded."

The relationship between the old woman and the young girl continued, based on small gifts and skills learned through imitation, almost entirely nonverbal, until three years later, when Miaba's grandson, the playmate of Chessalay's brother, died in a shooting incident. Miaba took to her bed, refusing to speak or eat. Chessalay agreed to stay with her while the family went to the church, and found her curled in a state of despair and withdrawal. After a few efforts to offer food or tidy the space, Chessalay ran to her own house next door and brought an old set of tempera paints. "I lifted her, quilt and all, and carried her out into the sun . . . and I began to paint our faces black, smearing the thick mess everywhere. I continued until we were covered, and I held her like a baby while she shook with her grief. Some time went by, and she rose. She returned with a picture of her grandson and some matches. I picked up the towel she pointed to and began to wipe the paint off as she searched through my childhood art supply bag. When I looked up, she was holding the jar of white paint. Slowly, she rinsed off all the black and replaced it with white. We turned into crazy white ghosts as she lit a match and put the flame to the picture. When it had dissolved into ashes, she spoke one word: 'Peace.' "

I love this story, because it shows two people of different ages, ethnicities, and religions improvising and making do with a limited set of symbols, creating commonality in order to reach out to each other. They draw on fragments from childhood or from past encounters, incompletely understood, and fragments from the new English liturgy of the Catholic Church, the passing of the peace, to use when language fails. I was nervous about repeating the story at Spelman, for the uses of "black face" and "white face" are sensitive matters—but both black and white appear as colors of mourning in many cultures, faces veiled or unwashed, smeared with ashes or clay that can both darken and lighten. Symbolism and ritual have a syntax, in which repetition and partial repetition create meaning and acknowledge similarity. My nervousness about telling the story to a largely black audience was a minor echo of the sense of risk that both women must have shared, not unlike the sense of risk we feel when we reencounter friends from childhood, perhaps on a first grown-up date, fearing rejection and afraid to give pain.

These two women, determined to connect across a gulf of unknowing, seem to me extraordinarily courageous, since neither had any way of being sure how the other would respond. In the first episode, I assume, Miaba was following a cultural script that would have made her ablutions intelligible and predictable, and allowed for the relationship between an older and a younger woman, perhaps some kind of initiation. But Chessalay could not know that script. In the second episode neither woman had a script. Chessalay improvised a makeshift ritual, built on their earlier relationship, and Miaba improvised an ending for it, her own transition to the next stage of grieving.

Each woman acted from a different continuity. Miaba is an immigrant, someone born in a different country and arriving without the knowledge and skills for the new one. But every newborn is also an immigrant, and our era is unique in that each new generation is born into a changing country. Each of us, as an adult, is an immigrant, for the country I was born into in 1939 was not the same as the country I live in today, though at least immigrants in time rather than space have the opportunity to adapt more gradually. The undergraduates in my Spelman seminar were born into a different country from the elders, but all of us bore the stamp of where and when we had matured.

This is why we so often face the choice between following old scripts that are no longer adequate and doing without. Yet, with goodwill, it is possible for individuals from different backgrounds to improvise together, to reach into their memories for materials from other settings and blend them together in a common performance. Many myths, like those of Genesis, and archaeological remains as well, point to a common origin of all human beings, long ago. More important is the convergence and overlapping of traditions. Children of any reader of this book might migrate to any country on the planet, might fall in love with men or women of any race or culture and raise their children. All of our children will have the task of inventing the future.

5 | *Adulthood–The Real of Me*

When Ama joined our seminar she described herself as standing "at a bridge called cynicism, struggling to cross over treacherous waters of fatigue, indecision, and sorrow . . . the business of aging, negotiating menopause, moving from mother to girlfriend in my daughter's life—a crossing of cultures, transitioning from known to unknown, from futuring to memory." A Spelman alumna approaching fifty, she had returned to Atlanta to begin the next phase of her professional life of consulting and counseling, but in the early months after her return she had to deal with one loss after another. Ama has worked with hospice patients, especially those with AIDS, but their deaths became intertwined with the deaths of friends like Toni Cade Bambara, the African American writer, and the process of planning Toni's funeral and clearing her apartment.

Ama did little writing for the seminar, although she had been present and engaged through all our discussions. "I couldn't write about my life," she told me six months later. "Right at that moment it felt so bad I didn't want to touch it. Only in the last month have I started feeling good. I had to come full circle with this. I did not recognize that I was just damn depressed until my daughter said to me, 'I want my mommy back.' I said, 'What are you talking about?' and she said, 'You are just . . . just relating to the *dog.* Just not wanting to give anything.' This has been one hell. . . . I have sorted big things out and declared different things about myself and my work to the universe." And begun another chapter of an ongoing story.

There was a time when most stories about girls simply ended with marriage: the princess and the prince were married and lived happily ever after, boy met/lost/married girl, romance bloomed and ended in. . . stasis, perhaps because there were so few choices to be made. Childbearing followed naturally on marriage, not a matter of choice or decision but a tragedy almost like early death if it failed.

We are still haunted by stereotypes and traditional expectations. Women are only just beginning to explore the range of alternatives that lie in our extended adulthoods, reaching into decades that were essentially unstoried in the past, often discovering more than one new plotline and startling their families. The sweeping away of the once necessary preoccupation of female adulthood with child rearing, leaving room for new possibilities, has given women the most vivid sense of the change that has occurred in the shape of lives and the creativity required to adapt. Many men are just beginning to wonder uneasily why the future flows so differently ahead of them and what is changing behind their backs, but men, too, are learning to live multiple stories. They used to joke, When Alexander the Great was my age, when Mozart was my age . . . they were dead. Neither men nor women now accept the notion that the chance for achievement or romance is past at forty or fifty, or that bearing and rearing children is the central task of life.

Ama, reaching menopause, spoke of discovering "the real of me." She is at the beginning of a stage of adult life that hardly existed for all the generations that have preceded us, almost like a second adulthood. Over the past few years I have begun to believe that it is important to live these years as more than a continuation or a repetition, to reexamine the past and to reimagine the future.

Through most of human history, adult work, marriage, and childbearing meant that the die was cast and fresh starts were a very rare luxury. Now, however, there is a substantial period when many women no longer find the meaning in their lives through their roles as mothers, and do not immediately segue into the grandparent role. Instead, this is a time for fresh starts. It corresponds to a period in the lives of many men, still healthy and energetic, when they realize that the limits of their achievements on a particular path are in sight and may feel futility or disappointment. Men sometimes respond to this mixture of restlessness and possibility by leaving their wives, marrying again, and starting new families—basically trying, with notable lack of imagination, for a second adulthood on the same plan as the first. Women cannot so easily repeat their childbearing years, so they more often start new careers, often going back to school for new degrees, released from caretaking. Meanwhile, some men find other and more imaginative kinds of new beginnings. Some husbands are rejuvenated by their wives' new energies, and more and more men as well as women are learning to reimagine themselves professionally.

The shape of lives is changing. It is changing for the young, whose bodies mature early but who must wait longer to take their places in the adult world. It is also changing for adults, whose lives are longer and healthier, with more opportunities for revision and second thoughts. The students in the seminar were still in a limbo, not yet full adults, while the elders were still making choices, busy with unfolding chapters of adulthood, not old age. Here we all were—alive, healthy, and looking ahead to new experiments and new learning. Adulthood has become a long era with freedom for multiple new beginnings.

You can think of lives and populations as having different shapes. The latest of these shapes, the template of our lives today and the responsibilities it entails, remains to be explored. Increased longevity—the way we manipulate biology—has an effect on every age and stage, as well as on systems of meaning and concepts such as maturity and childhood, love and family. We have not only added some fifty years to life expectancy since the invention of agriculture, thanks to increments of knowledge and control, but added twenty of those years since World War II. We need to develop new understandings of how adulthood must change as it unfolds over time, beginning later and lasting longer, and how this changed timing will affect the relationships between generations.

There are many species in which parents never meet their offspring, moving on or dying off before the eggs they have laid are hatched. There are others, closer to us in evolutionary terms, in which the young, newly born or newly hatched, require ongoing care, sometimes by one, sometimes by both parents, but have no continuing connection after maturity, except perhaps as members of a flock or herd. The pride and joy of becoming a grandparent may be uniquely human, but the dependence of one generation on another for memory and knowledge may play out in other species as a crucial role in the herd or pack for the oldest living member—the doe who knows where to find fodder in winters of heavy snow or the lioness who remembers where the game congregate during drought. The alpha male of pack or herd is likely to be challenged in old age by younger males, while the oldest females can continue to draw on their experience to offer an alternative kind of leadership.

Once upon a time, in deep prehistory, when those who survived until puberty could be expected to live only another fifteen or twenty years, human populations really did fall into two main groups, dependent children and mature adults, with a very few longer survivors. This is after all the pattern for most wild animals, individuals very rapidly dying off after the reproductive years. As the species that survives by learning and teaching, however, human beings have learned to rely on the knowledge of those who have lived longest, valuing them and respecting them for their contribution to the life of the group. For most of our history, human life fell into three periods, childhood, adulthood, and old age, three coexisting generations. Languages do have ways of talking about a fourth or fifth generation (*great-* and *great-great-*grandparents in English), but these so far are usually rather makeshift extrapolations from the basic three, with various terms for others already dead, progenitors, ancestors, forefathers and foremothers. Now it is more and more common to have four living generations, and families have to provide children with terms of address for unprecedented numbers of grands.

Two of the American life histories we read in the seminar continued past the birth of grandchildren, the life of Sarah Rice, a black woman in the American South, and that of my mother, Margaret Mead, and we had several grandmothers in our number. Sarah was born in rural poverty and had her early career as a teacher disrupted by two unhappy marriages. She finally hit her stride in her forties, however, when she married Andrew Rice, "the only real husband" she had. By the time she was recording her life history, cleaning houses for white women and a leader in her church, she was established in both communities and widely respected as a source of wise and trenchant advice. "I know who I am and what I want and where I'm going. If there's a problem to confront, get it over with, and love the people right on."

Marymal and Cheryl had to rediscover themselves more than once, first after becoming disillusioned with their early choices, and then to set new courses for later stages. For Marymal, as for Sarah Rice, transitions were organized around marriages and the moves these entailed. Cheryl was born two decades after Marymal, so historic events affected her differently, but when everyone thought she had everything she could possibly want, she went through a comparable transition of self-discovery. Childbearing came for her after first youth with the force of a revelation. What the two women have in common is not which choices each made when, but the fact of making choices and new starts.

Cheryl was reserved in the seminar, making a conscious effort not to preempt the voices of the students, but she was eloquent and outspoken when we sat down with a tape recorder. "The world had given me the best of what the world deemed possible for a black woman of that time," she said, "and people were so thrilled for me. In New York in the early seventies everyone was courting black people from the Ivy League and the Seven Sisters and you just had your choice, all these jobs that people thought were so fabulous. I had been in Europe after graduation, and I came back and got wooed by *Time* magazine. I thought I was supposed to know what I was doing, supposed to have it all. Yet I was deeply depressed and I did not have a clue. I had met lots of men working in New York, and I married at twenty-seven *because* I did not have a clue. Looking from the outside, people thought of me as a success, but from inside I felt like I had literally been going through the motions in this muffled kinda . . . nothing felt right. All of these things that I was supposed to value because the world valued them, I hated it all. Whatever it was that was acceptable and wonderful and that people wanted, I had it. I never experienced it as valuable."

Cheryl's voice trailed off as she thought back, and then she continued with firmness. "The great thing was, on my twenty-ninth birthday I gave birth to our daughter. You know? Starting back at the beginning to make a life that made sense to me."

I do know, because like Cheryl I have only one child, a daughter, born when I was twenty-nine. It is curious that so few life histories written by women dwell on the experiences of motherhood. One of the reasons I assign my mother's autobiography is because she does talk about these experiences, perhaps because by the time she had me she was thirty-seven, well along in a career that included the systematic observation of mothers and children and the study of child-rearing customs.

Cheryl's path to motherhood was different from mine, however, because the idea of motherhood came to her suddenly, and from that moment every step of the process was easy. "I was astonished. I never thought . . . I had a hundred-something dolls and a whole room to play with them. I did some serious playing up there, but I was not playing mother. I was directing and scripting, I was God, and they had adventures." Doll play was for Cheryl a preparation for the career she found later.

"I actually had one of those 'soul conversations,' when I would not have known enough to call it that. Something inside me, deep, I won't say a voice, said, 'Get pregnant,' and I said to my husband immediately, 'Let's get pregnant.' And everything turned from there. I came out of my depression, I had the best pregnancy, I was just in ecstasy. I thought I was the most beautiful creature that ever was. I was not one of those poor pitiful pregnant ladies who sit and act depressed. I was gorgeous, and I just made love all the way through pregnancy. I had a great labor and delivery. Everything about it was a total shock, surprise, and pleasure.

"It was astonishing that I became a mother with so much ease and pleasure. I often think . . . I wouldn't say I came into my womanhood. I came into myself. I came into the beginning of my self. I think it was the thrusting through the whole thing that had been given to me and created for me and that was supposed to be such a treasure, but which for me wasn't a treasure. There was something so deep, so literally visceral, so life and death about it, that I think it was the first—oh! you mean this is your one and only life and you can do whatever the hell you want with it? That!"

"That!" A transition that perhaps depends on the possibility of fulfillment and the awareness of choice. Many women are not yet ready for that transition when they have children, as Marymal was not, and make it in other ways later. Some make it in the discovery of a life's work outside the home. "That!" in its many different forms may be another name for freedom. Writing about her current choices, Ama spoke of discovering "the real of me."

My mother and I did not make careers of motherhood, but we were both baby carriage peekers, vividly aware of our desire for children for a long time. She had had repeated early miscarriages and had virtually given up hope. My husband and I had been finishing our degrees, and when we decided it was time I was slow in conceiving and gave birth prematurely to a son, who died a few hours later. Our daughter, Sevanne, who was born just before I turned thirty, was long hoped for.

Although the phrase "biological clock" was not yet current, I had begun to worry about ever having a child. So I responded to Cheryl's story by talking about late mothers I had known.

"I don't think of twenty-nine as late," she responded. "I have friends my age who are having their first child now."

"Having a first child in your late forties, even in your fifties, is common now," I pointed out, "but even thirty was old then. The whole legitimation of having a first child in your thirties or forties hadn't happened. You said your life as an adult woman began when you gave birth, right? But the interesting thing to me is, if you have a child at sixteen you do get reclassified as an adult for certain purposes, but you're still not. . . . It's as if the birth of a late child were a different kind of transition, a different rite of passage. Because that realization that you have one and only one life to live just doesn't happen at sixteen or even twenty."

Cheryl had described filling out a questionnaire that asked the question "What do you like about yourself?" and answering that she *keeps trying again.* Speaking of how important it had been for the students to get a sense of the lives of the elders, Iyabo had mentioned Cheryl when she spoke of the elders having to struggle, but she could not know the saga of how Cheryl has repeatedly chosen the risks of creative self-employment over the glamorous jobs of her youth. What most of the students could not yet know was the enormous privilege, because of the emerging shape of lives in the modern world, of recurring opportunities for choice and repeated chances not only to try again but to make a fresh start with new skills and a new vision.

Many of the books we read together focused on childhood and young adulthood, but Nisa was our example of the full sweep of a life as women's lives once were, constructed around motherhood. In class we followed her from childhood to old age, five husbands and several lovers, five babies lost to death in infancy or childhood, and a last child adopted after menopause. Nisa had considerable freedom in the choice of partners, but the shape of her life as a woman and as a mother was determined by the foraging lifestyle of the San, moving around for most of the year with a small band and very few possessions, living on wild food. As long as the San were hunting and gathering in the veld of southern Africa, with no domesticated animals to milk and little in the way of grains, extended nursing was a necessity for infants to survive. Mothers carried their infants with them, fastened to their bodies, nursing as often as several times an hour. This stimulation of the nipples, perhaps combined with hours of walking, suppressed ovulation as long as it continued, for four years or so, leading to a three- to five-year spacing of pregnancies.

If you play with the figures for first pregnancy and the spacing of births, the picture of what it meant to be a woman among the San is startlingly unfamiliar. Menstruation was a relatively rare experience, occurring two or three times before each pregnancy. The real constant of a woman's adult life was lactation. Menopause, somewhere between forty and fifty, was less clear, since often menstruation was simply never resumed after weaning a last child. Lifetime exposure to estrogen was low. In effect, these women spent up to twenty years of their lives nursing, carrying infants with them wherever they went, along with the nuts and roots they foraged in the veld, as well as water or firewood. This set a built-in limit on childbearing, with the average number of births at just under five per woman, spaced out in a way that made a nomadic life possible; you cannot pick up all your belongings and walk if too many infants have to be carried. For the San, child care was a necessary constant in the lives of women, but neither pregnancy nor child care kept them from the essential tasks of gathering.

When we discussed extended nursing in class, one student knew that she had been nursed for a long time, going to her mother and demanding "boo-boo juice," which broke the class up. At the same time some of the students were shocked, even embarrassed, as if it were immoral to breast-feed for more than a few months or as if the image of a three-year-old, able to walk and talk, stopping by and demanding a pick-me-up from Nisa's breast were somehow obscene. This was part of a broader discomfort with any hint that there might be a component of sexual pleasure in infancy for both mother and child, that both fathers and mothers might feel an erotic thrill at the delicious tenderness of young children without either acting on it or feeling guilty about it.

A more hazardous picture of human maternity emerged after the invention of agriculture. Settled lives and alternative weaning foods allowed the number of pregnancies to more than double. With constant childbearing women's lives came to be shorter than men's, with frequent deaths in childbirth, a pattern that can be traced in any colonial graveyard. Affluence and contraception changed the pattern again, creating the modern situation of women outliving men, but in the least developed areas of the world, one woman in 13 still dies of causes related to pregnancy and childbirth, compared with one in 3,300 in the United States.

As long as they retained their traditional customs, the San had healthy and adequate diets, and adults lived well into their sixties, spared the dangerous stress and squalor of contemporary life. But what with all the standard infectious diseases, including colds and flu, and malaria as well, nearly half of all infants died before they reached reproductive age. Virtually every parent experienced the death of a child; Nisa had seen the deaths, at different times, of all of her children. The San had a stable population, something few of us have ever seen. We know we need to work to stabilize human populations, but we hope to do so without depending on the subtractions of early death, whether from disease and famine or from war and violence.

Through most of human history adults who have survived until reproductive age have had an average life expectancy of thirty more years, to about fifty. The Biblical threescore and ten was an aspiration, not an average. Every woman in the class, elders as well as students, was younger than the average life expectancy for women today in the United States, but all of the elders had passed that landmark as it was for fortunate ladies of the Paleolithic and average ladies of the Neolithic. Furthermore, although family planning may have been limited when our first children were born, most of us had stopped with small families. The kinds of conversations we were having about lives have become possible only in modern times. For women living in the developed world in the late twentieth century, a mere fraction of a long adulthood is devoted to childbearing and child rearing. Even for those who choose to bear as many children as biology permits, there are many years to be lived when the nest is empty.

How will adulthood change as it becomes longer and longer? Increasingly it will be lived in installments, with multiple chapters and new beginnings, like those described by Marymal and Cheryl, like Ama's and Johnnetta's moving to Atlanta, or like my becoming a writer in my forties and finding a new academic home to accommodate that. There will be new understandings of marriage. Sociologists have pointed out that even with high divorce rates, marriages today last longer than they did two centuries ago—when death came earlier, on the average, than divorce does now. Surely an institution that evolved to last ten to twenty years must be reconsidered when it is likely to last fifty and when both partners have scope for new learning and freedom to express what they learn—especially if leaving a marriage does not mean becoming an outcast.

Nisa liked being married, following the pattern of "serial polygamy" that seems to be developing in many contemporary societies. She also liked the excitement of love affairs, talking candidly of the different pleasures of married and illicit love, and this led the seminar into a long discussion of how our ideas of marriage and of male and female preferences are shaped by the double standard and by economic systems that make women dependents. Iyabo and Johnnetta did a joint presentation on Nisa in which Johnnetta approached the material very much from an anthropological point of view, but Iyabo made it clear in a paper she wrote later that the material had run head-on into her value system and her hopes for the future. "Am I wrong to think that it is ridiculous to be with that many men in a lifetime? Is the idea of having one love a Western idea and could we as a society be much happier if we were able to choose the ones we loved according to what we needed in that particular time period?" Iyabo framed all the issues she found uncomfortable as rhetorical questions. "Is there a true belief in the sanctity of marriage with the !Kung?"

In class I had emphasized the difference between relativity as a methodological principle—not judging any custom until you see how it fits in with other aspects of the culture—and moral relativism as an ideological one, but the disadvantages associated with being a woman are so widespread as to be almost part of the human condition, something that must be resolved together now that the lives of all groups are so closely entangled. "I remember when Dr. Cole and I were putting together our presentation," Iyabo continued, shying away from the first name in an essay, "how she remarked to me, 'The beatings [sometimes following on love affairs] have got to go.' This practice seemed to be accepted, just by the way Nisa took it by saying, 'And life went on.' Trying to reconcile this is hard. Is it wrong for me to feel that this is wrong no matter what, or have I failed at being objective?"

When property increases, and the inheritance of land is central, in-laws and the surrounding community all stand together to preserve marriages, and divorce is not the private decision it has become in America today. In the seminar more than half of all marriages had ended in divorce. Several of the elders, like Marymal and Johnnetta, had blended families, and several were taking responsibility for the children of kinfolk whose families had fallen apart. Today, whatever the ideals we continue to cherish, we need models for marriages that end, without calling them failures, and models for humane divorce to give continuity to children when family constellations change, as they so often did in the past because of early death.

Ama had described her first marriage to an activist in the Civil Rights Movement as a "marriage of revolutionaries," a transient relationship that matched a moment in history. My mother called her first marriage a "student marriage," one that produced "neither a book nor a child." She wrote about "trial marriages," like those common among the San, and argued ahead of her time for the pattern that has become widespread today, of young people living together in easily dissoluble relationships before they have children—and for the need to approach childbearing with clarity and commitment, conscious choice. Yet another kind of pairing, sunset romance, is beginning to emerge after children are grown up and gone, and it may be displacing grandparental engagement.

Few of the life histories we read involved a youthful first marriage leading to "happiness ever after." If two people are to continue learning and growing throughout their lives, developing through multiple stages and chapters, only a combination of effort and luck can assure that neither of them will be stunted and that they will still be in harmony. Joan Erikson, one of the women I wrote about in *Composing a Life,* remained in a single marriage all her life, moving constantly to new places with her husband. Four of us in the seminar were still married to a first husband, including me, but my husband and I have reformatted our marriage repeatedly, sometimes commuting and sometimes living long periods apart. Adaptation ever after. In several of the lives we read, the last marriage of a series was finally the happiest. Sarah Rice and Le Ly Hayslip, the Vietnamese woman who ended up in America after turmoil and disruption, would both have argued for marriage as offering happiness—but not with the loves of their youth. Marymal and Johnnetta are both happily married, but not on the first try.

Others, like Ama and Cheryl, have been married and had children but today seem to prefer to be single, free to move to new places and explore new careers. When Ama was describing her own midlife transition, she said, "I have looked back without any anger at my two marriages, and I have recognized that I don't like being married. I started saying that out loud about three years ago and trying to look at it and figure out, Are those good reasons not to like it?" Ama's daughter came back to live at home for a time after college, leaving Ama vehemently convinced that she is no longer willing to play that kind of mommy role, so today she lives contentedly alone.

For most human beings the central constancy of adult life has been work. Just as changes in fertility and a longer life expectancy alter the meaning of marriage, changing technologies have required new ways of thinking about the nature and goals of work. Although they own so little, only what they can carry, Nisa's people have been described as the "original affluent society," for making a living was not burdensome for them. Men hunted only two or three days a week, and women went out gathering only slightly more often. Cooperation and sharing provided the basic fabric of security, so San life discouraged competition and was lived in daily contact with a small band, usually related in some way, and a looser relationship to a much larger group that gathered only when water was plentiful. There was a constant flow of food and small gifts back and forth, creating and reinforcing the obligation to share, for giving was literally the only way of keeping.

This changed as the San, partly because of external pressure, shifted into different economic and political patterns. Many of the San now work for the Tswana and the Herero, taller and darker-skinned peoples, who have moved into their territory and regard themselves as racially superior. Living in one place, paid for their services in money or milk or grain, the San can begin to accumulate property, although customs of gift exchange are still strong. With alternative ways of feeding infants, San women have one baby after another, without the recuperation for the mother and protection for the child offered by long and frequent nursing. Both infant mortality and maternal death have increased, but not as fast as population. As independent subsistence is replaced by the experience of differences in wealth, material improvement is framed by dependency and poverty. The San have more possessions now but less freedom, and both the status of women and the self-esteem of men are undermined.

The transition to settled living has occurred over and over again in the last ten thousand years as human beings learned to produce and store foods. The domestication of plants and animals has allowed the production of surpluses so that some members of society are no longer busy with food production and can live in cities and think deep thoughts. This is the beginning of civilization and the intensive cultivation of knowledge and the arts. Meanwhile, farmers become peasants: part of a larger economy, governed by beliefs and laws promulgated somewhere else. Just as the authors of the Book of Genesis saw childbearing as a curse, they saw work—the work of farming—as a curse, in ways in which hunter-gatherers usually do not. Thus the

San are now going through the transition called the Neolithic revolution, which began with the invention of agriculture about ten thousand years ago and has almost entirely worked itself out: today there are very few foragers left. Other, later "revolutions" in the economic basis of society continue simultaneously. Since the eighteenth century the transitions of the industrial revolution have swept an increasing proportion of humanity off the land entirely and into cities. With every shift the numbers of human beings have increased.

In speaking about the shapes of lives in farming communities, we could think about the backgrounds of many of the life histories we read, for there are similarities between Chinese and Vietnamese village agriculture, sharecropping in the American South, and farming among the Shona of Zimbabwe. I could also think back to what I knew of villages in Iran, where my husband and I encountered simultaneously a modernizing urban society, introducing technology on a Western model, and patterns centuries old, which continued to shape family life and the life cycle. The tension was played out in the Islamic revolution of 1979, which has attempted to continue some kinds of modernization while restoring orthodoxy and the kind of family life that developed when most people were farmers: lots of babies and very few choices for women.

New kinds of wealth increase the possibilities for inequality, and women have repeatedly lost ground during periods of technological and economic development. Gathering wild foods or working the soil with a digging stick or a hoe, women have often had near equality, with land and its fertility associated with their own reproductivity and passed on through the female line. When agriculture began to include domesticated animals as large as those men once hunted, they tended to become male property, and so did the machines that followed. Cash crops and the division of the household economy between a domestic sphere and an "export" sphere fitted in with traditions of greater male mobility. Even on Israeli kibbutzim, with an egalitarian ideology, there has been a tendency to assign women to traditionally female services like laundry, cooking, and child care, while those activities that produce significant cash income are more honored and give the men who usually manage them a greater voice. In many parts of Africa, farming for household consumption is almost entirely in the hands of women, with the men engaged in various forms of migrant labor, bringing back cash if the women are lucky. All these trends tend to limit the influence and independence of women, and it is taking the full benefits of modern technology to recover.

I would have liked to assign a Muslim autobiography, preferably that of an Iranian village woman, for my class, but no available book-length autobiography quite fit. At Mason I have sometimes assigned *Women of Deh Koh,* a collection of short first-person narratives collected by an anthropologist, which has led to impassioned debates in my classes about the difference between the idealized version of a tradition "as it is supposed to be" and what really happens. Ardent young believers argued passionately that "there is no beating of women in Islam," but the voices of village women were telling us differently; indeed, Islamic jurists try only to limit the beating of wives, not to eliminate it.

Islam is the most rapidly expanding religion in the world, worrying to outsiders because of its militancy but appealing to people of color because of the image of Islam as uniting peoples of many races in mutual respect (this too is an ideal not always realized). The Nation of Islam (Black Muslim) movement continues, and today there are substantial numbers of African Americans who have followed the path of Malcolm X in becoming Sunni Muslims. Their numbers are small at Spelman, with its Christian background, half a dozen students conspicuously wearing modern *hijab* head coverings, and there had been controversy about the chaplain's decision to put a copy of the Quran in the meditation room. The oldest of my Spelman students, Pat Bakr, had been married and then divorced from a Muslim man before she came back to school.

Even without a Muslim life history on our list, I made a point of drawing on Iranian examples from traditional rural communities when we talked about families and the shapes of lives where resources are controlled by senior men. In Iran, just as men have authority over women, older men have authority over younger men, and fathers over adult sons. Traditional Iran can be called patriarchal more accurately than Western societies. In San society, individuals have great freedom in deciding which relationships to depend on in a larger network, while Western societies allow young men and, increasingly, women, to strike out as individuals. In Iran there are fewer choice points in a lifetime, and freedom and authority come gradually. Inherited ties are treasured and maintained, while strangers are mistrusted and relationships between two people are seen as unstable. The man who tries to rely on himself alone is at a disadvantage and the woman doubly so, while the Western picture of a couple absorbed in each other and standing together against the world just doesn't fit. The ideal marriage in Iran is between cousins: the network is strengthened and the bride treated with greater consideration, for it is in everyone's interest to make sure both parties are content and property is kept in the family.

Kinship is the most basic form of social security. The shift from extended family households to nuclear families has often been cited as a necessity for modernization, because sharing with relatives limits labor mobility and retards capital formation, but there are great losses. There are societies in which the ideal is thirty or forty people, including half a dozen married couples, under a single roof or within a single compound, run rather like a corporation. In Iran one married son usually does live in a household with his aging parents and unmarried siblings, but often other married sons live nearby. Some of these now follow more or less the nuclear family pattern, but they are rarely isolated as an American nuclear family is likely to be, with husband and wife living far from their childhood homes and only able to "reach out and touch someone" over the telephone lines or at holidays. We use the term "extended family" loosely to refer to relatives, but the real issue is one of mutual support. Relying on kin for help, offering a home to elderly parents, and being willing to take in children in emergencies have been critical in the transitions of many immigrant and impoverished groups in the United States.

In Iran, even when a couple does not move in with the husband's parents, a son is likely to have a very strong emotional relationship with his mother and a tendency to defer to his father's authority. Week after week, sometimes day after day, he will go and visit his parents, accepting his father's guidance, praising his mother's cooking or bringing her flowers. The most important woman in a man's life is usually his mother; the most important man in a woman's life is her adult son. She may wait a long time for that sense of fulfillment, but waiting is easier than feeling that the best part of life is slipping away.

Iranians look back on their childhoods with a wealth of vivid memories of family life never left behind: the smells of rice cooking, of the walled courtyard cooled and wetted down for the evening, the taste of fresh bread and herbs, the constant back-and-forth to the homes of relatives. The transition from childhood to adulthood is smoother in Iran than it is in the United States, where the stage for adolescent rebellion is set in the treatment of toddlers, and autonomy and independence are valued from birth. In Iran a man becomes a true adult only when his father begins to retire, not when he marries or finishes his schooling. Young adulthood does not feel like dancing the limbo, it feels like retaining an expected place in the family, becoming more autonomous only very slowly.

Although it had begun to change before the Islamic revolution, the system looks somewhat different from the woman's point of view. Traditionally in Iran the family a woman married into has been more important than her family of origin: after all, daughters go away when they grow up, sons do not. Women married early enough so they would come to define themselves as "wife of so-and-so" and later as "mother of so-and-so." A girl might, in the old days, have become a bride at fourteen, with her first child at fifteen and others quickly following, and she would have needed the guidance of her mother-in-law, whether kindly or harshly given, in order to cope at all. A new bride (one speaks of a woman as the bride of her husband's *parents*) was assigned a position close to the bottom of the family hierarchy, given less affection because she was a newcomer, and expected to show great respect to those senior to her. This is a reasonable system for guaranteeing the wife's commitment to the relationship in a much deeper way than economic dependence, for even if she is unhappy that unhappiness will be part of who she is, and her acceptance of it merges with her sense of self, with a better future lying ahead.

Not only a woman's name but her official religious affiliation, her citizenship, and much of her legal status are still derived from her husband, and she is expected to join modestly with the family in its relations with outsiders, using the rich and ambiguous forms of public courtesy and hospitality, keeping up a carefully constructed public front, with little privacy. Traditionally, few women had the opportunity to become "independent adults." By contrast, even though most Spelman undergraduates are financially dependent on their parents and are surrounded by rules, they are being prepared for independence and will have to make their own decisions.

No woman in a traditional Muslim society has the choices that Nisa had of withdrawing from marriages that became unsatisfactory and making her own way, much less of pursuing multiple love affairs. Islamic family law gives men the freedom to take additional wives (if—and this should be a big if—they can do so equitably) and also to divorce, and ensures that most property moves from fathers to sons. Sometimes Westerners say, "They treat their wives like things—like possessions." A better way of putting it would be to say that men treat their womenfolk like parts of themselves (not of course the head or the family jewels!), for in the eyes of society individuals are judged and valued not for themselves alone but in a family context. If a man beats or even kills a wife or a daughter for compromising the family honor, it is more as if he had gouged out a right eye that offended him than as if he had taken revenge on an independent person.

In traditional Iran, bearing a child, especially a boy, was the most basic element in a woman's identity after marriage itself. As long as she had no children, a bride was seen as not fully adult, rather as "on trial" in her husband's household. Her position as a wife and her status in the family were strengthened by each new birth, but even today if she departs the children belong to their father. Youth is not the best time of life for either men or women, so life after thirty is not seen as a decline. Postponing independence until early middle age gives men time to develop and acknowledges their need to do so, while the increased freedom and authority of middle age make up for the ebbing of youth. Women too come into their own as sons mature and daughters-in-law provide grandchildren. They still have a satisfying role when their first beauty is past.

In the West new patterns of maturity are creating not only new satisfactions but a new kind of spaciousness in adult life, especially for women engaged in caring for others beyond a single family. "My ideal of relationship is great and long-distance," Ama said. "I mean, I want your ass in Africa or the Mideast or something like that. I want you to show up twice a year so I can do what I need to do in the meantime. Women's lives are jeopardized by all the things they find themselves entangled with doing for other people, so the more you construct a life where you don't have them around, the better. I may just want to wander around my house at night and sit from chair to chair and think and talk to myself." Earlier in the year Ama had decided that it did not make sense to have her daughter actually live with her and was still concerned that it might have felt like a rejection. But Ama, living alone, is still very much a caretaker, as are many women in their careers, creating a home with space for development and cherishing in laboratories and offices and factories. I had watched Ama playing a parental role in the seminar just as I had watched Johnnetta doing so on the Spelman campus.

"You parent a lot of people"—I laughed—"just not in the same house all the time."

"Yes I do, and I like it in that constellation."

There is a familiar feminist quip that "a woman without a man . . . is like a fish without a bicycle." This brought a laugh in the context of American culture as it was when I grew up, when a woman was supposed to need a husband or lover as desperately as fish need water; it was a new idea that women do not need mates to move ahead with their lives. Certainly there were strong examples of women making their own way in the world in our seminar. But women in strongly patriarchal societies can survive only in the shadow of some man, and indeed couples can survive only within the context of the husband's family, so that a couple without in-laws is like a fish without water. Within that matrix, households are organized with a division of labor that makes men dependent on women as well. Husbands and wives may develop a deep and steady love out of years of mutual comfort and shared labor, but the man dearest to a woman's heart is not her husband but her son, and the woman a man loves most is his mother. The effort to make marriage the most important of all relationships, stable for a lifetime, seems to depend all too often on constraint rather than love.

Iran, when my husband and I lived there, had a high birthrate but was gradually reducing it. Changes in family life and in the participation of women after the Islamic revolution halted that process until the Islamic government undertook its own family planning initiative. When the single stories change, the aggregates change too. Traditional peasant societies provided the model for the statistical presentation called a population pyramid, showing the number of individuals at any given age. The metaphor was once accurate, it did look like a pyramid: many births creating a substantial base, rapid narrowing as deaths occurred at every age, and a small number of survivors at the apex. With every technological advance the apex has been higher and the form has narrowed more slowly.

That basic form has two new variants. In the developing world today the impacts of technology are seen in a pyramid with a very broad base, reflecting huge increases in the numbers of children and in survival to reproductive age. In industrialized or modernized countries, life expectancies have increased even more dramatically, but at the same time birthrates have dropped, so affluent industrialized societies produce a "population pyramid" shaped more like a pillar topped with a small cone. Whereas Western societies look anxiously at the rising tide of elderly, the developing world is drowning in children.

Social scientists have described a recurring shift in patterns of population, called the demographic transition, which generally occurs in stages. First, the stage of dramatic increase, driven by declining mortality, primarily among infants and children. This process is already evident worldwide. Eventually this levels off and is followed by a decline in births, with increasing investment in the extension of adult lives. The education of women and their freedom to make choices about childbearing combine with the confidence that the children one has borne will survive to bring this shift about.

No one is very good at predicting the cultural impact of these shifts. In some European countries birthrates have fallen below replacement levels, and declining workforces are maintained by migration from less developed areas, with startling increases in the day-to-day experience of cultural differences and related social tensions, while young people have longer and longer waits for positions to open up. In China the effort has been to enforce a drop in birthrates without waiting for demographic transition to occur spontaneously, but now we hear of only children growing up like "little emperors" in a culture that has no tradition for handling them—and a huge disparity in survival of male and female infants, which will affect family life in the future.

It is not surprising that activism for full participation for women has been strongest in industrialized societies, but this is only one facet of the search for new meaning and new ethical understandings in the changing shape of lives—the realization, for instance, that human intervention around the natural processes of death is hubris without human responsibility for birth.

Demographic transition is probably a necessity for ecological survival. At the beginning of the Common Era, a doubling of the number of human beings is estimated to have taken 350 to 700 years. When an uncontrolled birthrate is combined with an emerging public health and child immunization system, doubling can occur in less than 20 years. Today the waves of migrants and refugees pressing against political borders are moving not into lands that can be cultivated for the first time but into lands already heavily exploited. There are now some 6 billion human beings on the planet. At current rates there will be close to 9 billion by midcentury.

Demographic transition also represents huge changes in individual lives, going beyond the benefits of longer lives or control over too many pregnancies. The tendency is to think of these changes in terms of addition or subtraction of numbers of human beings or years of life. Yet anyone who has had the experience of building a new room onto a house knows from experience that the result is much more complex and pervasive than simple addition. Adding a room can change the entire pattern of usage—where the family spends time, where things are stored, which doors and hallways are used—and often changes the system of relationships within the family as well. Not only is a building modified, but the meaning of home is modified. Adding a new member—even a pet—to a household has even greater effects on the patterns of life.

The "extra room" represented by extended life expectancy is far more than a simple addition or extension. If there is a new stage in adult life, it is more like an atrium opened up in the center than like a wing tacked on, a space for new and airier lifestyles and freer kinds of relationships. Time has been discovered in midstream, a second adulthood, while youth and aging both have changed in shape. Reproduction and child rearing, no longer the center of life, are becoming a passing phase. New kinds of couplings are evolving before and after and instead of those focused on child rearing, like Beverly's early marriage and many others without benefit of licenses. Learning, by contrast, is ceasing to be temporary and becoming lifelong. Work that continues over more and more years will either become more burdensome or—with luck—be scrutinized and reshaped to make it more satisfying. Fewer and fewer people will spend all of their lives on a single career or in a single relationship. Grandparents will often be too busy with their continuing adult lives to play traditional grandparental roles for young children, roles that will be played by great-grandparents if only we can bring them together. And the relationships between young adults and older adults who could be their parents will be newly egalitarian as everyone moves into a mode of lifelong learning. This was the process played out in our seminar, elders back in school as models and colleagues to younger women.

New beginnings and endings, new ways of centering and balancing the composition. Not every temporal work of art has a beginning and an end, nor does every work of visual art have a frame, but most do, and the frames and narrative styles of our era are new. Sometimes stories, like the film *Rashomon,* have multiple endings or begin at the end and return to the beginning. Sometimes compositions incorporate the accidental, like the works of John Cage, or create an unbounded dialogue with a landscape, like a line drawn by Christo across the desert. The line begins somewhere and ends somewhere, dividing the land, but the horizons are infinite, necessarily far outside the artist's scope and control, and so it is with the path of a life. Until they began to live in houses with walls, human beings did not think in terms of boundaries. Instead, home was defined by the hearth at the center, and territory by a central waterhole or mountain providing focus.

What is so striking about the emerging shapes of lives is the existence of repeated moments of choice, choice of who to love, whether and when to have children, choice of career perhaps several times in a lifetime. Eventually we will learn to make choices about dying as well.

We choose whether to continue on a given path or to turn off. We live with roads taken and not taken, like the novels now being written in computerized hypertext that can ramify into multiple paths and outcomes. The possibilities become so complex that it makes no sense to become preoccupied by any single "What if?" Losing the myth of happy ever after, we have gained a reality of multiple and creative beginnings and a new chance to be the artists of our lives.

6 | Commitment–Vision and Revision

One day I noticed a poster on campus for a panel discussion on whether the Spelman motto, "Our whole school for Christ" (which I still have near me, engraved on a presentation pewter plate on my study wall), should be changed. The discussion was dominated by a group of conservative students whose strategy apparently was to argue that either the motto should be changed, to fit the secular character of the school as it now is, or the school should be changed to conform to the motto. Take it or leave it, they were saying, consistency is all.

It could be disillusioning, one student said, to apply to a school with such a motto and arrive to discover it was untrue—but she was not ready to consider that the motto might be true in some new sense. Another student complained that in preparing remarks for a convocation service in Sisters Chapel at the beginning of the semester, she had been instructed not to refer to Jesus or Christ. This, she said, was a denial of her freedom of speech and belief. The student spoke as if there were a general rule forbidding all expressions of belief, ignoring the distinction between the Sunday chapel services and Bible studies that go on all over the campus, which students are free to attend or ignore, and an official occasion when attendance is obligatory. She was citing the Bill of Rights in a way that would have invaded the freedoms of others.

In any case, the same words may have different meanings for those who speak them and those who are listening. Two Spelman students were invited to sing gospel songs at the banquet of a conference of women fund-raisers held in Atlanta. Listening to the words and recognizing the students who were singing, I knew that for them the performance was a testimony of faith, a way of bearing witness to the souls of the audience—but I also suspected that for many in the audience the words were discounted or tuned out. They were acceptable as part of a cultural performance but would have been an embarrassment if spoken in conversation at the tables. Christianity has been a central commitment for many African Americans, yet in some contexts they are regarded, rightly or wrongly, as using Christian symbols much as secularized Jews use Jewish symbols, as expressions of cultural identity. When Spelman was founded there was no question that culture, literacy, and religion were expected to go hand in hand, as was true with the founding of such northern institutions as Harvard and Oberlin.

It is hard at times to know how to interpret religious language, but sometimes interpretations are so out of phase that it is almost insulting. A subtle kind of discrimination recognizes gospel music as high artistic achievement but seems to dismiss the belief that underlies it as a fossil or a childish holdover from the past. I met a High Church Episcopal priest once who insisted that when the liturgy was sung the words of the Creed should always be spoken, because words sung are too easily treated as metaphorical and the Creed should be taken as literally true.

Quietly listening to Spelman women debate their motto, listening to some of the less religious students arguing that it should be retained for its historical value, while others found the very notion offensive, I was struck that no one was noticing how profoundly the words of the motto had already changed in meaning over time. In 1881 "our whole school" meant two white Northern ladies, Miss Packard and Miss Giles, and eleven pupils, former slaves, learning the rudiments of literacy, gathered in the dank basement of Friendship Baptist Church, under the name Atlanta Baptist Female Seminary. This became Spelman Seminary in 1884 and Spelman College in 1924. Additional teachers and better quarters were found, numbers increased, and programs changed steadily. A School of Nursing was added and eventually closed, as was a Missionary Training Department. New ties were developed with other historically black institutions, and new solutions also brought new problems. When I was there "our whole school" had grown from these seeds into a flourishing plant that could not have been predicted, a liberal arts college consisting of more than fifteen hundred students and nearly a hundred and fifty faculty members.

Many would argue that while "our whole school" has changed in meaning, the last two words of the motto are unchanging. Christ is the firm foundation, the Rock of Ages, unaffected by time, whose words remain true yesterday, today, and tomorrow. I encounter this theme whenever I speak about the need to adapt to change and to be open to other cultural traditions; someone always stands up and asks, Aren't there some things that do not change, some things we need to hang on to? Yes, I say, and no.

Not only from the first day of Spelman's history but from the very beginnings of the Christian community, words like God or Christ have had different meanings for people who were nonetheless able to pray and sing side by side, although all too often they quarreled and defined competing orthodoxies. The New Testament records the different emphases in their perceptions, for instance the social gospel as recorded by St. Luke and the mystical fourth gospel attributed to St. John. When I assigned the two Gospels to a life history class at George Mason, as provocative examples of different points of view in biographical writing, one of the many students who had apparently never read any of the Old or New Testament said, "This Jesus, the one that Luke writes about, he's someone I'd like to sit down with over a beer." He shook his head. "This Jesus of John's, though, I don't even want to meet him." The Old Testament is even more diverse, an anthology of writings recording the changing understandings of the Jews as they evolved from a tribe of nomadic herders to farmers, then to a small empire, and then had to find ways to understand defeat and exile. Religious groups based on scriptures constantly recycle their understanding of texts as they apply them to a changing reality and a changing knowledge of that reality.

In the world we live in, Creator might mean "the one who gave the electrons flight and twisted the strands of DNA" or perhaps, "my best effort at the moment, using available and familiar symbols, to imagine and celebrate the sacred." Or, for many people, nothing at all. Willy-nilly, the meaning of the words changes in the lives of individuals, becoming more abstract with adulthood, more close and immediate, perhaps, in old age. Plato would have argued that there is an idea behind the usage that remains unchanged, but it also remains inaccessible.

Between the changing reality of the community, "our whole school," and a changing understanding of "Christ," there lies that little word *for,* which carries bundled up in it centuries of thinking about fidelity and service, about commitment and the willingness to gamble on faith and hope. What do we have for Christ today? The Looking Glass willingness to believe six impossible things before breakfast, the willingness to make war and to burn heretics, the willingness to fast or to make pilgrimages barefoot? Resilience in unbearable conditions and unreasoning hope when all seems to be lost? A willingness to live with ambiguity, to listen and rethink—something rare in theological circles in Biblical times and since.

Spelman women today can draw strength from the conviction with which the founders struggled against the odds to create an institution to educate black women, even though they might differ with them on other matters. Miss Packard and Miss Giles were ahead of their time, laboring at the moving edge of enlightened opinion. Even then many Christians still believed that slavery was part of God's plan; quite a few still believe today that women were not meant to lead or to speak in public. No one repeats those scriptures at Spelman, but you can hear Scripture quoted against homosexuality or the gradual exploration of other traditions by African Americans, substantial numbers turning to Islam, smaller groups drawn to Buddhism or Hinduism. The aboli- tionists who were committed to freedom for slaves would neverthe- less have preferred to limit freedom when it came to other choices. I wonder whether Miss Packard and Miss Giles would have made the stretch of believing that their students should be able to move on. They might have surprised themselves.

Miss Packard and Miss Giles were improvisers, coping and solving problems from day to day, using the models of Northern schools, the words of Scripture, and their own sense of possibility, the thrill of see- ing unlettered and traumatized children discover who they could be- come. By coping and making do, praying and struggling (and occasionally bending the truth), they built an improvisational institution. This sounds like an oxymoron but is not. Instead it means an institution able to change and adapt, just as Harvard and Oberlin and countless others have done. Even schools can learn. Spelman's growth was part of the rapid development of institutions after the Civil War to prepare the African American community for a shift from the improvisations involved in simply surviving and weathering losses to eventual full participation in society.

The process continues, for participation is still not complete, and the willingness to engage in simultaneous improvisation and learning is the only way to move forward. Every adult in America today has been challenged to revise assumptions and deeply held commitments. We can no longer follow the old formula "learn first and then act," for today everyone is learning on the job, making midcourse corrections, acknowledging incomplete knowledge. Anyone who asserts that "we hold these truths to be self-evident, that all men are created equal . . ." knows that to get beyond mere repetition the words have to be understood anew.

More and more frequently I have been wrestling with questions of the relationship between commitment and flexibility, for today all genuinely adaptive and creative behavior risks the *look* of inconsistency. Malcolm X is a heroic figure precisely because of his midcourse corrections, because he demonstrated the possibility of profound change twice in adult life, once in joining Elijah Muhammad's Nation of Islam while in prison, and once when he began to explore the meaning of orthodox Islam as a world religion and to imagine peace between the races.

Even a single conversion in a lifetime is difficult and frightening. When folk do change their beliefs and find new landmarks, they still often demand that those landmarks be fixed. However hesitant their path, they want the new belief to be absolute. This drives the rise of fundamentalisms and authoritarianism, rejections of pluralism. It also drives the easy solution of abandoning belief completely, which leaves some aspects of humanness unexplored and unexpressed.

The alternative is to develop a concept of fidelity that can accept new learning and changes of course yet affirm some underlying constancy. Survival requires adaptation, whether in business or in politics, in marriage or in friendship. But the very concept implies some sameness that continues through change; the difficulty lies in defining and affirming that which survives. There are forms of survival we would reject, persons or institutions no longer themselves. "Before I'd be a slave, I'll be buried in my grave." There are fates worse than death, though it does not do to be too facile in one's assumptions. More and more people reject extreme dementia or vegetative states as "survival," insisting, No, that would not be me. A degree of adaptability can surely be incorporated into the sense of constancy, as one can adopt the identity of an explorer or a wanderer. And over time we can refine our ways of thinking about survival, realizing that what survives is an organism in its environment, an individual in relationship, a community with at least some of its customs and memories.

What would happen if, instead of all the rhetoric and metaphors of leaders with fixed goals adhered to by followers, we could project a sense of responsiveness and learning along the way, making these our custom and our constancy? We would walk in wonder and humility, and only accept authority based in the willingness to learn. We are all immigrants today, because we are all learning to live in a world different from the one we were born in, strangers and pilgrims gazing at new worlds. We have all been offered miracles of emancipation, whether from slavery, ignorance, or pain and early death, and living with these gifts requires constant learning. Some of what has to be learned is very difficult: to live lightly on the earth and to hold our convictions lightly too; to go against ancient impulses to maximize our offspring and our accumulation and our years of life. To take care of one another in spite of profound differences.

Sometimes I say to audiences, "Isn't it scary to have a president who is learning on the job?" People nod uneasily. "Of course," I go on, "there's one thing that's even worse, and that's a president who isn't— and we've had a few of those!" Human beings, fearing their own transience, have always associated value with permanence and preferred to put their trust in those who were ready to claim an unchanging truth. But this is no longer a safe strategy. Instead of planning our futures around gold, valued not just for its glitter and rarity but for its chemical stability, we have to depend on electronically stored information, spun from the human imagination and potentially evanescent. Thus, our modern faiths depend on the most fragile metaphysics in human history.

Trust is no longer based on fixity. In many cities now, buildings are not built on rock, as they are in Manhattan, but are "floated," with multiple basements, as they are in Boston. As with ships built of iron, buildings that float must reach far under the surface, for buoyancy depends on depth. Sink and swim.

In learning, one is changed, becoming someone slightly—or sometimes profoundly—different. What is learned becomes a part of the self, a part of that system of self-definition which filters all future perceptions and possibilities of learning. When I learn and practice skills, becoming a doctor or a hunting guide or an astrologer, I become defined by my skills, dependent on them. Inevitably I will want to make the certainties I have built into my sense of self continue to be true, even if they keep me in a state of rage or fear or habitual subservience.

Yet changes in beliefs and assumptions are nothing new. In spite of

all the imagery of rocks and foundations, of unchanging and unques-
tioning faith, there have always been some commitments that involved constant change and learning. In fact, all the best relationships
have a degree of mystery, demanding growth and change, learning
moving between strangers. The best friendships, the most resilient
marriages, student and teacher, mentor and mentee. They float. The
most striking example is the commitment of parents to a child—
different from day to day and year to year, bridging shifting values and
worlds of experience. We love our children, we criticize and discipline
them, we keep trying to maintain mutual understanding, and we are
less and less able to predict who they will become or to make decisions
for them.

One of the characteristics of parent-child relationships is how
much we can learn from our children, if we will. We keep on growing
because we live with strangers. Faith, too, has this quality, for God is
never fully revealed. The deepest hopes are expressed metaphorically
in ways that only time can decode: "I want to be a fireman" turns out
to mean, "I want to be brave and strong and dependable like my
dad"—or, sometimes, "in ways that my dad has failed to be."

The same thing is true of all those commitments, made at one stage
of life, that reveal new facets and flaws over time. We all arrive at
adulthood with a load of promises, some parroted, some made for us
by proxy, and some we think are freely chosen. We have recited the
Pledge of Allegiance to the flag and sung patriotic songs. We have
joined organizations like the Boy Scouts or the Girl Scouts, with oaths
as part of the package. We have been committed to the faith of various
religious communities: if Jewish, then by circumcision to a covenant,
by bar and bat mitzvah ceremonies to the Torah; if Christian, then by
baptism, in the recited words of creeds and catechisms, in the recep-
tion of communion or confirmation. Spoken promises are no more

than outward and visible signs. We are also committed by the time and place of our birth, the gifts given to us before we can judge the debts incurred.

The most important covenants of life, whether in childhood or in adulthood, are accepted without understanding what fidelity to them will mean, for meaning never ceases to evolve with age. The Hippocratic oath; the vows of citizenship and office; and especially the vows taken in marriage are not, cannot be, made with full understanding. The bride and groom are in many ways strangers, and both will continue to change—who then is the "we" who promise to stay together, and how will we recognize each other across the vicissitudes of time? Perhaps couples should promise, like the Boy Scouts, to do their best or, more modestly, like the Girl Scouts, only to try. Perhaps, like one couple I know, they should review the terms of their commitment to each other at regular intervals.

No one at twenty or twenty-five has a real sense of the time that might lie ahead—especially since modern medicine has stretched that time to a possible seventy or more years. We do not really imagine, when we speak of sickness or health, the long, dragged-out loss of self caused by Alzheimer's or other degenerative diseases, when one partner ceases to recognize the other. Sickness is now taken to include many behaviors that disrupt marriages, like alcoholism, battering, or drug addiction, but it may not be possible to live with them. Richer and poorer have new meanings too, as when a poor couple lives separately to be eligible for public assistance, or a wealthy one juggles with ownership to avoid taxes or lawsuits.

Sexual fidelity is newly puzzling today, but it has always been a poor and inadequate measure of all fidelity. Under the old double standard the words of this portion of the marriage vows were not really regarded as binding on men and coexisted with the notion that normal women weren't much interested in sex, especially as they grew older. But the double standard did translate into a different kind of fidelity: men might have affairs or visit prostitutes, but they were not to embarrass or abandon their wives, who retained the honor and security of their position. Rejecting the asymmetry of the old double standard, we have also lost the basic idea that the sustained bonding of male and female parents is the central human issue, rather than perfect sexual exclusivity.

In recent years I have begun asking people, when the breakup of a marriage is attributed to adultery, whether there was not something deeply wrong before the affair was discovered. One after another of the women in the seminar who had been divorced referred to the womanizing of their partners as secondary to other problems or as fatal to the marriage only when it became a recurring habit. Only one of the elders spoke of deciding to end a marriage immediately when she discovered an egregious infidelity. Often, I believe, sexual infidelity is used by one partner or the other as a trigger to end a relationship that has already become unsatisfactory. I hear stories of letters "absentmindedly" left for spouses to find—or opportunities seized upon to put the other partner in the wrong. Marriages can survive adultery unless there is a will on one side or the other to get out, and sometimes the adulterous partner is heartbroken and the partner who has been betrayed is just a little smug. But there are also times when both parties would like to patch things up but feel somehow that they are expected to be unforgiving, and lawyers often make it so.

Perhaps we should get in the habit of asking more deeply what fidelity means in any particular marriage or to any particular individual, but we are nearly unable to discuss it. Even raising the issue feels like giving permission—the same problem parents encounter in discussing sex with children: how do you prepare someone to manage an impulse without somehow condoning that impulse? The only possible solution is to get out in front of it: for parents to discuss sex with children well before puberty and for couples in the first flush of love to try to define fidelity in layers. Couples need to understand that fidelity, even if it does not always mean abstinence, does propose some other standards: it may mean carrying the burden of secrecy and forgoing the pleasures of confession to a partner. It might mean the practice of safe sex only outside of the committed relationship. It will take considerable time and effort to find new and genuine ways of promising, in the words of the song title, to be "Always True to You in My Fashion." Fidelity surely means both more and less than who jumps into bed with whom, which is anyhow not the most important decision faced in life.

Choices about all the potential irrevocabilities of life—joining the army, committing a felony, experimenting with drugs, quitting a job—should logically be tested against prior commitments, just as the desire to mortgage a house is tested against prior liens. Fidelity must surely include discussing major career decisions that affect the security of a partner. Conceiving and bearing a child creates a new set of commitments, so fidelity should mean the agreement to have children only when both parties wish to and only within the framework of the marriage.

Then there is the question of becoming a different person. At one time I thought it would be interesting to go through the experience of a training psychoanalysis, but my husband argued that to do so would be to risk a personality change from the person whom he married and who married him, which should not be undertaken except perhaps as a last resort to address extreme suffering. Still, both of us have changed, neither of us is the person the other married.

People do change, often involuntarily, often in ways that simply come with age, yet no couple write into marriage vows that they will continue to love and cherish through weight gain or baldness, increasing stuffiness or conservatism. Perhaps they should, for no one can guarantee an ever-youthful body or endless idealism. There are people who treat the inevitable changes of aging as a form of infidelity or regard boredom as a reason for leaving a long-term relationship, and others who are terrified by the changes of new growth and development.

There are far more logical reasons to end a relationship than a casual adultery, yet many people live in marriages that can be seen as forms of desertion, separations unilaterally imposed and not discussed, or put up with physical and psychological abuse. Irrevocable or life-changing decisions made without consultation attack the grounds of a marriage far more than occasional extracurricular activities. Is someone who is "born again" to a new religious commitment released by that from previous commitments? Perhaps Jewish men should become Orthodox only with their wives' agreement, since they are in effect committing their partners to live in a radically different way. Perhaps we should consult before becoming vegetarians, a decision of some weight to the cook. What about going back to school and changing the way a household functions, or accepting a promotion in another city that will require a partner to abandon a career or a job? Traditionally in Catholicism, a married man or woman could not decide to become celibate because it was understood that a spouse had a right to sex, not on demand or taken violently, but as part of the ongoing texture of the relationship. What about those who suddenly feel they are called to begin again from scratch and assume that their spouses will be ready to do the same?

The familiar metaphorical language of marriage says that through it two individuals become one person, so real violations of that marriage ·

are attacks on the very being of the other. Marriage is a matter of coupled systems having to self-regulate jointly over time. The gift of sexual pleasure may be essential to the self-regulation. So is trust. But isolated sexual episodes destroy trust only if we teach ourselves that they shall.

Every covenant, every promise proposes limits on how life is to be lived, but every kind of fidelity has the potential for deepening and broadening, for projection out to larger communities, as individuals grow up and move in wider and wider circles of engagement and commitment. This is rooted in the patterns of the life cycle. "Our whole school for Christ" might come to mean "Our whole school for others . . . for peace . . . for social justice" rather than being a criterion for exclusion. Everyone who pronounces ancient words of promise is likely to find himself or herself later reinterpreting those vows as part of a search for deeper meaning.

Nevertheless, other kinds of fidelity cannot be entirely separated from sexual fidelity. Reading evolutionary psychologists who are discussing the traits that are important in mate selection, I have wondered whether humans do not seek out idealism as a sign of the capacity for commitment. It is interesting to think about the attraction of a young man speaking with passion about world peace or a young woman struggling to relieve famine across the seas. During adolescence, when courting becomes such an important part of life, "causes" also become important and young people anchor their identities in larger patterns of meaning. Henry Kissinger commented that power is an aphrodisiac, but it is also worth noting that vision is an aphrodisiac—that a Jack Kennedy or a Martin Luther King is appealing because of the stars in his eyes and the exultation in his voice. "Your old men shall dream dreams, your young men shall see visions." It is no coincidence that justice or liberty or peace is often symbolized in female form, perhaps to focus the commitment of young men growing up in their service.

Human fidelity is always subject to the vicissitudes of the past, the experiences of betrayal or abandonment over a lifetime. Often weaning is traumatic, casting a long shadow. Among the San, children of three or four have violent tantrums when their mothers begin to refuse to nurse them, and they rage at newborns. For foragers, breast milk really is a limited resource, and so is the amount of time a growing child can be carried. But even where there is very early pressure on infants to move toward autonomy, and breast feeding is terminated after a few months, as is true for most Americans, sibling rivalry is a major issue, endlessly discussed. The American solution is often to enlist the knee baby as a colleague in caring for the breast baby. In some cultures the involvement of other adults as surrogate parents buffers the sense of loss and banishment. A child who has previously shared the parental bed may now sleep with a grandparent or with older siblings, banished but not to solitude. Ama, the oldest daughter in a family that lost both parents, had spoken in class about how oldest children may be transformed into lifelong caregivers. Youngest children, like Hillary, may forever carry the glow of never having been displaced.

At some point every nursling loses access to the breast, every toddler is expected to pick himself or herself up and go on, and the props of childhood are gradually removed as the adults we have relied on urge us to self-reliance. Weaning, in its broadest sense, is an important part of every life history. Mothers prove all women inconstant when they give birth and put the infant's needs, at least for a time, before those of their husbands, and later when the needs of a firstborn give way to those of siblings. Children learn only with difficulty that when a parent seems to be abandoning them to go off to work this too is an expression of faithful commitment.

Survival has always required that human beings at least partly give up their ties to their families of origin and turn toward new families of procreation and creation. If we translate the problem of weaning into the problem of discovering a new center for loyalty, it is as if every human being spends a lifetime recovering either from being rejected or from having turned away, conceptually refugees or émigrés, victims or traitors, who must become immigrants committed to a new homeland. We can try to shape these transitions into graduations, but still there is a necessary departure and a necessary acknowledgment that return visits will be different. It is striking that the most loyal alums of any alma mater are the ones with whom the school has essentially failed, for if it had succeeded they would be too busy about their lives to come back for every football game and reunion.

My favorite starting point for thinking about weaning comes from a story I remember from childhood about a black bear that is probably legend. The mother has trained her cub to climb a tree when she warns of danger and to stay there until she gives the all-clear. But when the cub is old enough to survive on his own, she orders him up into a tree and simply departs. After hours of hunger and thirst, the cub's needs overcome obedience, and climbing down is the condition for emancipation and for survival. At least the bird that must be pushed out of the nest in order to learn to fly does not have to embrace disobedience in the process—but then bears are essentially solitary; their need for loyalty would not outlive childhood. Human beings could not afford so drastic a weaning because we survive through the capacity for cooperation and mutual trust.

One can defer weaning almost indefinitely. This seems to work for the Iranian man who lives most of his life as his parents' son. One can accelerate it, which is often the experience of girls in patriarchal societies, who may be weaned brusquely and early from the breast, before their brothers, and treated as transients to be sent out as child brides. One can take all the trauma of leaving home and blame it on some external force, like tribal societies that preface their initiation rites with abductions in which men masked as gods steal boys away from their mothers to offer them a new home among the men. Or, like many Americans, one can simply reinforce every sign of independence, almost from birth, and risk producing adults for whom leaving is easier than staying, for whom the only fidelity is to the self.

In every case there will be different attitudes toward the homes established in later life. Some people go through life willing to pack up and leave at the slightest discomfort, others make huge sacrifices to stay with what they have. Some create new households that will, as much as possible, replicate what they came from, while others do all they can to create contrast. For some, sameness is the very stuff of comfort, while others feel absolved from fidelity by boredom, pursuing variety as an expression of curiosity and the desire to learn.

Most people are more at ease when change is embedded in continuity and when continuity can still be recognized in change. When you want to help people be open to change and difference, you can ask them to delve into their own histories for the remembered experience of accepting something new. The experience of setting aside a long-held conviction has become universal, but it is not always conscious. Do you remember being told you would drown if you swam after eating? Do you remember being taught it was helpful to rub butter quickly on a burn? Everyone in my generation grew up believing these were scientific truths. Do you remember noticing for the first time your own unthinking prejudice? Remembering these things, we can remember going beyond them. Sometimes deeply religious parents avoid telling children about Santa Claus, lest the experience of learning to disbelieve become habit-forming, but understanding science requires the willingness to question and discard beliefs—and the awareness of having done so. Even our deepest commitments are honored by an understanding of how they have evolved over time.

After a lecture in North Carolina, a woman said to me, "I've been teaching in a small town where no one wants to know anything about other cultures, they don't see any point to it, what they have is best." I told her to go into the kitchens and look for corn and potatoes, cinnamon for apple pies, spaghetti, and soy sauce. Coffee and tea. Perhaps even tacos and Roquefort cheese dressing. The comfort foods we take for granted arrived as exotic novelties in other eras of borrowing and innovation, so the discomfort of remembering they came from elsewhere is useful.

What strikes me most sharply as an educator is that commitments can be transformed without being abandoned, expressed by extension rather than by contradiction. It is possible to take the love and loyalty felt for one household or person and extend it to all peoples or to transform love for one landscape into a concern for the planet. What is nearest and dearest to me—my own life and health and body, my family, my local place and community—can be either a reason for extending care outward or a reason for conflict and predation. We all come from cultures where the model was the family of origin. We are building a world where the model is commitment to the children of an unknown future.

In a democracy a leader must be willing to learn and therefore to take the risk of apparent inconsistency. We are fortunate to have a legacy of founding documents that reflect different styles, the Declaration of Independence and the Constitution, and founding fathers who argued far into the night. In any case these documents must be read in the context of current concerns and opinions. Narrow construction of the Constitution is much like fundamentalism in religion—it denies that the sacred texts are necessarily fluid, their meanings shifting and developing over time. Within our lifetimes Americans have had to give up a number of assumptions and fixed beliefs, so a historical perspective on past changes is helpful in facing those still to come.

Certainties are addictive, necessary to feeling right. For addicts, pouring a drink or taking a drug feels like coming home, for their bodies have learned to regard the presence of the drugs as a natural state and have adjusted to it. The loss of familiar certainties and habits of thought can be perplexing in much the same way, leaving us feeling like uncomfortable strangers in our own skins. The basic commitments of life are woven into the sense of self. Religious faith, a long-term marriage, even a familiar habit of hate or rage can be profoundly painful to lose, lingering like a phantom limb. Similarly, after a loss it is common to hear the echo of a loved voice or catch the glimpse of a face and feel haunted, and anxiety lingers when the reason for fear is past. What we see and hear is after all constructed in the mind, relying on clues learned from familiarity, and loss makes an accustomed world desolate and unfamiliar.

We are all creatures of habit, both in behavior and in thought, for no one can create a new world and a new way of living with every passing day. Even those who are proudly free from dependency on morning coffee or afternoon tea are likely to be habituated to exercise or a morning shower or moving their bowels at a particular time, all behaviors that become virtually a part of self-definition by long conditioning. Mind and body have learned to trust certain regularities in the universe, like the pull of gravity. Part of the modern condition is that these are increasingly subject to change, often replaced by conditions that depend on complex technology: dependence on an information-rich environment, on entertainment, on air-conditioning. After a natural disaster or a breakdown of social systems, the withdrawal symptoms could kill us and illness and death spread as the society struggles for some new self-regulation.

When Johnnetta announced, in the fall of 1996, that she would be retiring from the presidency of Spelman at the end of the following year, many members of the Spelman community were appalled. Part of Johnnetta's original understanding with the board had been that she would remain in the presidency for a decade and then step down, freeing the institution to regroup or to face the next cycle of changes. The decision was no surprise to me, because we had often discussed the multiple chapters of contemporary lives and the wisdom of moving on. When I conceived the idea of writing about my Spelman experience, I had proposed Johnnetta as the one who would review the manuscript, but now Marymal was concerned that Johnnetta's resignation might mean her commitment was insufficient, perhaps she would no longer put Spelman first. Working together, accepting her leadership, students and faculty had come to assume a permanency, to expect that the warmth of her greetings to everyone she passed would be an unchanging feature of the campus. Her commitment, it seemed to me, was in no way lost, but it was time for its expression to change, to step back. Similarly, during the period of working on the book, when my own health slowed my writing to a snail's pace and I could no longer travel easily to Atlanta or keep up with correspondence, I was concerned that my delay would also be experienced as an infidelity—as a betrayal.

These issues necessarily look different from the vantage point of different ages. The undergraduates had to know that they themselves would be moving on and away—I joked with them that it was time for Johnnetta to graduate—but like children growing up they wanted the home they were leaving to remain unchanged. The elders, more vividly aware of the losses of every departure, were also aware of how much their own convictions had evolved in their lifetimes.

During the seminar we read *When Heaven and Earth Changed Places,* by a Vietnamese woman, Le Ly Hayslip, whose own convictions had been wrenched and shifted as she tried to find forms of fidelity to her parents, her child, her self, and an eventual life in America. Two members of the seminar worked on presenting it together, Jackie Marshall, Johnnetta's assistant, who could remember the war and how it fit into the other issues of that era, and Celeste, for whom it was all new, just close enough in time not to have been covered by her high school history books.

"I did all this research," Celeste said. "This was all new to the undergrads, and the older women are sitting there like, yeah, and so? We started talking about where people were about the war, and to hear about attitudes in the African American community, that was phenomenal." Celeste had started from the assumption that of course the black community would have opposed the Vietnam War and recognized it as racist, but the elders leaped in, describing the black community as largely supporting the war—after all, the American military had been good to African Americans in recent years and there was little sense of solidarity with other people "of color"—that usage did not yet exist, nor did the notion of a Rainbow Coalition. Working-class blacks supported the war just as working-class white folk did.

"I never would have gotten that out of a history book," Celeste said. "Class differences in the black community are so not talked about— like the schism in my high school between kids who had lived in suburbia since childhood and people who had moved a couple of years ago? That was never talked about. So the fact we were talking about class in the context of the Vietnam War was like, wow!" Another shock wave went through the class when we discussed the angry sense of betrayal in the black community when Martin Luther King, Jr., came out in opposition to the war. His profound step in translating his commitment to social justice for black people in America, achieved by nonviolent means, to a commitment to all peoples suffering injustice and violence is a perfect example of the translation of a narrow commitment to a broader one, but at the time some of his followers felt abandoned. Today the rightness of that translation is taken for granted, so almost no one gets the benefit of knowing that Dr. King was learning along the way, taking decisions that looked inconsistent to some, broadening and deepening his own commitment, even as death approached.

7 | *Symbols of Connection*

When Johnnetta was inaugurated as Spelman College's first black woman president, Drs. Bill and Camille Cosby announced a gift of $20 million. Some commentators were cynical about whether such a gift would materialize, but almost a decade later, while I was at Spelman, the Cosby Building was dedicated. The Cosbys had specified that most of the money be used for a single building and the endowment of its maintenance. They wanted to build meaning and identity as well as classrooms and offices, and part of this was an emphasis on creating lasting quality rather than cutting corners to make the money go further.

In his speech "Dr. Bill" talked about how he had felt as a boy when, one by one, sports opened up to outstanding black athletes, like Jesse Owens, Joe Louis, and Jackie Robinson, and the whole African American community followed their progress and celebrated their victories.

He also spoke of how every black man had secretly worried that they might be shown up as not quite first-rate. The community worried again about figures like Marian Anderson and Thurgood Marshall and Barbara Jordan, each one bringing images of superb achievement to new areas of endeavor, each one at the top of her or his field regardless of race. Dr. Bill was capping his own achievement as an entertainer by setting a model for philanthropy within the black community. The most significant past philanthropy at Spelman came from the Rockefellers (Sisters Chapel was named for two Rockefeller sisters); the Cosby gift, the largest ever from the African American community, was itself an achievement and an example, like the television career of Bill Cosby. The building has a beautiful atrium with polished marble floors, rosewood paneling, and elegant stair rails of brass and chrome. Many small and subtle details were designed by its African American architect to refer to African traditional forms and symbols. The construction and interior design were also done by African American firms.

The day of the opening was a ritual of pride and shared achievement. Everyone moved and dressed with elegance that made me feel like a dumpy country cousin, with wimpy hair and dingy teeth, surrounded by royalty. The atrium and the auditorium glowed with huge arrangements of tropical flowers, Camille Cosby's favorites, birds-of-paradise, orchids, and bromeliads. A new art gallery opens off the atrium, displaying art by black women and adding the message of diversity to the message of pride: so many styles, so many different visions.

All the symbols evoked a heritage and a future that could not be celebrated without remembering suffering as well as achievement. As part of the day of ceremony and rejoicing for the opening, the college gathered in Sisters Chapel, singing the hymn by James Weldon Johnson that has sometimes been called the Negro national anthem, re-membering the sufferings of the past and drawing the contrasts of the changing times:

> *We have come over a way that with tears has been watered,*
> *We have come, treading our path through the blood of the slaughtered.*

When Spelman was founded in 1881, there were some 5 million freed slaves, 3 million of them women, most of them illiterate, and any education at all was the issue. Today, as in the Cosby Building, the affirmation and maintenance of quality are central. Later, in the audi-torium of the Cosby Building, students chanted an antiphonal text by a faculty member, Gloria Wade-Gayles, author of *Pushed Back to Strength*, dwelling on the future of "righteous, mighty Spelman women," single voices and chorus.

Even before that formal dedication, our seminar had been meeting in the Cosby Building, and later that spring I gave a public lecture in the auditorium, with a title inspired by artwork for the dedication, fea-turing symbols used in Ghana in fabric designs and in wood and met-alwork as well. The symbol that gave me my title was *sankofa,* translated as "go back and fetch it" and described as standing for "the use of traditions from the past in building the future" and, elsewhere in the materials, for "lifelong learning." They're singing my song, I thought. The symbol was new for me as well as for many at the col-lege, a piece of Ghanaian tradition to which African Americans were laying claim regardless of where in Africa their particular ancestors might have come from or whether their usage was ethnographically precise. My use of it was a way of responding to my experience at Spelman, the borrowing and reuse of a symbol bringing me into a di-alogue.

In my lecture I used the word *appropriated* to emphasize the active quality of taking up and utilizing an element from outside my own experience. African elements, brought and passed on by slaves, elaborated by subsequent generations, have become pervasive in American culture. Sometimes writers suggest that elements, like musical style, are racial property, stolen from black people by such as Elvis Presley. Elvis did make a lot of money, but in the meantime he destroyed himself while everyone learned to listen a little bit differently. The passing back and forth of symbols and art forms is an essential process in human culture. The symbols and those who learn to use them are changed, as the symbols of Judaism were reshaped by Christianity and reshaped again and deepened by each new group that has adopted them, Greek or Irish or African American. This is one of the ways we really can walk in each other's moccasins.

Earlier that spring First Lady Hillary Rodham Clinton had come to Atlanta to promote her book *It Takes a Village*. The title is from an African proverb become familiar in recent years, for the First Lady was not alone in using—appropriating—it to remind Americans that raising the next generation is a shared responsibility. One review of the book said snidely that we all know better than to look to Africans for a model for child rearing, but the things that go wrong in the development of some African American children have much to do with the way the majority culture fails as a village for all our children. We can learn ways to do better from cultures anywhere on earth, as my mother learned the value of breast feeding and the need to create a supportive network of adults from her fieldwork in the South Pacific. And then use what we have learned to benefit the children who are our responsibility.

Sankofa is an injunction to learn from the elders of one's community and from the past, to go back. But it suggests the need to adapt what is drawn from the past to the present, and to adapt the symbol to include learning from elsewhere as well. All around the student dining room at Spelman there are portraits of black women who have not only survived but left their mark on American society against all the odds. Sankofa—learn from the models of the past: Sojourner Truth. Fannie Lou Hamer. Marian Anderson. Harriet Tubman. And many more, some I had never heard of. To many who have no memorial.

Those portraits would not have been there when the elders in our seminar were students—even the building did not yet exist—but Marymal once pointed out a group photo of one of the earliest Spelman classes, which included the first woman in her family to get a formal education, Cornelia, for whom Marymal's daughter was named. "She finished Spelman when it was a seminary, I think it was the class of 1889. That Cornelia, because she was the first member of the family to have a formal education, she was the pride of the family. Her brother married my great-grandmother, so when my grandmother was born, she was named Mary Cornelia. She always wanted to come to Spelman herself but couldn't afford it—it was very hard to make a living then—so when I was coming up that's all she ever talked about. Then when I had a daughter, I named her Cornelia in their honor." That first Cornelia became a symbol of possibility for the generations that followed, but the meaning of the symbol has changed, as the education offered here has broadened to include learning from more and more sources.

Most women of my generation went to schools where the portraits on the walls were of men. We learned to use them, but we have benefited as women's faces have begun to be included and women's names have been acknowledged as belonging on the rolls of thinkers and artists. When Johnnetta became president, all the early portraits in Reynolds Cottage were of white women, followed by those of black men. "All the blacks are men, all the women are white" sums up the twofold problem for black women of finding models. That too is now changed.

What do you do when the available symbols suggest subjugation even as they speak of freedom and possibility? There has been debate about whether "jumping the broomstick," the custom used to indicate the commitment of slave couples to each other even though it had no legal standing, should be used as a wedding custom affirming African American identity or whether it is too evocative of pain and imposed separation. But virtually all traditional wedding ceremonies contain reminders—the father who gives away the bride, the veil that is lifted only for the new husband—that marriage was an arrangement in which women might be treated as if they were property. We use them gingerly, not to be trapped by them but to transcend them.

Again and again women speaking about their lives are caught between the desire to affirm the culture they come from and the fear that in doing so they are embracing a subordinate role. For women, sankofa necessarily means revision and reinterpretation. Maxine Hong Kingston is haunted by proverbs that compare women to maggots, and takes up the Chinese myth of the woman warrior, reshaping it into an identity that is both feminist and Chinese. Tsitsi Dangarembga, writing about the alternate paths open to women among the patriarchal Shona of Zimbabwe, opens her novel by having her narrator say she was not sorry when her brother died—if he had not, she, as a girl, would never have been educated. In many conservative Jewish congregations today, women have taken to wearing the prayer shawl traditionally worn by men. At Spelman College there is an impressive women's jazz ensemble, yet traditionally the role of women in jazz was limited to singing.

Hillary Clinton had the task of transforming available images and symbols to create a new way to act as the wife of a president. Some dozen nations have now had female chiefs of state, and eventually there will be a woman in the American presidency, a woman whose husband, if she has one, will have to invent his own role, as Art Robinson, Johnnetta's husband, did at Spelman, with generosity and flair. Eleanor Roosevelt is the best approximation to a model Mrs. Clinton has had, someone who was attacked and satirized also but who was less threatening to American men—how many wives in those days wanted to model themselves on Mrs. Roosevelt?

I had met with Mrs. Clinton, whom Johnnetta taught me to refer to as the First Sister, several times, so I called and asked if I could bring members of the class to her book signing. As many as could come bundled into a van and set off, timed to arrive when the line had ended and there would be a few minutes for conversation. I wanted my class to have her as a model, just as I wanted them to find models among the authors we read and to learn from one another.

Hillary Rodham Clinton and I do not belong to the same generation. Sometimes she has seemed to me very young, full of intelligence and high purpose but unprepared for the residual hostility against the participation of women and the tendency, which women of my generation know all too well, to misunderstand and demonize women in leadership roles. Born in 1947, she is a baby boomer, while I was born in 1939, a prewar product. Those who had been adults during World War II, often called the GI Generation, held political power for so long after the war, in steadily increasing geriatric splendor, that my own cohort came to be called the Silent Generation. Having the Clintons in the White House represented not only a transition from one generation to another but a generation skipped, which explains some of the stylistic dissonance between them and their predecessors. They must echo a past in which leaders always projected strength and superior knowledge, but also model the transition to a world in which the willingness to learn is paramount. For the president, Thomas Jefferson seemed to be a key figure, always learning, passionate in his convictions, yet curiously ambiguous. For the First Lady, living with the portraits of presidents and their wives, Eleanor Roosevelt was the best available model.

I believe it is important to learn from our own ancestors (literal and figurative), from other cultures, and from our children. Conversations with Mrs. Clinton ranged over the roles of women, the role of symbols in culture, and the cultures and religions of the countries she was to visit on her travels. On other occasions we discussed the travails of authorship and the fact that many creative people do their best work after experiences of rejection or denigration. When Mrs. Clinton was working on her book, we talked about the fact that both of us had raised daughters, both only children, who provide each of us with a sort of moral gyroscope, a way of thinking about all children and about the future. Whatever we do to ensure that all of today's children are adequately educated and nourished, that they reach adulthood untraumatized and able to face the future with resilience and a willingness to learn, is a means of shaping the world in which our own children must live. Human groups diverged a long and violent time ago, so we can fuel endless schisms and hostilities by looking to the past; the new convergence lies in the future, the possibility that our children or grandchildren may move to or marry into any culture in the world, the certainty that whatever individual choices they make, their lives will be intertwined with lives around the planet.

For now, African Americans are citizens of a country where skin color is loaded with symbolic meaning that is still being reshaped and reinterpreted. Even at triumphal moments like the dedication of the Cosby Building, when the African tradition is being celebrated, race, as Americans have understood it, is an inescapable theme. For Euro-pean Americans, even those who live and work in mixed groups, being "white" is not a matter of constant awareness but something taken for granted, along with the privileges that go with it. As a white person I want to believe that in my friendships with African Americans color becomes irrelevant, but that never quite happens, just as sex never becomes irrelevant between males and females, even in completely nonsexual relationships. Often enough conversations in our seminar were sufficiently intense that *I* became irrelevant and others went ahead with their business—but race was often central to their business.

One of the handful of white students from other countries on the campus, whom Johnnetta interviewed for her cross-cultural interview assignment, had described herself as feeling like a white ice cube melting in a black sea, and I wondered about the details of the metaphor—did she feel that she would ever be fully a part of the Spelman community? Did she feel that in being there she was surrounded by warmth that would dissolve something frozen in her? This is something white Americans quite often feel in their friendships with other groups. One of my Mason students, in her autobiographical writing, described her father, a career army officer who exemplified the ideals of reserve and self-discipline but was also limited by them, and frustrated and isolated in retirement. After she married a Latin American immigrant and lived for a time in his family home, she undertook a long and tactful campaign to lure her father out of his isolation and help him to be more expressive in word and gesture. Simple things, like "I love you, honey" over the phone, or "I miss you," that he would not have said before.

Often at Spelman I could hear, very clearly, allowances being made for my presumed ignorance, and often I got little lectures about things

I already knew but that many white folk are blind to, like color consciousness within the black community. But certain kinds of ignorance on the part of white Americans are not forgivable. No one is guilty of the crimes committed by others in previous centuries, but that kind of innocence does not justify the "innocence" of ignorance. We do have an obligation to be willing to learn.

Johnnetta and I have occasionally had conversations in which we disagreed about whether race was an important issue in a particular event. There was an episode at Emory University involving roommates, a black woman and a white woman, where the white woman's boyfriend had more or less moved in. When the black woman protested, the disagreement escalated to a fistfight between their respective boyfriends, black and white.

From my point of view, quite similar sequences were unfolding on campuses all over the country. Not only have chaperonage and parietal hours been abandoned, but young people have come to believe that they have a right to conduct their sex lives as they wish—often in a small shared room or apartment. Two women living together would not invite a third woman to move in without discussion—but one of them may bring a boyfriend to share her bed without considering the effect on the other, who is often expected to spend her evenings in the library or to buy earplugs. This can be pretty gross in a dormitory room and profoundly disturbing when roommates come from different backgrounds. This is one more of those situations where we no longer have a clear set of rules, where those who have different standards of morality need at least to work toward common standards of courtesy.

I argued that this situation could have developed as it did without a racial factor, everyone white or everyone black. Johnnetta disagreed but dropped the subject. (Can one hear a small, weary, unvoiced sigh of disappointment?) I realized I could actually see her deciding not to pursue the discussion, balancing the values of our friendship against an increment of awareness and honesty, so I gave it a good deal of thought afterward. The same sequence of events could and does occur without racial overtones, but whenever Americans of different races are involved in any kind of conflict, I had to concede, race is a factor, blocking attention to other and perhaps more significant layers of meaning, requiring a first analysis in terms of "us" and "them."

Two aspects of the situation, curiously intertwined, occurred to me immediately: One was the existence of stereotypes about the sexual proclivities of African Americans, stereotypes that, like any set of stereotypes, are sometimes acted out and sometimes passionately denied. I imagined a young African American woman who has grown up in a conservative religious home interpreting her roommate's behavior as implying that she, being black, would have no sexual morals or sensitivities, whereas she may be hypersensitive about such issues.

The second issue is harder to recognize, the experience of African Americans that they are unimportant enough in the white world to be invisible and what they see or hear does not matter. There is a long history of black domestics laundering adulterous sheets and clearing away revealing trash to reconstruct the facade of tidiness and respectability for employers they may see as slatternly and worse. So I imagined a young woman lying in her dormitory bed at night, feeling that her roommate and her roommate's lover are appropriating her space and invading her privacy because they do not care about having her respect; she is so unimportant in their eyes that she isn't really there.

What we have to learn is not only to respect the rights of others but to accept the salience of their experience and all the other experiences evoked by a word or symbol. Unless we work with that, we keep re playing the same scenarios. My daughter, a mature and competent woman, has pointed out to me repeatedly that there are situations in which I treat her like a child—and that if she puts up with it, it may get worse. There are also situations, however, in which she behaves with me like a child—and if I put up with it, I too will tend to reinforce it. So each of us faces decisions about how often to protest, how often to let it pass. Many women would say the same things about the assumptions of female helplessness made by men, even when the intention is to be helpful or protective.

The problems swirl around and around, for race, gender, age, and class all have resonances with one another. I remain mystified by the problem of finding a balance between giving too much importance to race and too little. At Mason I find myself in a quandary if an African American student gives a shoddy performance, arrives late repeatedly, does not finish assignments. If I "make allowances" for cultural differences, I risk drifting into liberal racism: I might come to assume that the poor performance of a few students is the best that can be expected from the others, putting them all into a marked and negative category, encouraging all to perform badly.

At Spelman I learned that one of the most important services a historically black institution can provide for its students, if it will, is to maintain an uncompromising demand for quality performance without having to negotiate racial differences at every step. When I was asked to speak to a large assembly of first-year students, several sections brought together, one of the section leaders halted my lecture to scold some students in the back at length for talking. Mindful of the background murmur of conversation I have heard in black churches, I would probably not have done that—certainly not with such vehemence, which felt to me uncomfortably authoritarian—but he may have been right, teaching a lesson more important than mine. We all arrive at every encounter shaped by our pasts and betrayed by our assumptions.

I treasure relationships of mutual respect and friendship with African American friends and colleagues. They "make allowances" for me, but only up to a point, because too much tolerance can corrupt a relationship and cut off the chance to teach and learn from each other. In the Philippines, a country where people will go far out of their way to avoid giving offense or creating conflict, I met foreigners who had lived there for a decade consistently violating some rule of courtesy. Because no one had ever warned them, they felt not protected but betrayed.

The nearest I have ever come to understanding the small, soundless sigh of disappointment I had begun occasionally to sense in my black friends was when my coauthor Richard Goldsby and I spoke at Dartmouth on the AIDS epidemic, he as an immunologist, I as a social scientist. After the lecture a member of the audience came up to congratulate us and enthusiastically pumped Dick's hand, full of praise. Then he said, "You really ought to go on tour and give that kind of talk in inner-city schools." Sigh. You can't even be angry because the intentions are so good. Often enough I give a speech and something similar happens, someone comes up to me, full of praise, and ends by saying, "Why, you almost reminded me of your mother." Sigh. Not that Dick is not concerned about AIDS in the black community. Not that I do not know the many ways in which my work echoes my mother's. But that those little add-on sentences tell each of us that we are not being heard as individuals.

I asked Cheryl one day about mistakes I might have made as a white person teaching at a historically black institution and about the sensitivities surrounding my writing plans. "I don't know if I'm stepping on people's toes or offending them, or look as if I'm in a plot or . . ." A run-on question to allow for reflection.

"No, I don't think you are," she cut in briskly. "But I do think you may underestimate the extent to which history affects people. The way the patterns of interaction between black and white affect people. There's a whole long history there just on this campus. I can think of white full-time teachers here who are very arrogant and patronizing, and people are conscious of it, but if you ask them they'll just say, Oh well, that's how white folks are.

"In a situation like our seminar, the interaction is intimate enough for people to take their own readings and decide how to be, and then it's okay. But otherwise you're just one more white person walking across campus. You have legitimacy because of Johnnetta, but there is a whole history of white people writing about black people. I don't think it has to be anything you do. I think it is part of the weight of the construction of race in this country, that you can be as much Mary Catherine Bateson as you want to be and you're still a white woman . . ."

". . . and every black woman can be totally herself and *she's* still seen in terms of a category."

"We know it as we walk in, out in the world, and you know it as you walk into a black situation. Very few white people ever have the experience of being in the minority. Fewer have the experience of being on black territory, on some bit of intellectual or philosophical or geographical space that really has been claimed.

"My friend from Radcliffe? After we read *Coming of Age in Mississippi* in class, I sent it to her and she said, I'm so sorry, I just didn't know, and I said, This is unacceptable, you have to go read some black history. You feel hip and liberal because your best friend is a black woman. Most white people say they *didn't know,* like that's a good thing? I said, I'm offended by your not knowing. You've known me since 1963, you read as much as I do, why have you never read any black history? When we met again in California, I said to her, Let's be friends, but it's gotta be on a different basis. You thought I was so easy to know because I've never put anything out there that wasn't part of your world. I don't feel comfortable in your world, I don't live in your world, learn something about my world. She is now one of my closest friends."

Cree Durrett was the only white woman among the elders, and in her writings for the class she kept coming back to the lessons of minority status. In her autobiographical paper she described the experiences of women in her generation (and mine—Cree is just seven years older than I am) of being in the minority in graduate school as women and, in effect, acting out the expectations and stereotypes of the majority.

Like me, Cree grew up in a family of liberal intellectuals whose opinions separated them from many of the prejudices of the time and left them nervous about the threat of McCarthyism. She went to Bennington College and found herself, in her senior year, quite unclear about her next step. "What to do next? What to *be* when I grew up? Simultaneously, I was all-knowing and knew nothing. I had tried teaching and worked in government. Neither was for me. The analytical discussions among friends who were law students appealed to me. I knew *nothing* about being a lawyer but thought I'd like to try it out. Harvard was just beginning to open its admissions to girls (we weren't 'women' back then), and apparently they were intrigued by this one-time dancer, switchboard operator, student government president, applying from Europe. I arrived in Cambridge in the fall of 1953 . . . the first female grads had received their L.L.B.s that June, and our class included 17 of us and 520 boys."

The women responded to their minority status by trying to become lost in the crowd instead of banding together and supporting one another. They were aware of the stereotypes, of the pointed questions the male students and the faculty would be asking. "How would they perform, these girls who were taking a place from someone who would stay and earn a living and not leave to have babies? Somehow we got through the year, I'm not mincemeat and have lived to tell the story. But by the end of the summer I had serious reservations about my career path. It was clear that the jobs open to women were in government, clerking for a judge, or hanging out your own shingle and scrambling for whatever clients you could get. Indeed only one of the twelve women who graduated in our class got a job with an established law firm. . . . I did not reenroll." Cree did marry a lawyer rather than become one, and moved with him to Georgia, still frustrated not to have made more of her talents.

When I asked the women each to do a life history interview with a member of another culture, many of them gravitated to foreign students or immigrants who described their early experiences in the United States. Cree interviewed a young Korean woman who had been plunged into an American public school, knowing no English, at the age of twelve, and heard about her friend's experiences of being a member of a minority, first in a predominantly black school, then in a predominantly white school.

"Kids don't know much about other cultures, just, you look funny, you talk funny. And I was tiny. . . . I went to a school where it was all big, huge, growing teenage African Americans, and I was their little toy. They'd never seen anything like me. They loved the reaction they got when they pinched me and poked and hit me in the back of my head and I'd turn around and start yelling in Korean language. They'd pick me up and twirl me around and just throw me to somebody else. I thought black people were all mean, all just awful people."

When she finally found friends, they were white students coming into the neighborhood by bus, "just like me. They were minorities too. We understood each other, we had to stick together because the black kids were intimidating all of us. I got to be friends with some of the white kids, and they really helped me a lot. When I left that first school, my impressions of American people were, Okay, black kids are bad, white kids are good. But we moved, and when I went to the next school, where there were more white kids than black, it was just re-verse and the white kids were rough, see, so then I had this . . . Wait a minute! I thought all the white kids were good? Well, they were just as bad. It wasn't over color, it was just teenagers.

"Those black kids, they made me realize that life is not what I want it to be all the time, that there are different kinds of people that you have to deal with. Because even though they were rough to me, I don't think they were really trying to hurt me. When it comes down to it, I think they were just more involved in what kind of fun they could have with somebody like me. It was scary, but I learned a lot from it too." Cree was concerned about discussing this interview in class. Would it be all right, she asked me, to describe it, or should she just avoid the issue? I said she should go ahead, but that day the students mainly spoke about the differences between writing their own experi-ences and eliciting those of others.

When I started asking about the sankofa symbol, someone loaned me a video with that title, *Sankofa,* for the injunction to look back to Africa and not forget the horrors of slavery. In this sense the same in-junction might be engraved on the Holocaust Museum. It took me several days to discover that the sankofa symbol, which I met first in its most schematic and symmetrical version, was derived from the image of a long-necked bird, looking backward. What caught my attention, however, was the notion that instead of simply accepting or remembering tradition, one should *go and get it,* take hold of it, to use as needed, an active rather than a passive approach.

When I was in Israel I read editorials that condemned rhetoric about the Holocaust as a human tragedy, emphasizing and reemphasizing that it was a Jewish tragedy, "our" tragedy. But Americans who have lived far from the killing fields need to make the effort of empathizing with the misfortunes of others, to take on both a degree of guilt and an identification with the victims. The native populations of the Americas suffered a Holocaust, as did the millions of Africans imported to be slaves. Hiroshima. Yugoslavia. Ruanda. We do well to appropriate these events from both sides, victims and victimizers, for no human community has clean hands. We can do little about the sins or achievements of our ancestors.

It sometimes makes academics uncomfortable when an ancient symbol is revived in a new setting—in fact, it made me uncomfortable to see three different explanations for the sankofa symbol, only loosely related, in the materials about the Cosby Building. But this is the human way with symbols. At graduation Spelman students wear woven stoles, orange, black, and green, of kente cloth, from Ghana—they wear them over academic robes, which are adaptations of the robes of celibate medieval clerics, and these in turn are worn over virginal white dresses, adding up to a veritable archaeological mound of layered symbols. But when we think of students and commencement, we don't think of monks and brides, and in recent years kente cloth has been integrated into the academic regalia of many African Americans as a statement of pride.

In the neighborhood of Spelman and the rest of Atlanta University Center, there are many "culture stores," selling, among other things, Afrocentric clothing that is mostly manufactured in Indonesia. Wonderful prints and copies of batiks that have long been imported into Africa are made up into robes, majestic and distinctive, like those Marymal wore, with no need to worry about current fashions or waistlines. This passing back and forth of patterns, adopting and adapting them to represent new meanings, is reminiscent of the way Chinese porcelains were copied in England and then the copies copied in China for export. I used to be a bit of a purist about all this, but today it strikes me as a way to think about how all these human creations can be playfully pieced together, enriching us all.

When I went on early morning walks with Johnnetta, she pointed out a large complex, the Shrine of the Black Madonna, which seemed to have the widest range in the store it runs—books, artwork, jewelry, and clothing. I learned later that the shrine had been a center of black separatism, and that part of its message was that African Americans should turn away from the culture of the white community. During the seventies a number of Spelman students who had been going there had decided to abandon their studies because the education at Spelman was too white.

One woman described the impact of the shrine on her daughter: "They kind of pulled her away from the road she was traveling. This was an awakening for her. She said she was too bourgeois and knew nothing about being an African American, so her involvement with the shrine helped her find out who she was, but she decided she didn't want any part of Spelman.

"She was very involved with them. I had real problems with that because I felt like they were exploiting our young black women, telling them, We are black brothers and sisters, we have our own black-owned businesses, we grow our own wheat, have our own banks, bakery, day care, bookstore . . . telling them not to deal with the white man, yet really building a structure within a structure." So are we all, I thought, living in a global economy where no community is autonomous and self-sufficient.

"They were supporters of Farrakhan, and everything at the shrine was totally black," she said. "They had the young people out on the street in every type of weather, canvassing and getting donations. They lock the door—at the shrine, once you're in, you don't come out until the service is over. They might have idols up there . . . I just don't know. I just disassociated myself from anything that was connected with the shrine."

By junior year, when her daughter was ready to drop out and was living with a man she had met at the shrine who had already been married and had two children, this mother said, "No way! You're gonna finish college and get that degree, what you do after it is your business. I offered to make the sacrifice and have the two of them live in my house although I could see what was going on. And they did, up until she graduated. I told that young man he needed to work. If you want to be in a marriage, each person has to contribute. Her father gave her a car so she could continue in school, living in my house. That man would take her to Spelman and take the car on the pretense of going to look for a job. In the evening I'd go to take out food to cook and he'd eaten up all the food and been in bed all day, asleep. That was his pattern."

After the daughter graduated, she moved out on her own. "I haven't heard too much about the shrine lately," my friend said. "I think the students are gravitating over to Morehouse for church, or into the city." In any case, the shrine bookstore was willing to deal with me, and I bought a long vest in a design based on mud cloth, batches of books, and dangling earrings. Was it okay to wear the vest, I asked Johnnetta, would people be offended? On the contrary, she was delighted.

All parts of Africa, south and north of the Sahara, are included in the culture stores. Ancient Egypt is treated as African just as firmly as Jesus and the early Christians have been treated as northern European—fair-haired and blue-eyed—in much of Christian art, and as firmly as men and women of many shades have been classified as "black."

A large number of Spelman students have African names, like Iyabo, and others derived from Arabic via Swahili, like Imani. I listened at commencement to nearly five hundred names and wondered at the choices they represented. What do you do when one dimension of slavery was the imposition of foreign names? Many recent names are made up, combining various models, sometimes scornfully called ghetto names, Tevin, Johnella. But there were times in the past when white doctors mischievously suggested to black women that they give their daughters "melodious" names like Gonorrhea or Vagina. Black men and women have had to find their own names. Sankofa, take them and use them—or take the initiative to create new ones. Joy San Brown, another of the women in the seminar, was named by her mother after a favorite character in a childhood book, a little Japanese girl, and this unusual name was for her the gift of a lifelong interest in Japan, a window through which to learn to look out at another culture.

The material of history and tradition is so rich, why not play with it for the building of identity and the exploration of difference? Scholars express curiosity and respect in their own way, but revisionist interpretations are no reason to abandon useful symbols. Sojourner Truth, a former slave, gave a speech famous for the refrain "Ar'n't I a

Woman?" Now scholars say this was inserted by the white woman reporting. Still, it remains the overwhelmingly powerful summary of
what Sojourner Truth had to say. We will not stop quoting it, just as
Catholics have not given up wearing St. Christopher medals just because scholars in the Vatican have determined that no such person existed.

Every society and every individual uses a version of the past to justify and inspire the present, and these versions are not always complete or accurate. Truth, after all, is elusive. Sometimes a historic
figure, like Thomas Jefferson or St. Paul, can be used to justify quite
contradictory positions by selective quotation, to affect the events of
the unfolding present.

Alternative versions of the past, including both myth and scholarship, need to be set side by side rather than set into opposition in a
storm of caricature and debunking. The self-reliance and loving virtue
of families in the last century; the peace and goodwill of rural life; the
heroism of the pioneers; the harmony of Samoan culture; the necessity of using the atomic bomb . . . none of these is entirely untrue,
none of them is complete. Any of these can be caricatured, presenting
a reverse image instead of supplementing an incomplete one, and
leaving us the poorer. Scholars, textbooks, and museums are needed
to present more nuanced and skeptical points of view, for alternative
versions are the pathways to wider understanding. Different people,
different peoples see the world differently—see past and future,
themselves and others differently. Curiosity and respect make it possible to enter into those alternative visions.

Trying to understand what their experiences of race had meant to
my Spelman sisters, I noticed that they resonated with the recurrent
experiences of teenagers of being singled out or excluded and that
some members of the seminar described experiences within the black

community with the same remembered pain and desire to belong. Fleda described going shopping with her mother for a particularly fashionable kind of blouse, the item that every girl her age wanted that year, and being snubbed in a downtown Atlanta department store uninterested in serving black customers. But she also wrote of her teenage agonies as a freshman at an elite black boarding school, stigmatized before the upper-class boy she was attracted to by the rule that forbade her to wear high-heeled shoes and stockings like the older girls.

Cheryl described the experience of shifting from a black private school to a segregated public school, where she was hazed by black students for her black bourgeois background and had to conceal her love for reading. She made that transition, learning to chat "with both the gangsters and the eggheads." But when she was selected to be one of the small group of black students to integrate a white high school in 1960, her mother was determined that this was an ordeal she should not have to face. "I had been taught that the segregated South was an anomalous whim of some ignorant white folks and that elsewhere we were accepted like everybody else. And I believed it, expected it. I even dreamed in the colorless rhetoric of the time."

Applying to the Northfield School for Girls in western Massachusetts, Cheryl and her mother, both carefully and elegantly dressed and wearing white gloves, presented themselves at the elite white school in Atlanta that was the testing site. After running the gauntlet of disapproving eyes and muttered comments, Cheryl was ushered, all by herself, into a separate room with a separate monitor. This was an omen of what was to come, for when she arrived at Northfield she found herself in a tiny attic room with no roommate, "literally singled out." In another time and place, a private room, generally available at Northfield only to seniors, might have felt like a blessing. The challenge that everyone encounters in growing up, that makes us acutely sensitive to nuances of meaning, is to find a way to be "singled in": acknowledged as part of a collective yet simultaneously treated as a unique individual.

Spelman students often spend a semester or a summer as exchange students. Celeste had spent a semester at Wellesley, Hillary spent a summer at Dartmouth, Iyabo a semester at the University of California at San Diego. In many cases they find themselves seeking out other African American students and taking black studies courses, as a matter of choice. For most of them the changed setting is a way of exploring the unavoidable issues of race from a different angle. There are very different experiences waiting at historically black colleges, colleges located where they naturally have a mixed applicant pool, and colleges that have traditionally been white and are seeking to enhance the presence of minorities. Colleges may slip, because of bad administrative habits, into filling quotas, but the real question is how students, white and black, can at the same time develop a center of identity and belonging and learn to live in a global society. Black and occasionally white women also come to the Spelman campus for a year, and they too are there to learn about the difference between being part of a majority, part of a minority, and, if they are lucky, being just folks.

It used to be quite common for idealists to speak of being "citizens of the world," part of the "human family." Increasingly I find myself emphasizing the idiosyncratic experience of each individual, along with the experiences of sharing that remain, always, only partial. Thought, like action, is always local at its roots, and an ethical commitment to the species and to the planet starts from the local turf, the air and water, as Iranians say, the touch and smell and voices of family, and the ways these combine in a single consciousness. They say that many of those who claim to love humanity hate people. More accurately, they may fail to come to terms with the individuals in their lives, the ambivalence and mystery of even their closest relationships, and instead prefer abstractions about humankind. But if we are grounded in a place and a time and a community, we can then lay claim to the entire human heritage. African Americans who claim Native Americans and Thomas Jefferson as ancestors are right, regardless of DNA tests. Le Ly Hayslip can claim Jefferson as well, or Maxine Hong Kingston. Anyone who celebrates the traditions of American democracy should be free to claim Deganawida and Hiawatha, the founders of the Iroquois Confederacy, for all Americans have been affected by their ideas.

I suspect that for Johnnetta not only Eleanor Roosevelt but also my own mother is an honorary ancestor—and so is Herodotus, the first European chronicler and explorer of cultural particularity. I have "ancestors" as well, that I have picked up along the way, like Ibn-Khaldun in North Africa, the fourteenth-century founder of sociology, St. Catherine of Siena, the first woman canonized as a "doctor of the church," and Sojourner Truth. Today many white folk have adopted Martin Luther King, Jr., as an honorary ancestor, sometimes sentimentalizing him too far and forgetting the outrage with which he spoke. I like to claim Malcolm X as well, along with two of King's ancestors, Mahatma Gandhi and Henry David Thoreau.

It is good that we surround both our children and our leaders with the reminders of history. The White House is full of the past. Some people claim that the Lincoln Bedroom is haunted—but I believe we are all "haunted" by the memories of assassination and the awareness that the wounds of slavery and of the Civil War are still not healed, still require action. It is important for young African Americans to learn about the achievements of their ancestors and their community. But it is also important for members of every community to be inspired by the words and works of those who live in other places on the planet and look different from them. And those who lived in the past as well. All human beings have a claim to the whole range of human creativity and imagination.

8 | Lucy's Children

During the early eighties, when I was just getting to know John-netta, before she became president of Spelman, we made a date to meet in New York and go together to the American Museum of Natural History to see the most important fossil evidence of human evolution, gathered from all over the world in a single exhibition. It was extraordinarily exciting in ways that were surprising to both of us—after all, we had seen the pictures and read the descriptions for years—to encounter the actual objects, bone and stone, the "hard evidence" of becoming human.

Johnnetta and I are both cultural anthropologists, so we have been most interested in that part of human behavior that is learned. But you cannot think about learning without recognizing that the capacity to learn and the readiness for particular kinds of learning are, at base, physical, and the products of evolution. You have to notice that learning is often blocked and that change, which reveals familiar intimates as strangers, is often frightening. Some scholars are convinced that all our social ills arise from biology, that we will forever see one another as strangers and be controlled by impulses of fight or flight. Most cultural anthropologists, however, look at the wide variation in human behavior permitted by biology and conclude it is possible to shape and cherish the learning process, guiding it in the direction of openness and lifelong learning.

The beginnings of hominid evolution in Africa have been accepted since the discovery in the 1920s of the remains dubbed *Australopithecus africanus,* sometimes called the killer ape. This discovery triggered a certain fatalism about human behavior, conjuring up an arresting picture of human descent from a violent and homicidal killer of large game—perhaps the same character so often depicted in the act of dragging a captive female into a cave. Since then, however, ongoing work in archaeology has combined with the study of contemporary foraging societies like those of the San and of our nearest primate relatives to show that this version of the human heritage is a gross distortion. As I remember that day I realize that Johnnetta and I were still largely trapped in the "man the hunter" understanding of our species. By now we know that our ancestors were not routinely homicidal and that they lived mainly on fruit and vegetables, the men doing some hunting but depending heavily on female gathering for subsistence, each helping the other.

In 1974 the gracile remains of a female the scientists called Lucy were discovered; she is now recognized as belonging to a different species, *Australopithecus afarensis,* an even closer relative to us. There she was, right there in New York City. Grandma. Eve. Johnnetta had recently had surgery on her foot, but instead of postponing our visit we had gotten a wheelchair that I pushed from hall to hall. There we were, two women, one black and one white, bonding together in mutual support and in the delight of learning and discovery, Lucy's children, come together in friendship after our species had learned its way around the globe. Upright posture was one of the breakthroughs of human evolution, but wheels are one of the great human inventions—and we can affirm now that mutual caring and cooperation are also part of our inheritance.

Historically anthropologists have combined evidence from archaeology with observations of contemporary human groups and of other primates to understand the relationship of human biology and the capacity for culture, evolving together. Differences of sex or age or race all have biological components and can be illuminated by comparisons with other species, but there is a constantly recycled debate about whether the characteristics of a given group are biologically fixed, socially constructed, or some subtle combination of the two, a debate that follows the process of learning from birth right on through the life cycle. Thus, we are beginning to know a great deal about the biology of aging and how different disease processes can cause it, but there is still much to be said about how social expectations of the elderly promote inactivity and dementia—and may bring about irreversible change. The same arguments about how much to attribute to biology and how much to environment turn up in relation to race and gender, along with the same fateful effects on expectations and on learning.

Similarly for many illnesses, it is hard to keep the two sides of pathology in focus and understand the relationships of biochemistry and experience. We have learned a lot about how depression, for instance, can be treated with medication, but our successes may lead us to pay too little attention to the effects of experience—and to the ways in which experiences of cherishing or trauma have different effects on young and old, male and female.

Over the period that I have been using life histories in my teaching, wherever I have taught, I have heard the life stories of students who found it almost impossible to study because of the grief and depression in their lives. A number of us in the Spelman seminar had gone through such painful periods, so that we had had to wonder about how much of the problem was within ourselves and how much an outcome of external factors. Cheryl had spoken of a long depression in early adulthood, Ama was struggling with grief deepened by her work with AIDS patients, and Imani had dropped temporarily out of college. I had my own memories also, the lingering effects of the steady, inimical pressure I had felt as a dean at a newly coeducational institution followed by betrayal by colleagues I had been close to—the discovery that those I had trusted were strangers. Early in that experience I became conscious that I was all too willing to internalize blame rather than label and struggle against the unethical behavior of others.

Imani had been raped when she was six by a friend of her brother, twice her age. She had the same experience of internalized pain, blaming herself as a child for the actions of someone older and more powerful. She did not tell her parents until some two years later. "The time line is hard for me," she said. "From the time that I was raped until the time that I told my parents, I can remember about three major events in my life, I was really . . . I can figure out when I told them because I started remembering my life again. I remember the first half of first grade, and then I don't really remember anything until the second half of third grade. It was a long time. Why is it that I get raped and *I* have to work it out? Where is the asshole that raped me—is he having to work it out?

"I was watching *Donahue* with my mom. I remember writing my mom a note saying, I have something to tell you, promise you won't get mad at me. Then I told her. She called my father in New York, and he came to Amherst. It's funny, we sat down at the table, and I remember I said to my father, Raymond [not a real name] raped me, and he said, I know. But I didn't know that my mom had told him, so I really thought he had known all those years that I was terrible and dirty and awful and he knew that it was all my fault, and all those years he was just waiting for me to crack under the pressure . . . and confess to him that *I* had done this awful thing."

Depression comes up often in life histories written by women. The most famous account occurs in a short story by Charlotte Perkins Gilman, but Gilman made it very clear in her autobiography, one that I often use in teaching, that her story of the paralyzing depression of a young mother was, like so much fiction, autobiographical—and that although she recovered substantially, she never again felt quite the same, mentally or emotionally; her resources were depleted forever. In our seminar we had started by reading Maxine Hong Kingston's *The Woman Warrior,* in which the bewildered grief and madness of women are a recurrent theme: "Within a few blocks of our house were half a dozen crazy women and girls, all belonging to village families," some who never spoke, some who growled or laughed, locked up in rooms or taken away to the "crazy house." Maxine worried about her own sanity and watched her aunt's breakdown. Her implication is that the cultural treatment of women destroys them, but perhaps it was the dissonance of traditional roles in a new country. The Chinese husbands went out and learned to cope. Their wives were shut up at home, perpetual aliens. But dissonant roles and the stress that goes with them are more and more common.

One reason we hear so much about depression today is that its social costs have increased as we move into the information age. Depression affects thought as well as feeling—it is not just that you feel sad, you also lose curiosity and problem-solving skills, while memory and other learning skills are impaired. You feel stupid and bored, weary and dreary and blurred. We may be entering the first era in the history of civilization when a mild state of chronic unipolar depression—"living and partly living," in T. S. Eliot's words—is not regarded as appropriate in the great mass of the populace. As more and more kinds of work require continuing learning and fine discrimination, resignation may at last have become less useful in society than mental agility.

Depression has been linked to brain chemistry through low levels of the neurotransmitter serotonin, and new medications like Prozac or Zoloft have been publicized in ways that encourage physicians to prescribe them and patients to request them. This trend has fostered the notion that depression is exclusively biological, but periods of depression are often triggered by experience. The brain almost seems to *learn* to be depressed, as the immune system learns to deal with new threats. Each subsequent round of depression, however, is more likely to be internally caused, with little or no external trigger.

The kind of society we live in probably fosters depression, for low serotonin levels have been attributed to stress and low self-esteem. It's a circular process. We have built an affluent, highly competitive mass society in which more and more people feel helpless or abandoned at some stage of their lives, and in which high levels of stress are not balanced by dependable cherishing. Low serotonin levels have also been linked to violence.

Cheryl talked to me one day about violence and crowding. "I love New York," she said, "but if I lived in the worst parts of Brooklyn or the Bronx I would have killed somebody by now. There's something about numbers and how people respond. The white survivalists—sure they're crazy, because they put ideological stuff above what they're feeling—but they're experiencing something real in terms of people, numbers, who gets what, how things are divided."

At least in this culture, depression and violence, as alternative by-products of low serotonin levels, seem to be linked to gender. Women and men deal with grief and suffering in different ways. Just as more males respond to stress and alienation with aggression, more females sink into depression, which has sometimes been described as internalized rage. And just as controlled aggression makes good soldiers, mild depression may make obedient wives and daughters, resigned to circumscribed roles. But not all societies have constructed the role of women to demand passivity, and not all societies have institutionalized violence as we have in warfare and the criminal justice system.

There are studies of patients in mental hospitals that suggest that boys and girls respond differently to abuse, often in ways that bring them closer to gender stereotypes than the rest of the patient population, abuse producing higher levels of depression, passivity, and withdrawal in the women, and higher levels of violence and aggression in the men. Both men and women who have been abused improve more slowly than others, less able perhaps to trust and therefore to move into the kind of learning that occurs in therapy. Many violent males with the same kind of history could no doubt be found in prisons, their behavior treated as crime rather than as mental illness; many depressed women have simply suffered at home.

There surely are biological differences between males and females, some of these in the areas of cognition and emotion. But many differences probably lie not so much in what *can* be learned but in what is *most easily* learned, contrasting reactions to similar experiences or contrasting traits acquired as a result of trauma. Healthy individuals may be more nearly androgynous than those who have been traumatized. All learning takes place in the context of variable biological potential, but it is easy to deform or stunt in the individual organism the potentials offered by the genes, and experiences, like genetic traits, may carry over from generation to generation, leaving potentials unused and undeveloped.

Many societies, including our own, seem to have organized child rearing to enhance the potential for violent and aggressive behavior in the males and to prepare females for life in a state of chronic mild depression, often through practices that we have only recently come to regard as abusive. Beating young children was for a long time standard in the Christian West and leaps out of classic autobiographies. Extremes of corporal punishment may affect psychological development the way foot binding affects bones and muscles. Only the worst cases of depression and aggression are recognized as pathological, however, the routine casualties having become part of the definition of normal.

The fossil evidence of human evolution that Johnnetta and I looked at that day, along with diagrams and photographs of skulls, has stimulated new thinking about development as well as about evolution, for the process of becoming human required a reshaping of the life cycle, with new eras of both potential and vulnerability. Over millennia of evolution, *Homo sapiens* has emerged as a species born strikingly immature and requiring extended adult care and protection, which allows for a lot of learning. When infants are isolated, lacking stimulation, or when they lack continuity of loving care, they do not thrive intellectually or emotionally. The extended childhood that makes culture possible depends on cherishing, touching, comforting. Growing up human is not easy, and many human societies make it harder.

Johnnetta and I are both mothers and teachers, teachers of young adults and increasingly of older adults, and for us as for many women traditional divisions have been eroded. We recognize the home as a place of work and have tried to make work a place of caring, and both of them places of learning. Educators trained in all-male institutions sometimes argue that nurturing approaches to college teaching subvert the process and make it insufficiently challenging. On the contrary, although challenge does promote effort, a degree of security is needed to promote creativity. In our era, as educational institutions try to encourage more independent and adventurous thinking rather than just exam results, they have begun to be more supportive as well.

Many cultures mark the transitions from boy to man or girl to woman with frightening or painful rituals and a drastic separation from the home. Initiation rites, which often include a period of intensive learning, suggest at their culmination that the basic learning tasks are completed and the loving care of parents is now unnecessary. But cultures vary greatly in when that transition occurs, and the timing is changing in our own society. Perhaps in reality that transition never does occur, since nurture and learning are never completed. Today, when we are increasingly concerned with supporting learning in forty- or sixty-year-olds, we should be asking how they will find the necessary cherishing.

Not only are human beings born extraordinarily vulnerable and helpless, but they retain some infantile characteristics throughout their lives, as Johnnetta and I could see from the fossils and the diagrams in the museum display. This biological trait, traditionally referred to as *neoteny,* is what lets us hope to "die young as late as possible." We are very similar to other hominoids at birth, but the various species of apes develop more rapidly, and over time their differences from humans emerge. The profile of an infant chimpanzee is nearly human, but the adult chimp has craggy brows and a protruding jaw. In effect, "man, in his bodily development, is a primate fetus that has become sexually mature." As the rigidification of human adulthood has been deferred, certain traits have been "driven off the time scale of development." We all die in infancy, however many years we live.

The term *neoteny* was coined to underline physical differences, but it underlines behavioral differences between humans and other mammals as well. Those who have attempted to domesticate or humanize wild animals often observe a transition when the darling wolf or lion cub, so like a pet, sloughs off most of its relationship to human foster parents. The attempt to raise chimpanzees like human children seemed to work well for a time, with the chimps more responsive and quicker to learn than human infants, but at a certain point the effort seemed to reach a dead end. With maturity, wild animals become less playful, less willing to learn, and less responsive to affection. Often domestication, both our own and that of other species, has involved selection for neotenous traits. Dogs, closely related to wolves but shaped by centuries of domestication and selection to fit human preferences, remain in some degree puppylike throughout their lives. Domesticated cats look more like the kittens of other feline species than do undomesticated adult felines, lions, lynxes, even bobcats.

What neoteny offers is the shift from a fixed adaptation to the vast range of human patterns and the possibility of choice. The rigidity that sometimes accompanies adulthood, however, burdens society as it freezes into prejudice and the inability to trust, while the capacity for delight and curiosity may be more central to humanness than we allow ourselves to acknowledge. Human evolution has deferred adulthood, maintaining both vulnerability and the flexibility that leads to cultural and technological development, allowing us to play the game of knowledge and thereby to push our dying later and later.

Neoteny is what keeps us adaptable, able, as Ashley Montagu puts it, to respond rather than simply to react.

We all know of adults who remain intellectually open, who seem to go through their whole lives with a quality of discovery that is sometimes called childlike. This is precisely the correct word for that innocence, playfulness, and flexibility to encounter new ideas, putting curiosity before control. This is a quality that lingers in many great artists and scientists into very old age and is, perhaps, the basis of what we call wisdom. We are now at a time when the need for these traits is greater than ever before, for we are constantly confronted with new and different experiences.

When adults return to the classroom, they are often concerned that they may have lost a necessary degree of mental agility and openness. More disturbing to many teachers, however, they may have lost the docility drummed into them in school and have become less tolerant of boredom and repetition. We did a lot of laughing in our seminar room. There seemed to be direct connections between the laughter that surrounded the passing of a fictitious ball of energy, the emotional intensity that followed, and the flow of ideas. Every week a different member of the class brought food to be shared in the break, a ritual of snacks and munchies and a period of gleeful gossip.

Schooling is often abusive, the pressure translated by some into competition and by others into apathy and withdrawal. Because of their distance from the classroom, the elders were freer than the undergraduates, for whom anything taken for academic credit retained an aura of coercion. Johnnetta was my mainstay, because although she groused about "this visiting professor who was forcing her to do homework," she made it clear that, for her, reading and coming to class were a pleasure, not a burden. But all of the elders brought the awareness of their common freedom of choice.

Human infants survive only if they receive loving care. The memory of that care remains as a basis for the ability to give and receive care, while trauma in childhood may produce adults with limited abilities not only to give and receive love but also to learn. Monkeys reared with adequate nutrition but without a mother's care have been shown to be unable as adults to care for their own infants or even to mate, and human beings abused in childhood are likely to become abusive.

Contemporary society has turned against many of the most punitive aspects of traditional child care, but debate continues about the importance of discipline, the hazards of permissiveness, the dangers of "coddling." Most of the world does not think children benefit from being made to cry or left to cry alone, but Western cultures come from a harsh tradition in which children, marked with original sin, were felt to start out evil and require correction. Furthermore, most of the world understands the vulnerability of an adult left alone all day with very young children, while our emphasis on privacy has probably made some kinds of abuse more likely. Judging by the accounts that have recently become available from adults growing up in those years, the fifties seem to have been a heyday of secret molestation. Sexual abuse certainly always existed but may have increased well before the sexual revolution and the vaunted decline of family values, following what might be called the privacy revolution, which isolated children in nuclear family households.

Within the wide diversity of child-rearing patterns in the United States, African Americans have often been regarded as suspiciously indulgent and sensuous in their handling of infants. Few black folk went as far as some white folk in replacing cherishing with rigid hygiene and scheduling in early childhood, but there has sometimes been a repressive discipline that followed the indulgence, in an effort to assert control over children whose world was extremely hazardous. This is what some members of the class emphasized when we talked about child care: being yelled at or slapped or insulted, called "out of their names." Some trauma comes not from family life but from early encounters with institutions like schools or hospitals or from historic events like conquest and captivity. Almost every African American life history I have read includes a memory of the early discovery that the warmth found within the home was not reflected outside. Pat Bakr, for instance, wrote about moving with her family to a new home in New Jersey. "My kindergarten teacher was a pretty white woman with long blond hair. I liked the way she talked to the children because she seemed to really like kids. I just knew that she would like me too because I was cute and special. All my family said so. My teacher asked for someone in the class to get her something from the play box, so I was the first one to retrieve it. I remember handing the article to the pretty blond teacher, but she would not take it from me. Instead she went past me and congratulated another little girl for being smart and helpful. I was furious. Why was this woman ignoring me? I looked at the other little girl to see who had outdone me. For the first time in my life I noticed that I was black. This little girl was cute too, but she looked like my teacher. She had on a very pretty pink dress that had ruffles on the sleeves and around the hem, and she had a head full of long blond curly hair. I now understood that there were two kinds of cute. There was a cute for whites and there was a cute for blacks."

Whole populations may be marked by conquests or ecological disaster and then pass on the results to subsequent generations as their pain resonates in the way they care for their children. Population growth and ecological changes may have been responsible not only for human migrations but for fundamental cultural changes in prehistory, including punitive practices of child rearing, institutionalized violence such as warfare, and the suppression of women. In a band stretching where the Sahara is today, across the Mideast and into the Gobi Desert in Asia, regions that were once lush and fertile became deserts around the fourth millennium B.C.E. Settled farmers could no longer support themselves and became migratory, spilling out in a series of invasions when carrying capacity was exceeded. Often the groups that were conquered had peaceful, cooperative cultures, while the invaders had institutionalized warfare and the subordination of women, a set of harsh traits that were then passed on through the experience of subsequent generations. These are the traditions that shaped Western civilization—Israel, Rome, Greece—and these are the traditions that have survived, although their harshest features have been moderated over time. Even as we hold on to what is most valuable in these legacies, it is time to change them even further.

We sometimes say, in referring to the aggression and competition of politics or the business world, "It's a jungle out there," but it may be that what is "out there" in our intensely competitive society is a recreation of the desert, with nomadic values embedded in our religions, laws, and institutions. We live not in a concrete jungle but in a concrete desert where little grows. Jungle—or rain forest—may not be such a bad thing for humanity, yet in this era we are steadily reducing the forested areas of the planet and increasing the areas of desert. When fertile green areas are turned into desert by misuse or climate change, human relationships are likely to become harsher and more competitive.

Conquest of any kind creates subject populations that have to learn to survive, but the displacement of the slave trade was extreme, more like abduction than like conquest. "The quintessential science fiction scenario has already happened to black people," Cheryl pointed out. "People with mysterious technology—men from Mars—came, scooped us up, we had no idea where we were going. We had no idea there even was someplace to go. In the bush in Africa there are people who had ancestors who were abducted, and if you ask what happened to them they say, 'We think those people ate them,' or 'We think they threw them in the ocean.' They know about the U.S. now, but the storytelling tradition stays the same." Cheryl has been involved with filmmaking on the griots, the traditional storytellers of Senegal, and with other African narrative traditions.

She went on to connect the patterns of survival that emerged with what has been called the Stockholm syndrome, especially as it might be played out over generations. "When you kidnap people, and get them under control, they begin to identify with the kidnapper and all that, you know? Nobody's ever studied that over generations: What happens when a whole bunch of people are kidnapped, denied their language, denied their religion—you cut them off, you mix them with other people whose language and rituals they don't share, you rename them, you beat, kill, rape, fell? Then there's a second generation, whose parents have been beaten down, but they've figured out what they have to do not to be killed, so they bring up their children to keep living. Those children have children.

"I think some of what we are seeing now, where black men are not only murdering and raping black women but are murdering each other, is new in this generation. They are staring right into the mirror of each other's faces and shooting each other as someone who needs to die, someone who is expendable. There are interesting dynamics that are going on there when you not only feel free to attack the Other, which seems to be a human thing, but you are so twisted inside that you attack the Same."

"You yourself are the Other," I said.

"And that perspective is actually integrated into you! This misrecognition, this mirror killing thing has been coming along. It probably happened some in the first generation, among the first slaves. There was probably some guy who was told, Kill that black man over there, and did so. He figured out the best way to stay alive and to keep the others alive. Then in the next generation people had figured out how . . . I think there is some reason, possibly our resilience that we're always talking about, that it has taken us this *long* to get to this particularly ugly place. People are people."

You can see it in playground rivalries and jingoistic politics, but people are not always and everywhere as suspicious and competitive as common sense has come to assume. Attacking the Other is one of our potentials but not a necessity. Banding together and muting rivalries by turning hostility outward is not the only way of organizing a community. Among other primates, alternatives to hostility exist also, especially curiosity, sometimes affection. Another source of new insight about our species is recent work in the rain forests of Zaire on my favorite relative, *Pan paniscus,* the bonobo or pygmy chimpanzee. Gradually the bonobos have stolen the limelight from the other apes and from more distant primates, like baboons, as models for understanding human behavior. Like the fossils, they suggest alternative ways to see ourselves.

Bonobos spend more time in mixed-sex groups than chimps do, and when tension arises it is resolved by mutual caresses in all possible combinations rather than by quarreling, love not war. Among bonobos the most important relationships are not between males but between sons and their mothers. In bonobo society, seed is spread so widely that everyone is everyone's child.

All human beings develop less fully than they might. A peaceful community, one in which no one's potentials were diminished by the need to recover from paralyzing trauma, would allow more learning and would allow individuals to remain open to new learning longer. Imani described how painful experience in childhood affected her learning and participation in primary school and later in college. Smart and caring as she is, she has had to invest a huge amount of energy in simply surviving, emerging courageous and thoughtful.

It may often have been true that a society was better off denying most curiosity and playfulness to prepare for a life that was necessarily both real and earnest, and that it has been sufficient for most individuals to live out their lives on the basis of a body of accepted cultural knowledge—indeed, the loss of playful curiosity may be the entry fee to adulthood. Much as we value the achievements of artists and scientists in the past, most of us would rather not have too many around, and certainly they would be troublemakers in many institutions, easily distracted, intrusively questioning in the classroom, subversive on the factory floor. All too many educational institutions aim for homogeneity and docility. Bullishness in the cultural china shop gives way to quiet and docile obeisance to sacred cows.

A great part of what is called education probably developed as a way of suppressing curiosity and ensuring obedience in the young, obedience given to elders who would be weakening their position if they revealed their own doubts and questions. This is explicit in some places, such as some religious schools, where curiosity and a readiness to question traditional answers are treated as sinful. It is implicit in all systems of tests, however, where students are expected to supply the answers that teachers regard as correct. Even while we are transmitting useful information we are often destroying the capacity to seek out new truths, and once the learning process has been too drastically slowed down it is difficult to resume.

The closing down of curiosity affects people at every level of society and may even become a precondition to positions of authority or power in the community. The greater the prestige attached to a position, the more important it is to seem to know the answers already, rather than to continue searching and questioning. When we speak of the necessity of gravitas in leaders, we are proposing a different mode of being, nonwhimsical, stable—and an extinction of neotenous traits. We look for the sculpted brow ridge or the forward thrust of the jaw. We admire the craggy face of a Lincoln, seemingly destined for carving in granite, while the softer, rounded face of a Clinton is less reassuring. A politician's popularity goes up when he "hangs tough" and thrusts out his jaw, eerily reminiscent of adult male gorillas or baboons, and we forget to ask about his willingness to continue to learn.

An interesting example of the incongruity of leadership and learning has been playing itself out with rapid technical change. Substantial numbers of executives who were well established in careers when personal computers became available were able to delegate all work involving them to technical staff. When they arrived at a point where their lack of computer literacy felt like a flaw, the process of learning had to be pursued in secret because it was so embarrassing. The CEO of a company, for instance, might feel quite unable to call on technically skilled underlings to teach him and watch him make foolish mistakes. For about a decade there was a boom in workshops organized away from the home office, to allow these movers and shakers to catch up without embarrassment to what has become a basic form of literacy.

When a CEO delegates the application of computer skills, he is taking advantage of his power, the kind of power that the political scientist Karl Deutsch defined as "the ability not to have to learn." The same kind of power is expressed when a parent or a manager says, "Do it because I say so." On the one hand, this can be very reassuring, and indeed there is a vertigo when such people admit to uncertainty and openness to new ways of seeing. On the other hand, taking advantage of power to avoid learning can ultimately be disastrous. Rulers put themselves at risk if they do not know enough about the lives and opinions of their subjects; so buffered are they by courtiers that they may long to walk the streets in disguise, as the caliph is said to have done in the Arabian Nights.

Today we live in a world where answers change steadily, enough so that it is important to be ready to revise opinions throughout a lifetime. New technologies offer new possibilities and demand mastery of new skills. Political shifts mean that yesterday's enemies are today's friends. New ethical understandings demand new attitudes and changed behavior. There is a growing recognition of the need for ongoing learning and revision of previous learning. We can no longer afford the association between leadership and the loss of a childlike willingness to play and learn.

The increasing need for adaptation to social and technological change throughout the life cycle poses the question of how it can be sustained. It may be that the cognitive and emotional openness of childhood need not be outgrown, molded into hostility, or muted by depression. It may be that we can learn to take the risks of learning in each other's presence and that, in the words of a bumper sticker, "it is never too late to have a happy childhood." What it takes is a combination of play and sustained and mutual cherishing.

There have been many societies in which age brought respect automatically. I believe we are moving toward a society in which, although authority is still associated with age in some contexts, age is respected only if it is accompanied by a continuing capacity to change and learn, since those who do not do so become incompetent in the face of change. As parents, teachers, or leaders we need to model the willingness to learn, even when learning involves confronting troubling realities. One wonders whether much of the panic about erotic material on the Internet originates with adults who feel less competent with technology than their children. By contrast, the openness and excitement of older students are inspiring, especially when you can see growth. At Mason a student in her sixties, a white woman from an elite family, was shaken by Audre Lorde's autobiography, by the searing details of an abortion and the evocation of lesbian sex. "It's so alien to me," she said, "but now that I read her writing I know this is someone I have to respect."

The other reason to conserve openness to learning is that it is simply more fun. The idea that what is pleasant, delicious, playful is bad for you does not make sense in evolutionary terms, for the capacity for pleasure has been shaped by natural selection. Once we notice the joy of learning, we can notice the interesting similarities between human learning and human sensuality, which also runs through the life cycle, disengaged from the limited seasons of conception. Pleasure acts as an innate teaching mechanism, a built-in reinforcement. Hormones and nerve endings are organized to make sex pleasurable so men and women not only recognize each other with desire but return to repeat the pleasure and associate it with each other, forming a basis for long-term bonding. The ability to enjoy a given activity is the kind of trait that develops when the activity confers an adaptive advantage. The sensory pleasures of infancy and childhood are folded into the pleasures of adult sexuality, making it playful and diverse.

Learning too starts out as its own reward. A child learning to walk or to put together a puzzle is visibly delighted not only by the new skill or the praise of adults but by the process of discovery, of making new connections, exploring a new kind of experience. The joy of learning leads to a different kind of relationship, the love for teachers who have opened up fascinating vistas of understanding.

Well before they have reached adulthood, most children have had the intrinsic joys of learning distorted by painful associations, clouded by anxiety, by coercion and loss. Because obedience has often been more important than understanding, and because it is important to prepare for the harshness of life, it has been said that children needed to be toughened up by discomfort and boredom. Perhaps because of generations of effort to prevent children from exploring and discovering the pleasures of their own bodies, learning too has been largely detached from pleasure and enforced by pain. In the struggle with natural sexuality, learning has been seen as drawing children away from an unregenerate state of nature into civilized and joyless discipline.

Instead, human beings learn to take pleasure in purely symbolic rewards, like money and titles, so these can become the motivations for a lifetime of effort. But such extrinsic rewards may obscure intrinsic rewards—it is easy to think that the pleasure of doing well in school comes from the gold star rather than from the activity itself. It is even possible to do something intrinsically rewarding without experiencing pleasure, only out of fear of punishment. Indeed, this is what has happened with work in many societies; whatever satisfactions work might offer are, for many people, obscured by the conviction that they work only for a paycheck. The longed-for reward of a pension replaces the satisfaction of work well done, and only the emptiness of retirement reveals the value of what has been lost. The same process can be seen even in scholars, who have studied for extra years because they continued to enjoy doing so. All too often the process of completing a doctoral dissertation or achieving tenure is so anxious and grim that the joy of scholarship is effectively destroyed. The extended initiation rite of medical training, with all of its induced stress and competition, is precisely calibrated to cauterize the emotional responses of physicians, lest they care too much for their patients.

Even as males are forced into an arid and rigid adulthood, it is common in many cultures to regard women as childlike and to keep them in a state of dependency, institutionalized and reinforced neoteny. It has, after all, been important to keep women "maternal," that is, to keep them capable of loving and caring for children who would not otherwise survive, maintaining the capacity for empathy. Women are often permitted a continuing closeness with their own mothers and continuing contact with children, both of which sustain the wisdom of cherishing. Psychologists have argued that cultural constructions of gender force males to distance themselves from the mothers who have been their principal caretakers and sources of warmth, leading to a degree of emotional inhibition and resentment. Yet when there are no women on the scene, as has been true in foxholes, men move into caretaking roles and cherish one another.

What is not so often emphasized is that mothering requires constant learning to keep up with the discontinuities of development. Although women have often been (and in many places still are) denied education, their very subservience has promoted a different set of skills of observation, sensitivity, and adaptation. Dominance may require desensitization: learning not to empathize with an enemy or a servant as a fellow human being. Cooperation requires sensitivity.

The ability to respond like a child may be the most precious inheritance of human evolution, one that is essential to the maintenance of the capacity to learn. If we want the adaptability, we may also need to care for one another in adulthood as we care for children. Instead of training males to be able to do without tenderness in many settings of their lives, we might choose to nurture and extend their playfulness.

For every member of society we should rethink the continuing need for cherishing, making that cherishing mutual so it is not an excuse to limit the choices of others.

At Spelman College I got a sense of what the words *alma mater* could and should mean, the image of a school as a nurturing mother. The institution is itself protective, sometimes overly so with its gates and walls, but I was reminded often that during the years of Jim Crow it had served as a safe haven from a hostile society in the same way that the black churches did.

There is also an ethos of mutual support among the students, and a strong tradition of female friendship that was in abeyance among the women I knew when I was in college in the fifties. Sisterhood. The women in the seminar cared for one another and for me, especially during a period when I was concerned for my husband's health. Throughout my stay in Atlanta, Johnnetta's household was a reliable sanctuary.

I had a small guest suite with a kitchenette in one of the dormitories, but I had made a promise to myself that for at least one meal a day I would go to the campus dining hall or the smaller faculty dining room and, if I did not see someone I already knew to join, would strike up a conversation with a stranger. Not at breakfast—I needed a solitary cup of coffee to start the day and open my mind to others— but most often at lunch. Approaching strangers is always awkward. Walking into a huge, echoing room, asking permission to join someone sitting alone, and starting a conversation was inevitably tense, especially since I knew there was good reason to regard me with suspicion. Some of those encounters were bleak, but once or twice a week politeness—it is still true that most Spelman women are ladies—would blossom into curiosity and lively exchange.

I brought the ease of having been both liked and privileged through most of my life, even as an outsider: a gentile in Israel, an American in the Philippines, a Christian in Iran, the only woman on many committees. Even with that background, socializing took a daily act of will. That's the kind of situation in which stress and anxiety can interfere with learning, but the warmth and cherishing I found at Spelman as I slowly got to know a group of people beyond the borders of the seminar permitted me to learn and wonder, to follow the urgings of curiosity and respect in the demanding process of sitting down with strangers and attempting to connect.

9 | *Deep River*

Increasingly I believe that coming to terms with death is the beginning of wisdom: not seeking it, not becoming obsessed with it, but affirming it as the completion of life and thereby including it in our sense of self. This is a gradual process that unfolds over time, but like other landmarks in the life cycle, death is changing. Many college students today have never suffered the death of someone important in their lives or been in danger of dying themselves. Few have touched a dead person or noted the natural colors of skin when blood no longer circulates. Even fewer have been present through the natural transition of dying. People my age are more acquainted with death in its many forms, but in trying to bring the end of life into focus, we face something like a Chinese landscape, with a misted gap between the detail of the foreground and the mountains beyond.

The remoteness of death is a recent problem. Death has been an insistent reality in most human lives, taking loved ones at every age and stage, visibly and intimately, with no smoke and mirrors to obscure the process. When the seminar discussed the losses Nisa had suffered, the deaths at different times of all of her children, it was very hard for us to imagine. Such deaths were beyond anything any one of us had had to deal with, as remote as Le Ly Hayslip's childhood in Vietnam, with the battle line moving back and forth through her village. Those of us in our fifties had encountered death through the loss of parents or grandparents, and we all remembered premature deaths, the assassinations of our youth and the casualties of the sixties and the Vietnam War. Every member of the group was aware of the toll of urban violence, but no one ever becomes accustomed to the death of young people in the prime of life, and sheltered students are stunned when one of their number dies.

One Sunday halfway through the semester, arriving for a service in Sisters Chapel, I learned that news had just come of the death of a Spelman undergraduate, killed by a drunk driver, and the entire student body was shaken, many turning out in black for the memorial service. Such deaths, like the suicides of young people, although they occur at a steady rate, feel like exceptions, events outside the normal. African Americans tend to avoid the words for death, but they live with a nearer sense of mortality than many whites. Statistically, black life expectancies, although they have increased since World War II along with those of whites, have tended to run some ten years behind.

Most of us, I believe, can trace a series of steps to the awareness that death is part of life. There is a sequence of transitions in adulthood when we realize at the deepest level that our own time and horizons are limited, that we have to set priorities in casting the final message of who we are. Often the sign we encounter is the death of one or more contemporaries at a time when death no longer seems like an anomaly but begins to present itself as part of a natural process, or the death of parents, which makes independent adults feel suddenly alone in the world for the first time, a very different transition at different ages. Sometimes there is a brush with illness that threatens death or chronic disability, an end to a familiar way of living. The preparation for death begins with any step toward closure on adulthoods that now extend so long they are taken for granted. Sometimes the end of a career or the departure of grown children signals a break in the pattern, intimations of mortality. New responsibilities appear. Instead of a focus on the imperatives of making and doing, we begin to think about the ethics of passing on what we have and passing away. Those who are sick and dying can try to accept care with grace and to offer the next generation a bearable vision of their own mortality. Traditionally, dying well was more important than struggling for a brief postponement of the end.

For Ama, the first steps in coming to terms with the reality of death went back to childhood. Ama's mother was widowed at twenty-nine with four children, the youngest only ten months old. "I grew up with somebody still absolutely bemused and paralyzed by having lost her husband. My dad died when I was three, and my memory started from that day. It was very traumatic. I was able to crawl under the table, and the house was just full of people. That really stays with me: that you might not want to get married, 'cause they just up and die. But low and behold, look at me, who's made thousands of friends the world over, and they die and they leave too.

"I think I just got marked very early. So even though I ended up as a child of the revolution getting married at twenty and then having a child at twenty-one, nevertheless I always had that feeling, This is nice, but . . . an uneasiness. Someone's just gonna call up and say that they died."

Ama's mother lived with the fear of bereavement, as most of her generation did, even before Ama was born. "My dad was in World War II, in the navy, probably as a cook because that's what they let us do, and I remember being at the table and my mother recounting what it was like and how scary it was to have my dad in World War II and gone and not know where they were. She was very frightened of somebody named Pearl Harbor. I thought Pearl Harbor was some woman for the longest time and somehow my daddy had some relationship to her— 'cause, you know, girls listen differently—and it was very frightening to my mother. Whoever Miss Pearl Harbor was, a lot of damage had been done by her! That is how I appropriated World War II in my understanding."

Then when Ama was twelve, already moving into adolescence, her mother died too. "She was thirty-seven. Her last words were, 'Oh I have such a tremendous headache,' and she never spoke another word. She had a seizure and we took her to the hospital, and she was dead by the next day. She had remarried and had two more children. My baby brother was just three months old. I was watching my stepfather when the phone rang, and he picked it up and I saw him recoil, so I knew, coming of age right in that instant. Then we went from Connecticut to live in North Carolina, where we knew our family already because as northern children we'd go south for the summer. It was so dizzying for my mother to die, November 29, 1960, that was a Tuesday, and by Monday morning to be in North Carolina, moved lock, stock, and barrel, the funeral having been held on Saturday. We got on the train and went to live with my mother's sister in North Carolina and never went back, all four of us. My stepfather and his two sons went to his brother and sister-in-law in Washington, D.C., which would produce two different lifestyles and two very different sets of lives. I did the *rest* of my growing up in North Carolina. I'm very careful to make that difference, because otherwise it would dismiss my mother."

At every moment of transition, earlier transitions are revisited and the transition ahead may be anticipated. Ama has gone through her life treasuring what she knows of her parents, her artistic father and her mother of "blue-flame lipstick, Lucky Strike cigarettes, and black Coty-girl hats, she who made dessert every day, adorned in flowered dusters," but she has felt marked by loss and by the experience of being the oldest girl in an orphaned family at such an early age.

When Ama joined the seminar, she was at the transition of menopause, which marks the end of a certain kind of possibility but sometimes also the end of some of the limitations imposed on women. For women today menopause is a kind of new beginning, when they can launch into a new freedom or start a new career. At one time, however, when the contribution of women was defined as childbearing, menopause could be regarded as the end of productive membership in the community. Menopause can feel like a death to a woman for whom life is synonymous with motherhood. It is an important reminder for all women that they are more than their reproductive capacity and that in order to give they need to develop themselves. Even today becoming an elder proposes both growth and loss.

I was thinking and writing about aging even before I reached menopause. After I wrote *Composing a Life,* although I was still in my forties, I found that what I had written about adapting to change over the course of a lifetime was proving useful to men and women further along, and I began to be invited to speak to groups older than I was. America was gearing up, because of increased longevity, to think new thoughts about aging, and we were hearing the first murmurs of concern about the retirement of the baby boom generation. As my hair began to turn, it reminded me of a time in my mother's life when silvering hair made her newly radiant, and I joked with audiences that I was into grow-it-yourself silver jewelry. Knowing my interest in lifelong learning, when I told her I was getting hearing aids Vanni said, "That's going to be really exciting for you." It seemed clear to me that adulthood had become so long, with so many choice points, that we needed to search out moments of punctuation and invent new rituals. Suddenly it was newly fashionable to celebrate fiftieth and later birthdays, and women in many places devised "croning ceremonies," proudly putting a positive twist on an old negative and reclaiming ancient images of wise old crones. Medical institutions were beginning to take the health issues of menopause and aging with fresh seriousness, and part of the new punctuation was a shift in lifestyles: "lite" eating and drinking, exercise, giving up smoking. Simplifying.

By the time I went to Spelman at fifty-six, all of these trends had begun to affect the elders in the seminar, several of whom were active in thinking about health issues in the black community. Aging was beginning to look like a challenge to new learning. Joan Erikson, in her eighties, sending her greetings to a conference she could not attend, remarked on "how remarkably *interesting* [my emphasis] it is to be old. Older than you thought you would ever be. It is not in the least like sliding downhill, as I always anticipated. But much more like plodding up a mountain, the pathway getting narrower and steeper. You learn to watch your step, keeping as aware as possible of footholds. You lighten your backpack. So many things are dispensable . . . in order to free your hands, as a safeguard against your upsetting imbalance."

Everywhere, as people grow older, they shift into new styles of participation, sometimes gladly and sometimes with greater reluctance.

Among the San, men who can no longer run as swiftly as they once did become more involved in making and maintaining tools, an honored role: the meat brought back from the hunt is said to belong to the maker of the arrow, so it is he who begins the process of dividing up the kill. When women have borne their last child, they may join men as healers, moving into a relationship with the world of spirit that would have been inappropriate during their childbearing years. Most of those who have children will have the experience of seeing grandchildren, but with only 10 percent of the population over sixty years old, few will see great-grandchildren.

Within the pattern of three living generations, there is often an alliance between children and their patient and indulgent grandparents, with the parents of young children busier and stricter. Folk wisdom has it that grandparents and grandchildren can be especially close because they have a common enemy. Sometimes, when a couple lives with the husband's parents, the grandmother may claim all the pleasures of a new baby and none of the chores. When I was living in Tehran and teaching young Iranian women, I could observe a shift toward living closer to the bride's parents, whose role in child care would be supportive of her rather than competitive. Where the ideas and interests of parents and grandparents match, it is relatively easy to pass a child from lap to lap. Where styles of caring differ, as they have in the United States all through this century, it gets much harder.

The old are not only loved among Nisa's people but also treasured, necessarily so, for a society without writing depends on memory. These are healthy old people in moderate numbers. Acute illness, when it comes, runs its course quickly, since no one can be kept alive beyond the ability to take food and drink, and other kinds of illness either improve or are worsened by the distances walked. The role reversal in old age, when the young may care for the old as intensively as for a newborn, may be unique to our species. It matches the extreme helplessness of human infants and the human dependence on learning. But for a migratory people it cannot endure for long.

When a subsistence community with little in the way of reserves is struck by drought or famine or particularly difficult conditions, the very old and the very young often die first, for they could not survive without the foraging of strong young adults. It is a foolish sentimentality on the part of some Western societies that decrees that aid should go to children while the adults on whom they depend are allowed to despair or die—sentimentality, or the belief that the adults are to blame for the disaster. But the San and other foraging peoples cherish those who survive into old age. They make great efforts to protect and help the sick and the wounded and grieve for them when their lives end.

It is possible for the San to struggle against death, to dance and chant for the sick and lay on hands, but it is not possible for them to pretend that death is not close and real. Just as conditions of life among the San kept population nearly steady, so death was a reliable enemy. Unlike us, the San in their traditional lifestyles could maximize both survival and reproduction without damaging their environment, and these are the conditions under which human beings evolved.

Among foragers survival depends on the energy and skill of the young in combination with the experience and judgment of the old. This balance changes when the old own or control all the resources that matter. When human beings learned how to cultivate and store food, they settled down into long-term communities and domesticated themselves as they domesticated wild plants and animals. Birthrates went up with changes in diet and decreased mobility, and elders were able to survive longer with chronic complaints. The status of the old was often enhanced in settled communities, but attitudes toward them grew more ambivalent, for the elders became increasingly the owners of land or animals or access to water for irrigation. When there is more to own, it is likely to be owned unequally, with some members of the community made into dependents. Sometimes even knowledge is hoarded by elders until the moment of death. With increasing longevity we all need to review what we pass on and when, since the same inheritance that would be momentous at twenty can be a mournful irony at sixty.

In Iran there are tribal groups that migrate between summer and winter grazing grounds with vast flocks of sheep and goats. The right to passage and the right to graze at appropriate times of year belong to the entire tribe, but equipment and livestock are owned by separate households. In many cases a father gives to his son, at the time of the son's marriage, the fraction of the herd he would receive were the father to die at that moment. With this anticipated inheritance, the son establishes a new household—but the father has by no means retired and will keep his last son, along with the son's wife and children, with him until his death.

It is harder for farmers to have their cake and eat it. An old man dozing by the fireside, clinging to control as long as possible, may still be the owner or the leaseholder of the land worked by his son. Because land cannot be repeatedly divided and recover, like a herd, there are often rules to keep the inheritance undivided, putting it intact into the hands of the oldest son. Failing such rules, when penury is produced in a farming economy by subdivision over time, the land may be reconcentrated in the hands of a few, who then regulate leases and sharecropping agreements.

A different pattern of anticipated inheritance developed in some parts of rural Ireland after the famines of the nineteenth century. In order to avoid subdividing the land, only two members of a family would remain in farming to the next generation; one son would inherit when he married a wife with a dowry, and one daughter would be provided with a dowry and therefore able to marry a farmer herself. The future taken care of, the parents would sign over the farm, not without putting their continuing rights into writing, and retire to the "west room," facing the sunset and musing on the hereafter. They contributed some labor and no doubt a lot of advice, but the new owner was now no longer a "boy" but a "man." For the young the system meant a lot of dutiful waiting around. The average age of marriage for sons was nearly forty, for daughters, about ten years younger. Yet even with delayed marriage and many long evenings spent in the pub, the population pressure was relentless. All the other children— as many as six or eight—would have to "travel," often to America.

Any reader of literature and folklore is familiar with stories that begin with younger sons forced out to "seek their fortunes" or fretting for the day when they would inherit. The development of a range of livelihoods restores to young adults the kind of flexibility that foragers have, for young people can leave home and support themselves. Without that freedom one wonders how often the plot of Shakespeare's *King Lear* has unfolded in actuality or in the fantasies of aging parents, sure that if their children gained control they would be abandoned. In the effort to avoid an impoverished old age, parents make sure early on that habits of respect and obedience are well and truly ingrained, and they cling to their control.

In Iran, even in urban settings where households are smaller and the young have a variety of employment, extended families have recognized elders. These elders may not have economic control, but they do have authority in certain types of family crises or decision making. Long after their sons are married and have children, they expect younger relatives to visit and consult at major feasts and transitions. The head of the family is not necessarily the oldest member but must be someone with age and education, and also someone with relatively great resources, who has earned respect for wisdom and good sense, perhaps even a woman. In a crisis a man might turn to the head of his mother's family rather than his father's family. The respect for the old and the expectation that they will share a household with one of their sons' families, usually cared for by a daughter-in-law, continues, but a distinction between age and wisdom is there as well.

The basic human rhythm of relations between young and old is a three-generation one. The period when adults begin to age perceptibly and cannot fully take care of themselves has corresponded to the childhood of their grandchildren, so care for the generation above and the generation below could be combined and sometimes one could look after the other. But today the need to care for aging parents waits in ambush until a time when their children have lived independently for decades and established patterns of their own, often until after the next generation of children have grown up and moved out. Meantime, that most ancient of alliances between grandparent and grandchild often never comes into being, not because the grandparents are in a nursing home but because while the children were young the grandparents were carrying on with their own lives, sometimes continuing to earn, sometimes spending their savings on travel or retiring to age-segregated communities. Distance has been the result of increasing choice.

Some two decades ago, when a member of the Saudi royal family who had eloped with a commoner was executed by stoning, a Saudi diplomat said on television that Americans have no right to criticize— Americans, he said with horror, who actually put their aging parents in institutions rather than care for them! He was making an accurate connection between different aspects of culture—freedom to marry as one wishes goes along with increased freedom from obligations to parents, while economic independence also often involves following employment to a new location, weakening family ties.

In the United States we do have an institution of anticipated inheritance, not unlike those of the Iranian sheepherders or the Irish countrymen, but the asset that is passed on is not livestock or land but an expensive education. Couples who have achieved home ownership (often trading up several times), and gradually paid off most of their mortgage as they approached middle age, often remortgage their property for their children's tuition, to equip them to be self-supporting. Some twenty years later, equity rebuilt, those homes can be sold to provide nest eggs for retirement.

The system works well only in an expanding economy, with real estate increasing in value, and has never extended to the working poor. In the meantime what the older generation is not passing on is jobs. They still have them. It is true that certain kinds of production jobs are scarce because they have been eliminated or exported. But high-level jobs have become rarer because those who have them are living longer and remaining healthy and so are newly tenacious of power and privilege.

The World War II generation reinvented old age, raising it from the time of greatest want in the United States, and developed an altered vision of retirement into an entitlement. Specifying a mandatory retirement age for healthy elders has come to seem discriminatory, while beginning times for pensions and social security have only marginally been adjusted, out of sync with contemporary patterns of aging. Retirement was once a period when work was no longer possible; now it can become an extended paid vacation, often ironically frustrating, sometimes lethal. It is not easy for those who have been told all their lives that work is a burden to realize their deep need to do something useful.

This is a new kind of generation gap, not the cultural conflict that developed in the sixties between parents and college-age children but a gap in timing that affects the way generations interlock for caretaking and for learning. Some of this is settling down as young people defer marriage and childbearing; like Irish "boys" and "girls" in their thirties, they quite often live with their parents or are supported by them until they can move up, so there is a better chance that grandparents will be "old" when grandchildren are little.

The increase in longevity is greatest for women. Around the world in traditional societies, old age has come early for women, marked by the physical wear and tear of bearing babies. Even so, wherever marriage patterns assume that husbands will be older than their wives, old men have been cared for by wives, not necessarily the first or even the second, and widowhood has been a common fate. Women prepared for old age by establishing themselves in new roles as mothers-in-law and grandmothers, not by launching forth on new careers. But these are societies in which age is revered, which put less value on youth and make it less pleasant, so age is more inviting. Iran is one of the better places to grow old, for the old are held in honor, most of them respected and cared for in their children's homes. No one who has been a member of an Iranian household, bearing several children and looking after aging in-laws, is likely to face a solitary or abandoned old age. Infirmity is sweetened by tenderness. Life ends with the body washed and swiftly buried, wrapped only in a shroud, the reading of verses from the Quran, sharp and dramatic grieving, and mourning ceremonies spaced out over ten, then forty days, then a year—but this is the appropriate end to the story.

In a society where the old are respected, it is easy for the young to defer gratifications and freedoms, confident that they will someday be enjoyed, while in a society where aging is pictured as dismal and un-inviting, the young are likely to want their pleasures and privileges as soon as possible and to resist maturing beyond that early fulfillment. Negative stereotypes of old age make us do some pretty silly things to defer it. In the same way, societies where aging brings increased status are far less likely to breed rebellion than societies where young adults feel they have little to look forward to. I have always felt sorry for Iranian women whose sons become westernized and bring home foreign brides who refuse to act like proper daughters-in-law, for these mothers are cheated at both ends of the life cycle. But the world gains by the Western wives and mothers who start out to live independent lives and stay with them, growing and productive.

San women who become healers, Iranian parents who manage their children's lives, Irish couples who move into the west room to meditate, are they necessarily wiser than their children? Probably so. But in a society undergoing rapid change, earlier learning becomes less valuable, while the retention of power may actually work against the willingness to learn. I have sometimes asked audiences whether they expect to become wise as they grow old, and everyone seems to nod emphatically, without noticing the changes in the meaning of *old*. The longer old people survive, however, and the more active and able they are, the more important it is to make real distinctions rather than see age as a halo around all of a handful of survivors. It may be important not only to compute health care costs but also to understand the sense in which elders are or are not wise. Wisdom may be another of those concepts that has slipped our grasp. Virtually everywhere except in modern America the wisdom of age is associated with an acceptance of the approach of death.

Human beings have the potential for learning at every stage of the life cycle, but there is certainly a slowing down of the process, and all too many people make up their minds to be old dogs unwilling to learn new tricks. It is not uncommon to think of adult character as fixed. Americans are now demanding increasing numbers of life sentences and the abolition of educational programs in prisons, on the assumption that once a violent criminal, always a violent criminal. Yet only a fraction of violent crimes are committed by individuals over fifty. "Life sentence," like life itself, has shifted in meaning, and now means parole in about twenty-five years, usually after the age when most kinds of violent crime are likely, but at an age when it will still be necessary to earn a living for some time. In a new millennium how many people are thinking, Once a twentieth-century person always a twentieth-century person, quite unwilling to adapt to the changes that lie ahead?

It has been relatively harmless for human beings to believe that death was somehow unnatural, the product of evil sorcery or a punishment for original sin, something not intended by the creator, for it was unnecessary to learn to welcome so reliable a guest. In societies living by foraging, no amount of care and struggle and magic could prevent death from happening according to ancient rhythms, while the alliance against death brought people closer together.

Today we need to reaffirm that living includes dying, that even at the level of cells, dying is part of the program of life. The only cell cultures that live forever in vitro are cancers. In the contemporary world, both reproduction and death are areas where technological progress has created choices we are barely beginning to face. I believe that the possibility of choice creates the responsibility for choice, that ethics follows efficacy. The second era of adulthood is enriched, often triggered, by the clarity that comes with an awareness of death. As human beings we have the obligation today to control our reproduction and eventually to choose our dying. This means making choices against the grain.

Choices about how to deal with reproduction and with dying are connected in their consequences, so it is unwise to address them separately. It is probably a mistake from the very beginning to separate the knowledge of death and the knowledge of sex, whether by dwelling on death and concealing sexuality or, as we do today, concealing mortality and flaunting sex. We need to let the emotions of the one balance the emotions of the other so that both are rightly honored.

I learned about death as an event early on, but death as an extended process in the experience of living beings was an abstraction to me until the death of my father when I was forty. Then I had an experience that had become rare for Americans, of sharing in the physical care of someone dying and laying out a corpse. In the last decade, as more and more people either choose to meet death at home or are forced to do so by the policies of institutions, we are reestablishing the human intimacy with natural death.

My father was fortunate in having been able to express his wishes so that he was not in a hospital. Without intravenous feeding and irrigation, biological life did not last long beyond his capacity to participate, and we could affirm his presence and participation even as bodily functions shut down. I was surprised to find myself thinking of dying as a maturation that spanned the technical moment of death. Death was something that Gregory was learning and grew into gradually, passing into unconsciousness, breathing more slowly and then ceasing to breathe, losing color and warmth, then passing into rigor and beyond it. I was surprised to discover, as with any intimate form of caregiving, that tending and cleaning a dying body could be deeply

satisfying. The process should not lightly be short-circuited, but neither should it be indefinitely prolonged. It also should not, like the
processes of birthing and being born, be mystified and concealed, for
human beings are equipped, probably genetically, to learn deeply from
these transitions, even as we build different superstructures of inter-
pretation upon them.

When I was pregnant for the first time, I gave birth prematurely,
aware during labor and in giving birth that for this infant, being born
and dying were the same thing, and I was exulting and mourning at
the same time, as I concentrated on my breathing. Probably being
born is more like dying than dying is like being born, but sharing in
either of these processes is a profound intimacy. The committed,
overwhelming acts of birth and death, like those of sex, are the great
moments of bonding in our lives. Tragedy, like conflict, offers opportunities for learning if only we use them. One of the paradoxical gifts
of the AIDS epidemic has been allowing discussion of the meaning of
caring for a dying lover. The AIDS epidemic has also meant that loving parents must bring the issues of sex and conception into the same
conversations as those of illness and death.

Over the two years after my time at Spelman, a series of events that
I had recognized in the lives of others as intimations of mortality happened in my own life. Early in 1997 a beloved sister-in-law, a little
younger than I, was diagnosed with brain cancer that took her life
some nine months later. At Christmas 1998 my daughter and the man
she had been seeing for a long time decided to get married and began
to plan a wedding for the fall of 1999. The world was gearing up for a
new millennium with excitement and trepidation about the disrup-
tions that would go with it, and I was beginning preparations for the
centenary in 2001 of my mother's birth. Parental and filial responsibility were doubling up in a new rhythm.

In the winter of 1997 I was in Virginia, excited about a new teaching semester at Mason with newly designed courses, including a version of the life history course that included almost all new readings—four Native American life histories, Zora Neale Hurston, Sister Souljah, and one of May Sarton's journals. In January, however, I returned from a speaking engagement with a "cold" that wouldn't let go. I stayed in bed, aching and woozy, and Vanni brought me chicken soup and vitamin C. I dragged my way through most of my classes, collapsed again, and did two rounds of antibiotics. Back teaching, I kept losing the thread of the discussion and forgetting details of the new books I was using. One evening I invited a student to walk me to the parking lot after class, secretly afraid I might not make it. Another evening I got lost going home and circled hopelessly in my car.

I told myself I had been doing too much, gotten up too soon. I told myself, as the cold symptoms faded and the exhausted aches and pains continued, that this was old age setting in and I'd better get used to it. I told myself that this must be a form of depression expressing itself physically rather than emotionally, so I spent some hours with a psychiatrist and took antidepressants, but nothing helped. Finally he said he didn't believe I was depressed and advised me to find a doctor who knew something about chronic fatigue syndrome. I was skeptical—after all, the popular media had branded CFS "yuppie flu" and dismissed it as malingering.

In any case, I was much too tired as the semester ended to look for another doctor. Instead I asked for a leave without pay, doubting that I would ever come back and beginning to assume that my problem was permanent and probably degenerative. I promised myself that at least I would finish this book, shaping it slowly in preference to other work.

I was keeping quiet about how ill I felt, but Johnnetta visited me in

New Hampshire, and after twenty-four hours she got on the phone to locate the appropriate doctor. Eight months and many tests after getting sick, I was finally diagnosed and knew that the illness was not degenerative and would gradually improve. Chronic fatigue syndrome had in the meantime finally been recognized and defined by the Centers for Disease Control, where some officials had been overinvested in the *Time* magazine point of view and the scientific effort had bogged down in politics. I was very lucky to get appropriate care, to have a mild case and the resources to slow down, healthy enough to cope from day to day, unlike the hundreds of people who have been effectively crippled, have lost jobs and been denied disability coverage and seen their lives collapse around them. Two years in, I have limited energy and must husband it carefully, but I survived a joyous family wedding. My concentration and memory are back to normal, so I can write and lecture with confidence and pleasure. With all the misunderstandings of CFS, I avoided long explanations, but there is, I believe, a need for openness in discussing lives, especially when there has been a history of mixed and disingenuous messages.

This episode has marked for me a transition to a new and visceral sense of limits. It will be hard to know what changes to blame on the disease and what changes to blame on the time elapsed between fifty-seven and sixty. In the meantime I have had two years of imagining what different paths into old age might be like, how it would feel if every day were only half or a quarter as productive or if learning yet another software program were suddenly an overwhelming task. If learning, all learning, were suddenly to become a forgotten skill.

Disease has become a political matter in the United States, surrounded by financial implications, not an act of God. Instead of recognizing a vulnerability we all share, we are busily apportioning and localizing blame—maybe there is someone who can be sued for negligence or the government can be forced to pay compensation, maybe the person who is ill has become so through some moral fault, promiscuity or drug use or even smoking. Maybe it isn't a real disease at all and can be mocked out of existence.

To be fully human is to accept human frailty, but such frailty is met as a strangeness within the self. I have come to believe that there is a direct connection between our denials of the body and human violations of the biosphere. The denial of mortality builds a fundamental dishonesty into the relationship between generations and at the same time makes us unable to read the texts offered by the landscape as we pass them, for these texts speak as much of decay as of new life. The rejection of death leads to a fundamental disdain for the biological world and its limits. Steadily, routinely, we refuse to play by the rules of nature.

Whether or not death is a logical necessity of any complex life, it is intrinsic to the biology we live in. Bisexual reproduction implies a reshuffling and checking of genetic material against the template of another genome, eliminating errors and eventually replacing the parent generation. Sexual reproduction is the protection against entropy, death is corollary, and together they make evolution possible.

You cannot affirm the biological order and reject death as the afterthought of a punitive divinity, just as you cannot appreciate the Greek tragedies if you insist that at the end "they all went to the seashore," for the tragic destiny is inherent in the entire plot, and denying it requires a misreading from page one. You can have love without marriage, but you cannot have either without death. Valuing love, valuing friendship, we need to encounter death with curiosity and respect.

It has often been seen as self-evident that whatever could change or perish was inferior to that which could not. E. F. Schumacher said that "the central concept of wisdom is permanence." Yet wisdom must include the awareness of transience and change. The dying god or the god who goes through countless cycles of death and rebirth is a very old idea, for the gods reflect all the strengths and all the follies of human experience. Just as we must read forests and lakes for their testimony about death and the limits on our aspirations, so we must read the documents of other cultures for their testimony about the relativity of our understanding and sense of responsibility.

We have to assume that the struggle to keep on living has been ingrained in human beings through evolution, useful as long as it could not fully succeed. Surviving infancy, even surviving the process of birth, requires a certain determination, and no doubt leaves a residue of learning. In earlier generations the experience of almost dying from an infection like scarlet fever was common, reinforcing the will to survive through the fogs of fever. But then the will to survive lingers, like other organs that outlast their functions. It has never before now been necessary to have what Freud intuited as a death instinct: death, like the pull of gravity, has been something reliable in the fabric of life, something that would "take care of itself." We have never needed an instinct to fall down, only one to get up—yet now in space travel it is necessary to provide for the sudden absence of what had been taken for granted. We are going to have to learn to manage the choice of dying at the end of life as we are learning to manage the choice of reproduction at the beginning. In both cases we have learned to block and resist an immemorial sequence and find ourselves responsible for fashioning a new one.

All the capacities to learn and manipulate that characterize our species carry the possibility and then the obligation for making choices. Only those things we can both notice and change have moral value. Today technology allows us to defer or avoid childbearing, to abort a particular conception, and to impose fertility when biology is recalcitrant. It allows the separation of sexual activity from conception so that now there are two decision points, whether to have sex and whether to reproduce—or rather, a whole sequence of decisions—where once there was one. Under these circumstances the failure to decide becomes immoral, for wherever choice is possible it is obligatory.

Once the existentialists could argue that not choosing death signified choosing life by default, the moral dilemma implicit in the existence of alternatives. Today we can argue similarly that, whether a child is conceived or not, whether it is aborted or carried to term or not, whether nature "takes its course" or not, there has always been choice. There is choice in the use of technologies to defer death as well, yet sometimes the most elaborate and expensive technological sequences are set in motion automatically, as if they followed as immutably as a reflex, for instance when the most premature infants are constrained to go on living.

As a result, for more and more people death must be chosen. We have the new and painful burden of rejecting medical intervention when reason suggests that a few additional days or weeks would have little to offer a dying person, or that the life saved might be unduly burdensome. In the moment my husband and I would passionately have wanted to save our premature son with technologies that exist today, not available at that time or place—but in retrospect, knowing the problems that sometimes haunt the lives of preemies, I am not sure that would have been the right thing. The normality of parenthood in the past was producing a number of children, some of whom lived and some of whom died, and perhaps this variability is why we have no definitive word for a bereaved parent as we do for a widow or an orphan.

The experience of almost dying of infectious disease in childhood has been reduced by immunization. Instead, more and more people have the experience of disease and recovery later in life, heart conditions or malignancies that would once have killed them and now send them back to their lives with the knowledge of mortality in their bones and a new way of thinking about time and about what really matters. To celebrate their return, we need to bring some new understanding to the word *survivors*, asking what wisdom survival brings, along with other experiences that speak of death and offer evidence of a new way of valuing life. Perhaps one reason for American skepticism about leaders who have not served in the military is the old saying "There are no atheists in foxholes." Perhaps a close brush with death, often just hearing the simple word *cancer*, demands a new perspective and a new humility. Medical intervention may eliminate a particular threat completely or stave it off for a period of tying up loose ends, repairing past wrongs, or simply listening to music, but the familiarity with death remains. Death is no longer completely alien but one of the strangers we live and negotiate with.

Living as long as we can expect to do, we need to reconsider both those things that are done again and again to sanctify the continuities of life—for we must expect to do them more often and to maintain them over longer periods—and the way to bring them gracefully to an end.

These were the issues Ama was dealing with during the seminar, and as she struggled with the deaths of her friends, she started emphasizing the connection between making choices about death and affirming life. "You know," she said to me, "that class was a self-help group. I'm already in a self-help group, but I seem to need one of a different depth, one that is purposefully reflective. I'd come back talking about our seminar, how miserable I was feeling so I just broke down in class, and they were right there." The effect of Ama's describing the seminar to her friends was that she decided to organize something like it, but her imagined translation to a new form was particularly interesting to me. "All my friends were clamoring, Are you gonna have that class again, I didn't have a chance to get in. The form that it has assumed in my thinking is to gather a circle in Toni Bambara's memory and let them begin the process of writing the stories about their lives by talking about Toni's life and death. She always used to ask us, Did you write that down?

"We could start with so simple a device as a 'pre-need' statement, that's what you give to the people who are going to be planning your funeral or doing something in your memory, and it's tied to your will or health directive. What you're gonna wear, what colors you like, who you wanna speak and who you don't wanna speak, what not to play . . . to push them into the kind of reflection that has to take place to do this.

"This will help everybody clean up her act. Lots of us are saying we've now been through one-two-three-four young women trying to take care of all their mommas' stuff. Momma didn't leave anything to say what she'd want. Me and Toni, twenty-four hours before she died, are talking about trying to get her will together. She had admitted they had found polyps on her colon, but that's as much attention as she would give." The legacy of mortality denied was quarreling afterward about how to deal with the apartment and how to organize the memorial service. Ama plunged in. "I said, 'Look, don't mess with me, I knew Toni too: we're having *food*.' We served three hundred people. I said, 'Let's get this done.' But it's done now."

Wills, living wills, pre-need statements—these are the preliminary steps toward accepting the fact of our dying and, when necessary, rejecting interference with that process, making choices. Cleaning up our act. We also need to start the process of passing on whatever we can, knowledge or property or keepsakes, while it still has value. Putting experiences on paper, giving memories a beginning and an end, is another way of imagining the rounding off of lives fulfilled, while sharing these narratives is a way of connecting the generations.

10 | Full Circles

When I went to Spelman I went with curiosity and respect, hoping to learn from the experiences of familiarity in the strange and strangeness in the familiar, both in myself and in the people I would meet there. At one level, certainly, I went hoping to move toward a better understanding of America's perennial perplexities about race, but the women I met there represent far more than an instant in a particular historical scandal. I went with a special interest in the cycles of learning and teaching and the ways we empower others—especially the young—for adapting to a changing world. Gradually I have come to regard the spiral of lifelong learning and the double helix of learning across generations as pathways that circle back and around, leading through the perplexities of lives and the estrangements of rapid change.

"My mother did not believe in change," Cheryl had written, describing her school years. "That is, she did not believe the world could change or should. The world was static, complete, and absolute: everything already decided, settled, understood. All a person had to do was understand, find their place, hit their marks, and learn their lines. People were infinitely malleable, empty when they were born and ready to be filled with the reasons of the world."

How distant this sounds today, an echo of the fifties. The world Cheryl's mother lived in was flawed in many ways, unjust and often dangerous, but it felt knowable. A world in rapid change is not knowable. Within a decade an entire generation had become committed to belief in change in every area of life—change for the good, change as liberation, change that makes us perpetual strangers in a new land.

Today we both believe and disbelieve in change. We talk about it constantly, but we have lost the certainty that change will be for the good and become aware of its paradoxical effects. Those who struggled passionately in the Civil Rights Movement have seen major improvements in the lives of about a quarter of the African American population, real but incomplete improvements in the middle, and worsening and a loss of optimism in the bottom quarter, along with a loss of solidarity in the whole. Integration no longer seems synonymous with justice. Those who became deeply involved in the peace movement have watched a domino effect of ironies, as Ronald Reagan's extravagant militarism ended the Cold War by driving the Soviet bloc into economic burnout. We have seen efforts for air quality lead to acid rain, and we have seen efforts to protect the poor vilified as weakening them. After every liberation there seems to be a backlash. So we believe, oh yes, we do believe that there is change all around us. But we do not believe *in* change, for we cannot trust it. We are beginning a new millennium in the awareness that unless we become better in many ways, life may become a great deal worse, but we also know that every change will have unpredictable costs and come freighted with alienation. The hope that has replaced change and liberation is the more gradual concept of learning, but learning is of many kinds.

My Spelman sisters who appear in these pages represent different stages in the American love affair with change, at the same time that they represent different stages in their own development and learning. No group this small can be used to prove any generalization, but attention to them can provide takeoff points for reflection. First and foremost, they could teach me because they are so much like me— intelligent, thoughtful people, like other men and women whose education places them in the middle class of an industrialized country. They are Americans who share most of the values and visions of other Americans, notions of fairness and integrity as well as tastes for Levi's or Coca-Cola or corn dogs. But like all other Americans, they differ from their fellow citizens in their allegiances to more particular communities. Their experience has been shaped by the facts of being female and black in American society and by the specific households and regions they have grown up in, whether in Atlanta or farther away, in Ohio or Florida, in the country or the city. Their advantages in life make them, relatively speaking, more representative of America in general and less representative of any minority group. Out of these complex ingredients the members of the seminar will have to compose their lives.

Every reader can learn in different ways from the stories here, sometimes saying, I have had that experience exactly, sometimes saying, Every day I encounter others who have had that experience, strangers to me whom I need to understand. We have been shaped by individual history and the histories of our communities. The past affects these women, as it affects all of us, beyond the circle of our personal experience. All Americans are affected by the nation's era of slavery, just as all Americans are affected by the War of Independence and the Civil War, even if they have immigrated within the last century or the last year from China or Eritrea or England.

We are all both representative and unique. Writing this, I have a sudden vivid memory of my mother exclaiming in exasperation, "Why is it you keep wanting exactly what everyone else your age wants? The only difference all this wonderful education makes is that you can invent more elegant reasons for why you have to have it!"

I had no plan to write about Spelman when I went there and did no systematic note taking, but I did go expecting to be changed by the people I would meet and the stories I would hear, as I have been in each new environment I have entered. Several months after I left, however, as I reflected on my time in Atlanta, I found myself deeply uninterested in another writing project I had planned: too abstract, too short of human voices. The voices of my Spelman sisters were echoing in my head, and I realized that my own learning at Spelman needed to be expressed, so I wrote to the members of the seminar, now scattered, for their permission to use their words and their names.

The following November, when my husband and I came to Atlanta to spend Thanksgiving with Johnnetta and Art, I met with as many as I could for interviews to compensate for my lack of systematic recording. Johnnetta gave a reunion dinner at Reynolds Cottage, the presidential residence, which she would be leaving at the end of the academic year, so that the students and elders who lived locally could discuss their qualms and questions. They had had the chance during the semester to consider the way I worked on *Composing a Life* and the decisions I had made in writing my memoir of my parents, and we had discussed interviewing, oral history, and alternative ways of reporting. I would not, I said, be writing a portrait of Spelman College or full histories of any individuals but would be drawing on the experiences of the group, weaving together examples of the ways lives have changed and the way this plays out in the relationships between the generations.

Jacqueline Marshall, Johnnetta's personal assistant, had been the one who coordinated arrangements for my coming, as she had on several previous visits. Jackie is a petite, dark, meticulously groomed woman from a West Indian background, reticent in our classroom and warm and welcoming to me elsewhere. She told me firmly that she had known from the beginning that I would write about Spelman, as Howard Zinn did when he taught there in the sixties, but that had not kept her from signing up. "Well, you were ahead of me," I said. "You knew me better than I knew myself."

After a moment's thought, however, I agreed with Jackie that in fact everything in my life goes into what I write in one way or another. I am one of those people who reflect most fully on experience with a sheet of paper or a keyboard. I find that I learn more from writing than from any other activity, because the process forces me to recycle experience, harvesting the learning in what I already know. Becoming a writer has meant for me learning to learn from experience, often by ruminating on past events and encounters and rethinking them, getting more and more juice out of them, as they open up a spiraling cornucopia of vision. One reason it is so satisfying to return over familiar ground is that there remains so much to be discovered. At the same time it becomes clear that time is recursive, turning in on itself, spiraling outward as well as back to the center of the nautilus.

Jackie was concerned that the Spelman faculty, dedicated to giving to their students, would be uncomfortable about any faculty member using that experience and writing about students as taking something, as a form of exploitation. Because I believe that learners teach and teachers learn, I do not see a contradiction between giving and taking in order to give again. Instead, it is my way of honoring my students. The process is circular, a double skein of sharing: curiosity and respect. Because we live in a time of rapid change, no teacher knows enough to teach without continuing to learn. So if I can draw on the experiences of Spelman or Mason students, or of the members of my family, in ways that enrich the experience of others, I think it right to go ahead.

Participation, observation, reflection. We are often uncomfortable at the idea that one can observe a nurturing relationship even while participating in it. When I described the systematic note taking and photography that surrounded my earliest years in *With a Daughter's Eye,* some reviewers were repelled, as if clarity of vision could not be loving. The insistence that any loving gaze is by definition blurred and rosy-tinted, however, becomes a prescription for bad marriages, brittle friendships, and ineffective parenting.

When one reviewer said that my mother had exploited me like an experimental animal, the image in the back of his mind was perhaps a laboratory rat that is used and finally "sacrificed" for the sake of science. But what I had described my mother doing was no more than intensifying and making systematic the observing that every mother does in order to understand the responses and needs of a given child.

As parents we gaze in wonder at our children and ask them, again and again, to teach us to be good parents, improvising and learning along the way. Like composing a life, child rearing is an art form that has no single formula. We all experiment in the sense that we try different approaches gleaned from a multitude of sources—magazine articles, the advice of neighbors, our own memories. An anthropologist who becomes a mother has skills of observation to draw on and a knowledge base that allows her to set her choices within the wider range of human experience. By breast-feeding me, a departure from the standard advice to middle-class American women at that time, my mother was "experimenting," drawing on her knowledge of mothers around the world. How, as a loving parent, could she not draw on all the knowledge and skills she had available, including keeping a record that allowed for self-correction? And if, in the process, she learned to understand child rearing in new ways, how could she not share that learning? Did the reviewer believe that all parental love should be blind, or did he assume that fuzzy-mindedness was a maternal trait only?

Wisdom surely requires a transcendence of the artificial line we sometimes draw between thought and emotion. Reading Pascal's saying that "the heart has its reasons which the reason knows nothing of," we imagine not two processes going on separately forever but the possibilities of conflict and convergence, with intuition and emotion sometimes forging ahead of rationality, sometimes nipping at its heels and slowing it down, sometimes converging in new radiance. Committed love can focus both passion and intelligence, the lover gazing into the reasoning hearts of others for learning and self-knowledge.

The learning and teaching involved in the very earliest days of caring for a child are a model for all teaching and learning, a circular relationship in which mother and child both gradually modify biological patterns. Human beings are not "empty when they [are] born and ready to be filled with the reasons of the world," as Cheryl had said, describing her mother's views. Infants arrive as distinct individuals with organized patterns of behavior ready to emerge but also flexible. Child rearing involves finding a harmony between the innate patterns in each infant and the unfamiliar patterns of a culture, as these are reflected in the behavior of others.

Biology frames the pattern, but humans adjust it. If an infant is given an old-fashioned feeding bottle, its sucking motions, preadapted to the breast, begin to change within twenty-four hours. A mother may simply nurse whenever the infant whimpers; this seems to correspond to the model of child rearing that is called *permissive*. Or she may follow the kind of *authoritarian* child-care manuals common in the first half of the twentieth century, immediately imposing a strict feeding schedule. Or she may start out feeding on demand and gradually ease her child onto a standard schedule, which she then enforces. Dr. Spock has been caricatured for advocating permissiveness, but when I was reading Spock, it was this approach that seemed to be what he was advocating, which is rather close to what is meant by *authoritativeness* today—a degree of flexibility and patience moving toward very clear boundaries set from outside, rather than an authoritarian imposition. Each model proposes a theory of the universe: it may be warm and undifferentiated, endlessly giving; or harsh, imposing its own standards for survival; or welcoming but finally inflexible.

An infant's hungers are not random, however. Within a week or so one can discern patterns of appetite over a twenty-four- or forty-eight-hour period, and these too can be confirmed as a model for an orderly universe. Discovering such patterns is part of the intensive learning from the newborn stranger, but it helps to have a notebook and a watch. It may be useful to speak of *evocative* parenting to underline the process of discernment and affirmation, the drawing forth that is the root meaning of *education*. At some very abstract and unconscious level, perhaps, the infant learns that there are both internal and external orders and it is possible to coordinate them. The beginning, perhaps, of wisdom, at the very dawn of the life cycle.

We continue learning from one another at all the stages of development, growing toward wisdom, the path never completed. I am not sure that wisdom even exists apart from the willingness to continue in that cycle of interacting, observing, reflecting, and passing it on. Spelman has a motto based on an African proverb, "Those who learn must teach," which encourages students to go out and work with younger members of the community. Johnnetta also argued that "She who teaches must continue to learn" and initiated programs to emphasize the other side of the coin, the need for continuing faculty development. These same processes can occur together, replacing the hierarchical conventions of the academy. Those who teach or learn must learn and teach at the same time.

Rev. Carolyn A. Knight, a professor of homiletics, spoke at Spelman's baccalaureate, very much in the tradition of African American preaching, offering one model for interactive teaching. She built her address around a Biblical text, speeding up and slowing down dramatically, sometimes punctuating her words with gasps for air, turning the audience into a congregation united in enthusiasm and affirmation after every sentence. The text, Joshua 17:14–18, describing the allotment of territories to the tribes of Israel, reports the protest of Ephraim and Manasseh, the progeny of Joseph in Egypt, at receiving an up-country share. It did not strike me as promising, but she elaborated it as a challenge: "*If* you are a great people," she said, go to the hill country and prove it. Prove your greatness by your own energy and effort, in spite of difficult conditions and delays. She was, it seemed to me, preparing the students for lives of change and challenge by evoking an energy already there and waiting to be called forth, an indignation that would not wait on fairness. The congregations in white churches tend to be passive and polite, but this is not true in most black churches. Black preaching evokes and incorporates the antiphonal responses of the congregation, building an interactive rhythm that may continue from week to week, with a potential for concerted action. It is not unlike jazz in that the preacher improvises around a theme that has been practiced and elaborated.

Often, the business of a teacher is to help others discover what they already know, still unarticulated, and how to use and share it. My mother, Margaret Mead, did a lot of public speaking of a very different kind. She was immensely popular at it, big laughter and big applause (she complained about the passivity in white churches, where she disliked speaking). She was funny and incisive and occasionally shocking, but the paradoxical secret of her success was that often she was proposing ideas right at the threshold of what her listeners already knew, evoking an awareness ready to crystallize. They would leave the hall enlivened, and a week later they would be repeating what she had said as if they had always known it. What had been strange became familiar overnight. Her students hung on her words and generally forgot to footnote them, for the words were quickly digested and integrated to enrich their own assumptions. The cycle of teaching and learning went on beyond the single occasion, for she had members of the audience write questions down and took the slips of paper away with her to study, providing the grist for *Redbook* columns directed to what people had on their minds, matters on which they might move a little deeper, a step forward. She read and graded every student paper or exam herself, so she could learn from them, and could refine and amplify her words.

My father, Gregory Bateson, seems to me to have been a speaker and teacher of a very different kind, proposing Otherness. He would slump on the platform, often seeming to be thinking aloud at some remote level of abstraction. What he had to say often subverted common sense and familiar assumptions. Some listeners said, That was amazing but I didn't really get it. Others said, Wow, that was awesome. And a few found their habits of thought overturned, learning to move in a vertiginous new world. Because his ideas were unfamiliar, they remained associated with him in memory and required ongoing effort, turning up in footnotes but also producing disciples. His thinking is still only slowly being assimilated. He was gurulike in the habit of offering seeming paradoxes, enigmatic comments for further reflection. He seemed dedicated to that other task of teaching, helping students to discover what they *don't* know, and offering only vague hints of how to find out and fit it in, so that the extended process would make it part of them. In doing this he evoked an awareness of how to learn.

Three different kinds of teaching, each addressing an audience in motion in a world of change, and each evoking a different and unfolding responsiveness. Teaching, governing, and leadership all build on models set in early childhood, so we need words for styles of teaching like those we use for styles of parenting. Each of the styles I have described is in some sense evocative, proposing self-knowledge and setting a process in motion for at least some of the listeners, a process that will come to fruition quickly or slowly and that may lie latent for a long time.

What many academics do when we present our work, however, is to lecture from a prepared text, citing data that are unlikely to stick in the mind and using abstract jargon that stakes out a position in the currently fashionable geography of theory. The conclusions are meant to be retained, not the process of reaching them, so when they become obsolete they are useless. Yet when scientific findings are being passed on, the goal is also to propose a circular process whereby errors can be winnowed out and tested, and ideas can rapidly be raised to new cycles of understanding.

There are ways of transmitting knowledge that feel like intellectual rape: so much logic and such powerful statistics, so many footnotes, that resistance is beaten down. But oddly, overwhelming logic and data often fail to convince. A friend told me that no one would ever appreciate what I was writing and saying unless I changed my presentation: "You've got to impress people. Go for Big Data, like American academics, or Big Theory, as the Europeans do." It sounded all too much like little boys, boasting, Mine is bigger than yours. "Stop sounding like a little girl just wondering about things," he said.

"I wonder." Those are the words with which Anne Moody ends her book, more powerful than more explicit conclusions. Perhaps persuasion depends on leading the listener to discover the truth of what is being said somewhere in his or her own experience. If you want people to change their minds, you have to address them as minds in motion, not as static receptacles, and help them acknowledge that every opinion has a story. If you want them to embrace strangeness, you can help them connect it to analogues of widening familiarity. There is a huge gap between offering the gift of an idea and claiming ownership of the mind of another. The listener or student needs to move slowly to the conviction that a new idea is one she or he may gradually decide to embrace and own and act on, in a mutual dance of gifts given and gifts received. We learn from the familiar in the strange and the strange in the familiar.

More and more, schoolteachers are told to have highly specific goals laid out in advance for every lesson, not to explore tangents or be distracted. Not to let themselves or the class wander into the world of analogies and loose ends and spontaneous curiosity. This narrow kind of presentation blocks the path to deepened understanding, which requires letting each new encounter resonate with earlier experience through reflection. Information, skills, specific strategies, all these can be conveyed in bullet points, but the encounter can never lead to wisdom.

All pulpits are potentially bully pulpits—it's part of the design.

Podiums too. Traditional styles invite a class or audience to be passive, just a step away from being bored, with the emphasis on knowledge moving in a single direction.

As the relationship between the generations shifts, such top-down models become less useful. One alternative is to start with a dialogue that engages listeners and takes them out of passivity, inviting them to share experience and creativity of their own. Sometimes I open a discussion of change and learning with high school or college students by asking them to give examples of things they have taught their parents. I have done this often enough so that I know how the answers develop, but there are always some I have never heard before, which open out into new explorations. When a group is challenged to speak instead of listening passively, they take a few minutes to get beyond wondering what they are supposed to say and begin to think new thoughts. On the first day of our seminar, poor Jackie, back in the classroom after many years, happened to be standing next to me and was caught off guard when this eccentric new professor tossed her a nonexistent "ball of energy." For a minute she simply froze and then passed it to the next person, who had had an extra few seconds to process the invitation and realize there was no single right answer she was expected to produce. There was then a double process of learning and liberation as responses developed in transit and each woman took account of what her predecessors had done.

Groups of students freeze in the same way, each person hiding out in the crowd, when I ask them what they have taught their parents, because teaching is supposed to move in the opposite direction. I let the silence extend. In our time technology has created an area of accepted expertise for the young: using the VCR, using E-mail, and surfing the Net are the examples that come up first today. The examples will change as particular kinds of equipment become more user-friendly, but there will never now be a time when there are not innovations demanding that skills be passed from the young to the old, if only the old are ready to learn.

Typically, there will be some examples of traditional knowledge that a parent missed and studies side by side with a child, sometimes now in the same college classroom: "I helped my mom learn French along with me." Then there are examples from the evanescent world of fashion and popular culture that offer an opening for discussing the unfamiliar tastes and preferences of a new generation: "I got my dad to sit down and listen with me so he'd understand why I like rap music."

The next kind of comment I get requires more delicacy, for it involves children teaching their parents new ethical standards, something that is not supposed to be necessary. In many households parents are taught by their sons and daughters to recycle and avoid waste. I can remember my daughter saying to me, "Don't tell me you're still using paper napkins!" She was right. I had been thinking and talking about environmental responsibility for years, but I hadn't learned to walk the talk in the kitchen and the dining room. Napkin rings appeared on the table with no-iron patterned napkins, changed weekly as they were in my childhood.

Other children say to their parents, "I can't stand it when you make remarks about women drivers." "Don't say Japs." "I just really don't like to hear cracks about people who are gay." My daughter, Vanni, looked at an early draft of this manuscript and said, "Why do you use the word *folk* for blacks and not for whites?" Well, I picked up the phrase "black folk" from W. E. B. Du Bois, but I'm glad to have the word for referring to other groups, getting away from the obsolete use of *men* or the clumsiness of using *people* too often.

Recently I spoke to an auditorium full of middle school students at a private school in Oregon. A girl said, "I taught my dad not to clap between movements at concerts." That's a minor bit of savoir faire, except that it suggests she had been giving her father the chance to learn about a different kind of music and the people who play it, like the boy who taught his father about rap. When I commented, she mentioned that the concert was at the school; parents not only learn from their children but also learn through their children from the children's school.

Recently a boy in Ontario said, "I taught my mom to be independent." Teaching, surely, through his own transformation as well as his words. I find it useful to explore the examples offered so the students can understand the power and significance of what they are doing— not just asking parents to behave in ways their children find more comfortable but opening up new worlds of possibility. My task is to provide the opportunity for reflecting on these exchanges. I took that group in Oregon through the issue of messy rooms: "How many of you get grief from your parents for having your rooms in a mess?" A big majority raised their hands, I know I can't fail with that one. "Well, can you find what you want when your room is messy? How about if your mom has cleaned it up?" Vanni used to have a complex filing system for her clothes and other possessions, spaced out and carefully differentiated—the only trouble was that they were filed in little heaps on the floor, which didn't work well over time. But a filing system that seems self-evident to its creator may be totally opaque to an observer. There may be some parents in Portland discomfited by the invitation to see order in their children's aggregations, but it seems to me that any attempt to negotiate the appearance of a child's room has to start from the awareness that there is always a degree of order, just as there is in the rhythm of an infant's hungers. It may not occur to children being scolded about messy rooms that their pattern is invisible to their parents—and it also may not occur to children or parents that the way we feel about "messiness" is a cultural construct rather than an eternal truth, for even though the search for order is universal, its manifestations vary.

A girl said, "I taught my dad not to interrupt." Since we live in a culture where males feel free to interrupt females and adults to interrupt children, she was teaching a new kind of respect. Then a boy offered an example of an even broader kind of respect: "I taught my dad not to keep comparing me with other people."

Someone is sure to ask me for examples of what I taught my parents and what I learned from my daughter. In infancy, of course, I taught my mother the proper use of a rocking chair and how to hold and nurse me, but that is further back than I can remember. I was blessed with growing up in a household where the adults took for granted that they could learn from me. My father wrote a series of father-daughter conversations, part fact and part fiction. I had conversations with my mother over the years about nuclear weapons because she was convinced that they must look different to a generation that has grown up with them. I remember saying to her and hearing her repeat for years that the ability to make bombs is not something that can be forgotten, that even though it represents a grave danger there is also a dignity to be grown into in the fact that we are now responsible for the whole of our species and the whole of our world. But she also listened carefully when I talked about the racial and religious tensions in my school and when, as a teenager, I lectured her on lipstick and bras.

Teenagers used to love to hear how I asked Vanni at the age of ten to take me to a video arcade and teach me to play Pac-Man, but many now don't know what it is. When I was living in the little guest suite at Spelman, I invited Johnnetta and Art to dinner and then, with limited equipment and no cookbooks, couldn't think what to prepare. So I called Vanni. "My mom is actually calling me for a recipe?" she said. "That's a switch! Well, I've made up this great new dish, chicken breasts cooked in apricot juice with branches of rosemary." It was a success, and I've served it since. That kind of switch is part of the circle of life. There are things that I have learned as an adult that she knows to the bone, so that often I find my acquired convictions strengthened when I meet them in her assumptions.

Stories evoke participation, spoken or unspoken. Personal anecdotes invite the listener to reflect on the familiar and turn it through different angles of refraction, perhaps many times. In the Gospel we hear of Jesus interpreting the parables to his disciples, but perhaps these decoding sessions were added later; better to leave the seed to grow. Stories remain in memory and open over time to multiple interpretations, rather than to a single correct reading.

Exercises like passing a "ball of energy" or introducing oneself in the third person are ways of drawing listeners into participant observation of themselves and others, modeling reflection on experience. Asking for examples of a previously unremarked-upon phenomenon from personal experience has the same effect, for every example is a capsule story, a possible pathway to wisdom, something beyond cleverness or encyclopedic information.

It is often said that experience is the best teacher. It is not so often pointed out that if this is true, most of us are poor students, and that it is our schooling that makes us so. Schools rarely teach how to reflect on lived experience outside the classroom in order to draw out the many possible levels of learning. They do not teach us to look at piles of toys and clothes spread out across the bedroom floor and wonder about the principle of organization involved. On the contrary, they teach children to abandon spontaneously created order and accept patterns imposed from outside, losing their earliest intimations of civility. It does not do young people much good to be told they are slobs or sinners. It may be helpful to understand their own impulses and ways of functioning and—we must never forget this—to realize that some compromise must be reached between these and the demands of the wider culture.

Teaching at Spelman often involves handing down received knowledge, with tests and exams to prove it has been properly absorbed. Yet many of the women in our seminar brought habits of reflection with them, and the course was designed to carry these further. Several are writers, accustomed to musing and remembering, while several look back on years of activism in changing environments. Some of the elders have been involved with thinking about education or mental health in the black community. Fleda has been engaged in recent years in exploring the levels of stress that characterize the lives of affluent, educated black women. Imani writes poetry. Beverly and Johnnetta are writing now as academics about gender relations in the black community, and Pat was planning to explore the same issues in fiction. Self-consciousness has costs. You go from a kiss to questions that won't be answered by plucking petals from a daisy: What is really going on? What are the assumptions underlying each person's behavior? Reflecting on experience, you cannot fail to realize that friends and lovers are always in many ways strangers. It follows that there is something to be learned from every encounter.

To become wise, I believe, one must have cared deeply about someone or something that could not be controlled or predicted, like a child or a lover or the fate of one's own body. Wisdom follows the realization that all commitments, even commitments to oneself or to God, involve moving targets. Wisdom comes not by accumulation of more and more experiences but through discerning pattern in the deeper mystery of what is already there. Even the self is no fixed constancy but changeable, moiré in motion, like a pool reflecting passing clouds and stirred by underwater springs.

Wisdom, then, is born of the overlapping of lives, the resonance between stories. To become human our species had to evolve a distinctive rhythm of development that allowed for this interaction, especially our long childhood and the survival and engagement of elders with the young. As we extend learning and cherishing throughout our days and as we take increasing responsibility for giving and relinquishing life, we are fulfilling the distinctive potential of our species. Lives follow different rhythms in different times and places, and fit together in different ways, and this is especially true today. Lives take new shapes as we live longer and try out multiple paths and roles, move around the world, make new starts. The statistics are familiar, but coming to terms with them is personal, as individuals recognize and work creatively with the changing contours of their lives and the shifting ways they overlap.

Hope for a sustainable future depends on reshaping the life cycle—not the individual life cycle alone but the overlapping and intersecting cycles of individuals and generations, reaffirming both the past and the future, not only in families but in the institutions we build and share. Such a reshaping would not only provide the wisdom for a reduction in numbers but could alleviate the injustices caused by shortsighted competition and consumption. Many of our problems stem from the neediness of infancy, while others stem from the denial of aging and death, yet life without need and without limits is outside the natural order and permanently at enmity with it.

Human beings have, for centuries, used metaphors in thinking about time that also describe objects in space. A journey or an exile. The bridge to a new century. A turning wheel. A tree reaching both roots and branches outward into earth and sky. Metaphors like these allow people to see pattern in their lives, brave beginnings and despairing falls, changes in direction, brief crescendos, and long sections of monotony. Wherever there is pattern there can be framework for meaning.

Even in developmental psychology we find a wealth of metaphor, for scientists of every stripe drift into metaphorical explanations, often without being aware of the assumptions they bring with them or using them consistently. But every metaphor, although based on a similarity, makes a connection that goes beyond it and draws in dissimilarities as well, which is why bad metaphors may be dangerous. Even the more carefully neutral terms are evocative: the *span* of life suggests a bridge, a way to get from one shore to the other without pausing in the middle; the life *course* suggests a river held between banks. Many peoples, thinking about lives, divide them into stages, and so have many investigators, but stages suggest demarcation. When the metaphors slip and slide and no longer seem to fit, there is growing unease. What lies on the other side of that bridge? What is that sea to which the rivers return?

Full circles. The wheel of life. The cycle of the seasons. From the myths and rituals of ancient peoples to the most modern nuclear physics, the circular recurs and becomes the cyclical as it moves through time. Cycles suggest inevitability, but they also suggest completeness and turn up in models of deepening or spiritual return to recognize the place of origin for the first time.

The maps and diagrams of lives, literal and metaphorical, might look different if we moved freely in three dimensions, like birds or fish. We still have the stereoscopic vision of predators and of our tree-dwelling ancestors, which allows us to judge distance, but we have spent most of the millennia of humanness walking on a flat earth.

Conventional diagrams suggest linear development, but the basic structure is, at the very least, a dizzying spiral. We move outward as we grow, but we carry a lifelong need for a center—or perhaps for a process of centering. The widest circle of movement and awareness is global, when finally all the circles are made one. Perhaps the image of concentric circles should give way to the three-dimensional image of a spiral moving both outward and inward to a center of some kind, a focused ending or homecoming. In African American spirituals, death is often expressed as going home, implying a return to Africa, even though, for the descendants of slaves, the only home they could remember was also a site of alienation. Going home is always both the same and not the same, so perhaps the life cycle has a twist in its return, like a Möbius strip.

In recent decades a proverb of circularity has spilled out of the African American community into common use. "What go 'round come 'round" was the way I heard it first, from black friends quoting it in the pronunciation they remembered from wise elders in childhood, and I prefer it in that form, so that even as it is appropriated and given wider meaning we can acknowledge where it comes from. Proverbs have layers of meaning. This one has often enough meant that those who inflict injustice will suffer in turn, but it has also meant that good deeds return to reward the doer, and sometimes it is said with a shrug of fatalism that suggests that the patterns of causation are beyond understanding. For me it reflects all the other images of circularity, drawing both good and evil within their circumferences, the spreading and overlapping circles of fulfillment and interdependence over depths of knowing and unknowing.

The stages of the human life cycle are prefigured and echoed in one another, but this quality is lost in the journalistic versions that caricature them, turning the developmental stages into tasks that must be completed—or achieved. The issue of identity never goes away, nor does the memory of helplessness in infancy, or the need to continue learning and the need to receive—and give—a combination of love and care that allows for play and dreaming and deeper growth, the combination that is best called cherishing.

Changes in the shape and interdependence of lives are part of a larger pattern of change that has been progressing at different rates in different parts of the world, hastening or delaying the transitions and shifting the ways in which generations interlock and the representation of age groups in the community. The changed timing of puberty, the reduced infant death rate and lowered birthrate, and the extension of adult life expectancies are only the most obvious. We are in trouble, our minds clogged with obsolete metaphors, unsure when life begins and when it ends (with plenty of controversy still to come), how to recognize and support adulthood, what freedoms to give when. Ancient biological rhythms are conflicting with new cultural landmarks, and the biological rhythms themselves are altered by technology. All the world's populations, at whatever stage of technological development, are increasingly linked. We have begun to recognize the need to limit population, strike some new balance between the different stages of life, and think again about making all our beginnings and endings carry the blessings of choice and fulfillment.

In the search for new metaphors we will need to emphasize the way lives mesh, transmitting direction and power. As important as the metaphor of a cycle or a wheel has been in thinking about lives, we would do well to extend it and think in terms of gears, circular forms with varying radii, the ratios shifting and energy newly applied. From the shriek of gears grinding together at times of rapid change, it seems clear that our species does not come equipped with synchromesh. We have absentmindedly abandoned many of the traditional ways in which the cycles of lives meshed across generations, creating new overlaps and convergences. These must be explored in art and science and resolved in new institutions.

Stories of individuals and their relationships through time offer another way of looking, but we need ways to tell these stories that are interwoven and recursive, that escape from the linearity of print to incite new metaphors. I believe that the choices we face today are so complex that they must be rehearsed and woven together in narrative. The decisions we make cannot be those of "economic man," rationally and shortsightedly pursuing self-interest, but those of an artist, composing a future of grace and truth. We will need new kinds of listening and looking to be open to new styles and harmonies. Listen to the change between Bach and Beethoven, for instance, and imagine this difference in sensibility applied to daily encounters. Follow the development from canon to fugue to the rhythms of jazz to see how lives fit together. Compare a tapestry of dozens of carefully worked figures with an equestrian statue, or contrast the larger-than-life protagonists of Rembrandt's *Night Watch* with a Balinese painting of a cremation. Perhaps the arts can teach us how to include both individual fulfillment and a greater harmony within a single composition. Perhaps, like systems of gears, they will renew our strength.

Meanwhile, we must all conserve the freedom to experiment and play, both tentative and committed, learning and teaching, from infancy to old age. Shaping friendships of intimacy and strangeness. Composing lives. Making our vows and pledging faith to unknown Others.

Appendix

About the Seminar: The Women and the Books

Most of the direct quotations in this book come from interviews or from papers written by members of the Spelman seminar who agreed to the use of their words and names. An additional quotation, included by permission, is from a George Mason student paper. These quotations and extracts have been condensed and copyedited. Where they refer to other living individuals in ways that might invade their privacy, names have been removed or substituted. When occasionally I have wanted to include anecdotes about persons whose permission I had not obtained, I have done so anonymously and in paraphrase. The elders were all Atlanta residents and relatively easy to reach, while two undergraduate members of the seminar did not respond to letters after the year ended and one asked not to be included. There were eighteen women in the seminar, including me, but fourteen are named below.

Some of the women in the seminar are quoted repeatedly, in different contexts. I have tried to include here some background or a description for each one, so the reader can connect the words to a person, and listed the pages on which each is introduced or quoted at length. Some women, including several whom for one reason or another I was unable to interview in the fall following the seminar, are quoted only once or twice, but this reflects the process of collation, not the force and value of their contributions to the discussion.

THE STUDENTS

Patricia Bakr (Pat) 20, 188
Hillary Ferguson 20, 24, 56, 60, 78–79
Iyabo Morrison 33–34, 79, 112
Imani Romney-Rosa 24, 35–42, 179–80
Celeste Watkins 52, 75–76, 88–89, 148–49

THE ELDERS

Joy San Brown 170
Cheryl Chisholm 34, 105–7, 162–64, 172, 181–82, 189–91, 225–26
Johnnetta Cole 7, 147, 177–78, 217, 228
Marymal Dryden 20, 24–29, 58–59, 82–85, 154–55
Lucretia Durrett (Cree) 21, 47, 164–66
Beverly Guy-Sheftall 64–65, 85–86
Fleda Mask Jackson 20, 172
Jacqueline Marshall (Jackie) 148, 229, 237
Ama Saran 48, 55, 100–101, 102, 113, 122, 202-4, 222–23

THE BOOKS (IN THE ORDER READ)

Maxine Hong Kingston. *The Woman Warrior.* New York: Vintage, 1976.
Anne Moody. *Coming of Age in Mississippi.* New York: Dell, 1980.
Sally Morgan. *My Place.* New York: Arcade, 1990.
Audre Lorde. *Zami: A New Spelling of My Name.* Freedom, CA: Crossing Press, 1982.
Margaret Mead. *Blackberry Winter.* New York: William Morrow, 1974.
Marjorie Shostak. *Nisa: The Life and Words of a !Kung Woman.* New York: Vintage, 1983. This book contains an extensive bibliography and background material.
Sarah Rice. *He Included Me.* Athens: University of Georgia Press, 1989.
Le Ly Hayslip with Jay Wurts. *When Heaven and Earth Changed Places.* New York: Doubleday, 1989.
Tsitsi Dangarembga. *Nervous Conditions.* Seattle: Seal Press, 1988.
Mary Catherine Bateson. *Composing a Life.* New York: Plume, 1990.

Acknowledgments

This book was made possible by the faculty, students, and administration of Spelman College, who allowed me to join their community of teaching, learning, and friendship during the spring semester of 1996. Johnnetta Cole, who was president of Spelman at that time, not only took the initiative in inviting me to come and teach a seminar but agreed to review the manuscript (twice) on behalf of the members of the seminar, and answered endless questions. Members of the seminar not only shared their memories and insights within the course framework but met with me for extended interviews afterwards and took me out to explore the city of Atlanta. Many others helped me in various ways, from the maintenance staff of the residence hall where I lived to the campus police. Special thanks to the Department of Sociology and Anthropology, the Women's Studies Center, and the Provost's Office.

Many of the ideas in this manuscript developed in the course of my teaching women's life histories at George Mason University, so I am grateful to the students there who shared some portion of their lives, as I am to the authors whose works we read in the seminar, to my parents, and to Erik Erikson for the long-ago experience of leading sections of his Harvard course on life history. Mason granted me a study leave for my semester in Atlanta and additional extended leaves to complete the manuscript, for which I am grateful.

The decision to draw on my Spelman experience in writing about changes in the life cycle and in the relationship between generations was made at the MacDowell Colony, where I spent two fruitful months in the summer of 1996, occupying a studio previously used by Tillie Olsen and Audre Lorde, whose friendly spirits kept me company.

I would like to thank my longtime agent, John Brockman, my publisher and editor, Ann Godoff, with whom I worked on *Composing a Life,* and Susan M. S. Brown, who deftly and tactfully cleaned up this manuscript, as she did *Peripheral Visions.* Mary Durland, Iris Knell, and Rev. Gail Bowman contributed needed references. I had the benefit of thoughtful readings of the manuscript from family members—my husband, Barkev Kassarjian; my daughter, Sevanne; and my son-in-law, Paul Griffin—and from friends Richard Goldsby and Barbara Kreiger.

Notes

1. OVERLAPPING LIVES

p. 5   Annie Sullivan: In William Gibson, *The Miracle Worker* (London: Samuel French, 1959), p. 25.

p. 7   I wrote about her: Mary Catherine Bateson, *Composing a Life* (New York: Atlantic Monthly Press, 1989).

p. 9   one "race": Anthropologists and others have taken to enclosing certain words in quotation marks, to emphasize that these are cultural constructs rather than scientifically based technical terms. Let this note warn the reader instead that she or he is in the presence of ordinary American English, with all its riches, fluctuating courtesies, and distortions. That this is the only logical way to handle the difficulty was suggested to me by Matthew Frye Jacobson, *Whiteness of a Different Color: European Immigrants and the Alchemy of Race* (Cambridge, MA: Harvard University Press, 1998).

p. 11   a memoir of my parents: Mary Catherine Bateson, *With a Daughter's Eye: A Memoir of Margaret Mead and Gregory Bateson* (New York: William Morrow, 1984).

2. ONCE AROUND

p. 23   San (Bushman): Over the long period of ethnographic research in the Kalahari, there have been several shifts in terminology. Early publications used the term Bushmen; when this was felt to be demeaning there was a shift to referring more locally to the !Kung or !Kung San, which Shostak uses. Subsequently the people themselves asked to be referred to as the Ju/'hoansi (the symbols !, /, and ' are used to transcribe sounds unfamiliar to English speakers), and most recently they have shifted toward a rehabilitation of the term Bushmen (*Anthropology Newsletter*, May 1996, p. 15). The term San includes but is not limited to the Bushmen, but, since the situation is still in flux and I have used it in previous writings, I have continued that usage here. Portions of Shostak's work incorporate the work of other ethnographers, all of whom are fully referenced in *Nisa*.

p. 24   "the birds of the heaven": Matthew 13:32.

p. 27   "Well, Son, I'll tell you": Langston Hughes, "Mother to Son," in *The Collected Poems*, ed. Arnold Rampersad and David Roessel (New York: Alfred A. Knopf, 1994).

p. 32   "now we see through a glass, darkly": 1 Cor. 13:12.

p. 32   Erik Erikson: The work of Erik and Joan Erikson pervades my thinking about lives. Variants of the diagrams referred to appeared in Erik H. Erikson, *Childhood and Society* (New York: W. W. Norton, 1950).

3. YOUTH—DANCING THE LIMBO

p. 49   reflect on and use our own experience: Mary Field Belenky, Blythe McVicker Clinchy, Nancy Rule Goldberger, and Jill Mattuck Tarule, *Women's Ways of Knowing: The Development of Self, Voice, and Mind* (New York: Basic Books, 1987).

p. 49   cultural anthropologists collect first-person: Lewis L. Langness and Gelya Frank, *Lives: An Anthropological Approach to Biography* (Novato, CA: Chandler & Sharp, 1981).

p. 53   helplessness of infancy: Jerome Frank et al., *Persuasion and Healing: A Comparative Study of Psychotherapy*, 3d ed. (Baltimore: Johns Hopkins University Press, 1993).

p. 55   "acquired insipidity" and "This business of womanhood": Tsitsi Dangarembga, *Nervous Conditions* (Seattle: Seal Press, 1988), pp. 116 and 16.

p. 56   as among other hunter-gatherers: Ashley Montagu, *Adolescent Sterility: A Study in the Comparative Physiology of the Infecundity of the Adolescent Organism in Mammals and Man* (Springfield, IL: C. C. Thomas, 1946).

p. 62   In a fixed economy: Peter Laslett, *The World We Have Lost* (New York: Charles Scribner's Sons, 1965), p. 94.

p. 69   teenage mothers: Steven A. Holmes, "Public Cost of Teen-Age Pregnancy Is Put at $7 Billion This Year," *New York Times,* June 13, 1996, p. A19.

4. IN THE HEARTLANDS OF UNKNOWING

p. 86   Stand on your own two feet: Beverly Guy-Sheftall, *Words of Fire: An Anthology of African-American Feminist Thought* (New York: New Press, 1995), p. xxvi.

p. 92   Ruth Benedict's first descriptions: Ruth Benedict, "Psychological Types in the Cultures of the Southwest" (1930), reprinted in Margaret Mead, ed., *An Anthropologist at Work: Writings of Ruth Benedict* (Boston: Houghton Mifflin, 1954), pp. 248–83.

p. 92   research in New Guinea: Margaret Mead, *Sex and Temperament* (New York: William Morrow, 1935); Gregory Bateson, *Naven* (Cambridge: Cambridge University Press, 1936).

p. 92   her book about Japan: Ruth Benedict, *The Chrysanthemum and the Sword* (Boston: Houghton Mifflin, 1946).

p. 93   debate about how much diversity: Arthur M. Schlesinger, Jr., *The Disuniting of America: Reflections on a Multicultural Society* (New York: W. W. Norton, 1992).

p. 94   nostalgia is delusory: Stephanie Coontz, *The Way We Never Were: American Families and the Nostalgia Trap* (New York: Basic Books, 1992).

p. 96   a story I have told repeatedly: Extract from a paper written in 1993 by a Mason student, Chessalay Blanchard, now Zimmerman; also quoted in part in M. C. Bateson, "Ordinary Creativity," in Alfonso

Montuori and Ronald E. Purser, eds., *Social Creativity* (Cresskill, NJ: Hampton Press, 1999), vol. 1, pp. 153–71.

5. ADULTHOOD—THE REAL OF ME

p. 104   survived until puberty: Ester Boserup, *Population and Technical Change: A Study of Long-Term Trends* (Chicago: University of Chicago Press, 1981), p. 37.

p. 104   hit her stride in her forties: Sarah Rice, *He Included Me* (Athens: University of Georgia Press, 1989), pp. 139, 152.

p. 110   one woman in 13 still dies: Barbara Crossette, "New Tally of World Tragedy: Women Who Die Giving Life," quoting UNICEF figures, *New York Times,* June 11, 1996, pp. A1, A10.

p. 111   thirty more years: Boserup, *Population and Technical Change,* p. 13.

p. 111   marriages today last longer: Stephanie Coontz, *The Way We Never Were: American Families and the Nostalgia Trap* (New York: Basic Books, 1992), p. 16.

p. 114   "original affluent society": Marshall Sahlins, "The Original Affluent Society," in Sahlins, ed., *Stone Age Economics* (New York: Aldine, 1972), pp. 1–39.

p. 117   Israeli kibbutzim: Melford E. Spiro, *Gender and Culture: Kibbutz Women Revisited* (New Brunswick, NJ: Transaction Press, 1996), p. 329.

p. 117   *Women of Deh Koh:* Erika Friedl, *The Women of Deh Koh* (New York: Penguin, 1991).

p. 123   Islamic government undertook: Statement by the Islamic Republic of Iran delegation, International Conference on Population and Development + Five, The Hague, 1991, http://www.undp.org/popin.

p. 124   demographic transition: For a discussion and critique of the theory of demographic transition, see Michael S. Teitelbaum, "Relevance of Demographic Transition Theory for Developing Countries," in Scott W. Menard and Elizabeth W. Moen, eds., *Perspectives on Population: An Introduction to Concepts and Issues* (New York: Oxford University Press, 1987), pp. 29–36.

p. 124   doubling in 350 to 700 years: Boserup, *Population and Technical Change,* p. 43.

p. 125   9 billion by midcentury: United Nations, "Revision of the World Population Estimates and Projections," http://www.popin.org/pop 1998.

6. COMMITMENT—VISION AND REVISION

p. 130   "our whole school": On the history and development of Spelman College, see Florence Matilda Read, *The Story of Spelman College* (Atlanta, GA, 1961). Also Spelman College Office of Planning and Institutional Research, *Fact Book 1995–96.*

p. 138   sexual exclusivity: See Meredith F. Small, *Female Choices: Sexual Behavior of Female Primates* (Ithaca: Cornell University Press, 1993), which suggests that for humans and many of our primate relatives, pair bonding accompanied by occasional outside forays has been the pattern: "Because most human sexual activity was, and still is, nonreproductive, quick matings outside the pair may have been inconsequential to the bond within which children were nurtured" (p. 199). Small goes on to say, "Cross-culturally, women engage in extramarital affairs almost as often as men, or they wish they could. And most societies disapprove of such behavior" (p. 216).

p. 139   "Always True to You in My Fashion": Cole Porter, *Kiss Me, Kate* (1948), in *The Complete Lyrics of Cole Porter,* ed. Robert Kimball (New York: Da Capo, 1992).

p. 141   traits important in mate selection: Robert Wright, *The Moral Animal: Why We Are the Way We Are: The New Science of Evolutionary Psychology* (New York: Vintage Books, 1995).

p. 141   "Your old men shall dream": Joel 2:28.

7. SYMBOLS OF CONNECTION

p. 152   the Negro national anthem: James Weldon Johnson, "Lift Ev'ry Voice and Sing" (1900), in Erskine Peters, ed., *Lyrics of the Afro-*

American Spiritual: A Documentary Collection (Westport, CT: Greenwood Press, 1993), no. 291.

p. 152 Gloria Wade-Gayles: Gloria Wade-Gayles, *Pushed Back to Strength: A Black Woman's Journey Home* (Boston: Beacon Press, 1993).

p. 152 symbols used in Ghana: Kwaku Ofori-Ansa, "Meanings of Symbols in Adinkra Cloth" (poster) (Hyattsville, MD: Sankofa Publications, 1993).

p. 153 First Lady: Hillary Rodham Clinton, *It Takes a Village and Other Lessons Children Teach Us* (New York: Simon & Schuster, 1996).

p. 155 "All the blacks are men": Gloria Hull, Patricia Bell-Scott, and Barbara Smith, eds., *But Some of Us Are Brave: Black Women's Studies* (New York: Feminist Press, 1982).

p. 156 GI Generation: See William Strauss and Neil Howe, *Generations: The History of America's Future* (New York: William Morrow, 1992).

p. 162 my coauthor Richard Goldsby: Mary Catherine Bateson and Richard Goldsby, *Thinking AIDS* (New York: Addison-Wesley, 1988).

p. 166 loaned me a video: Haile Gerima, *Sankofa* (Washington, DC: Mypheduh Films, 1993).

p. 170 "Ar'n't I a Woman?": Nell Painter, *Sojourner Truth: A Life, a Symbol* (New York: W. W. Norton, 1996). The famous 1851 speech was probably invented in whole or in part by Frances Dana Gage.

8. LUCY'S CHILDREN

p. 176 bone and stone: Eric Delson, ed., *Ancestors: The Hard Evidence,* Proceedings of a Symposium held at the American Museum of Natural History to mark the opening of the exhibition "Ancestors: Four Million Years of Humanity" (New York: Alan R. Liss, 1985).

p. 177 fatalism about human behavior: Robert Ardrey, *African Genesis: A Personal Investigation into the Animal Origins and Nature of Man* (New York: Atheneum, 1961).

p. 178 learned a lot about how depression: For an effort to bridge biochemical and experiential theories of unipolar depression, see Peter

C. Whybrow, Hagop Akistal, and William T. McKinney, Jr., *Mood Disorders: Toward a New Psychobiology* (New York: Plenum Press, 1984).

p. 180   depression comes up often: Charlotte Perkins Gilman, "The Yellow Wallpaper" (1892), in *The Norton Anthology of Literature by Women: The Tradition in English,* eds. Sandra M. Gilbert and Susan Gubar (New York: W. W. Norton, 1985). See also Charlotte Perkins Gilman, *The Living of Charlotte Perkins Gilman: An Autobiography* (1935; rept., Madison: University of Wisconsin Press, 1991).

p. 180   "Within a few blocks": Maxine Hong Kingston, *The Woman Warrior* (New York: Vintage Books, 1976), p. 216.

p. 181   "living and partly living": T. S. Eliot, *Murder in the Cathedral* (1935), in Eliot, *The Complete Poems and Plays* (New York: Harcourt, Brace, 1952), p. 180.

p. 181   linked to violence: Robert Wright, "The Biology of Violence," *New Yorker,* March 13, 1995, pp. 69–70.

p. 182   respond differently to abuse: E.(H.) Carmen, P. P. Rieker, and T. Mills, "Victims of Violence and Psychiatric Illness," in Ann Wolbert Burgess, ed., *Rape and Sexual Assault,* vol. 2 (New York: Garland, 1988), pp. 27–39.

p. 184   "die young": Ashley Montagu, *Growing Young* (New York: McGraw-Hill, 1981), p. 6. "a primate fetus": p. 6, quoting Bolk. "driven off the time scale": p. 12, quoting Huxley.

p. 185   chimpanzees like human children: Cathy Hayes, *The Ape in Our House* (New York: Harper & Row, 1951).

p. 187   monkeys reared without a mother's care: Harry F. Harlow and Margaret K. Harlow, "Social Deprivation in Monkeys," *Scientific American* 207 (1962), no. 5: 136–46.

p. 187   a harsh tradition: Peter Greggs Slater, *Children in the New England Mind: In Death and in Life* (Hamden, CT: Anchor Books, 1977).

p. 189   regions that were once lush: James DeMeo, *On the Origin and Diffusion of Patrism: The Saharasian Connection* (Ph.D. diss., University of Kansas, 1986).

p. 189   conquered had peaceful, cooperative cultures: Riane Eisler, for instance, writes in *The Chalice and the Blade: Our History, Our Future* (San Francisco: Harper San Francisco, 1988) of "partnership" societies invaded by "dominator" societies.

p. 191   the bonobo or pygmy chimpanzee: Frans de Waal, *Bonobo: The Forgotten Ape* (Berkeley: University of California Press, 1997).

p. 193   "the ability not to have to learn": Karl Deutsch, *The Nerves of Government: Models of Political Communication and Control* (New York: Free Press, 1966), p. 247.

p. 197   a continuing closeness with their own mothers: Nancy J. Chodorow, *The Reproduction of Mothering: Psychoanalysis and the Sociology of Gender* (Berkeley: University of California Press, 1978).

p. 197   force males to distance: Lillian B. Rubin, *Intimate Strangers: Men and Women Together* (New York: HarperCollins, 1990).

9. DEEP RIVER

p. 201   black life expectancies: K. G. Manton, C. H. Patrick, and K. W. Johnson, "Health Differentials Between Blacks and Whites," *Millbank Quarterly* 65, supp. 1 (1987): fig. 1, p. 140.

p. 205   "how remarkably *interesting* it is": Letter from Joan Erikson, late 1980s, undated.

p. 208   tribal groups that migrate: Fredrik Barth, *Nomads of South Persia: The Basseri Tribe of the Khamseh Confederacy* (Prospect Heights, IL: Waveland Press, 1961).

p. 208   rural Ireland after the famines: Conrad H. Arensberg, *Irish Countryman: An Anthropological Study* (1937; rept., Prospect Heights, IL: Waveland Press, 1988), p. 96.

p. 211   time of greatest want: Michael Harrington, *The Other America: Poverty in the United States* (New York: Macmillan, 1962).

p. 214   only a fraction of violent crimes: Hugh F. Cline, "Criminal Behavior over the Life Span," in Jerome Kagan and Orville G. Brim, Jr., eds., *Continuity and Change in Human Development* (Cambridge, MA: Harvard University Press, 1980), p. 645, table 13.1, "Reported Arrests by Age Groups, 1977."

p. 217   almost all new readings: The new readings in 1997 were Virginia
          Lee Barnes and Janice Boddy, *Aman: The Story of a Somali Girl* (New
          York: Vintage Books, 1994); Janet Campbell Hale, *Bloodlines:
          Odyssey of a Native Daughter* (New York: HarperPerennial, 1993);
          Zora Neale Hurston, *Dust Tracks on a Road* (1942; rept., New York:
          HarperPerennial, 1941); Chan Khong, *Learning True Love: How I
          Learned and Practiced Social Change in Vietnam* (Berkeley: Parallax
          Press, 1993); Polingsi Qoyawayma, *No Turning Back: A Hopi
          Woman's Struggle to Live in Two Worlds* (Albuquerque: University of
          New Mexico Press, 1964); Sister Souljah, *No Disrespect* (New York:
          Vintage Books, 1996); Anne Truitt, *Daybook: The Journal of an Artist*
          (New York: Penguin Books, 1982); Ruth Underhill, *Papago Woman*
          (1936; rept., Prospect Hills, IL: Waveland, 1985); Margery Wolf, *A
          Thrice-Told Tale* (Stanford: Stanford University Press, 1992). May
          Sarton published a number of her journals, and I have taught *Jour-
          nal of a Solitude* (W. W. Norton, 1989) repeatedly.

p. 217   CFS as malingering: The popular media began to dismiss chronic
          fatigue syndrome (called by various other names in the early years)
          as "yuppie flu" in 1987 and continued to do so until the early 1990s,
          as increasing evidence and statistics were published. Hillary John-
          son, *Osler's Web: Inside the Labyrinth of the Chronic Fatigue Syndrome
          Epidemic* (New York: Crown, 1996).

p. 219   "The central concept of wisdom": E. F. Schumacher, *Small Is Beau-
          tiful* (New York: Harper & Row, 1973), p. 33.

10. FULL CIRCLES

p. 229   write about Spelman: Howard Zinn, *The Southern Mystique* (New
          York: Alfred A. Knopf, 1964).

p. 230   my earliest years: Mary Catherine Bateson, *With a Daughter's Eye: A
          Memoir of Margaret Mead and Gregory Bateson* (New York: William
          Morrow, 1984).

p. 230   like an experimental animal: Jim Miller, "The Guru of Anthropol-
          ogy," review of *With a Daughter's Eye, Newsweek,* August 27, 1984,
          p. 74.

p. 231 "the heart has its reasons": Blaise Pascal, *Pensées,* iv, 277.

p. 232 models of child rearing: Diana Baumrind, "Current Patterns of Parental Authority," *Developmental Psychology Monographs* 4 (1971): 1–103.

p. 232 Dr. Spock: the edition of Spock's famous handbook that coincided with my daughter's infancy was the third: Benjamin Spock, *Baby and Child Care,* 3d ed. (New York: Hawthorne, 1968).

p. 233 "Those who learn must teach": This slogan may be derived from an Ethiopian proverb that is quoted in Charlotte Leslau and Wolf Leslau, *African Love Poems and Proverbs* (White Plains, NY: Peter Pauper Press, 1995).

ABOUT THE AUTHOR

MARY CATHERINE BATESON is the Clarence J. Robinson Professor in Anthropology and English at George Mason University in Fairfax, Virginia, and divides her time between Virginia and the Monadnock region of New Hampshire. She has written and co-authored eight books, including *Composing a Life* and *With a Daughter's Eye: A Memoir of Margaret Mead and Gregory Bateson* (named one of the best books of 1984 by *The New York Times*), and is president of the Institute for Intercultural Studies in New York City.

ABOUT THE TYPE

This book was set in Bembo, a typeface based on an old-style Roman face that was used for Cardinal Bembo's tract *De Aetna* in 1495. Bembo was cut by Francisco Griffo in the early sixteenth century. The Lanston Monotype Machine Company of Philadelphia brought the well-proportioned letter forms of Bembo to the United States in the 1930s.